AF743335

ROUTLEDGE LIBRARY EDITIONS:
MONETARY ECONOMICS

Volume 4

EQUILIBRIUM CREDIT RATIONING

EQUILIBRIUM CREDIT RATIONING

WILLIAM R. KEETON

Routledge
Taylor & Francis Group
LONDON AND NEW YORK

28 JUN 2017

First published in 1979 by Garland Publishing, Inc.

This edition first published in 2017
by Routledge
2 Park Square, Milton Park, Abingdon, Oxon OX14 4RN

and by Routledge
711 Third Avenue, New York, NY 10017

Routledge is an imprint of the Taylor & Francis Group, an informa business

© 1979 William R. Keeton

All rights reserved. No part of this book may be reprinted or reproduced or utilised in any form or by any electronic, mechanical, or other means, now known or hereafter invented, including photocopying and recording, or in any information storage or retrieval system, without permission in writing from the publishers.

Trademark notice: Product or corporate names may be trademarks or registered trademarks, and are used only for identification and explanation without intent to infringe.

British Library Cataloguing in Publication Data
A catalogue record for this book is available from the British Library

ISBN: 978-1-138-73264-3 (Set)
ISBN: 978-1-315-16457-1 (Set) (ebk)
ISBN: 978-1-138-63364-3 (Volume 4) (hbk)
ISBN: 978-1-315-20722-3 (Volume 4) (ebk)

Publisher's Note
The publisher has gone to great lengths to ensure the quality of this reprint but points out that some imperfections in the original copies may be apparent.

Disclaimer
The publisher has made every effort to trace copyright holders and would welcome correspondence from those they have been unable to trace.

332.1753015I
KEE
(1)

Equilibrium Credit Rationing

William R. Keeton

Garland Publishing, Inc.
New York & London, 1979

William R. Keeton © 1979
All rights reserved

3847093

Library of Congress Cataloging in Publication Data

Keeton, William R 1947–
Equilibrium credit rationing.

(Outstanding dissertations in economics)
A revision of the author's thesis, Massachusetts Institute of Technology, 1976.
Bibliography: p.
1. Bank loans—Mathematical models. 2. Credit control—Mathematical models. 3. Monetary policy—Mathematical models. I. Title. II. Series.
HG1641.K4 1979 332.1'753'0151 78-75066
ISBN 0-8240-4142-9

All volumes in this series are printed on acid-free, 250-year-life paper.

Printed in the United States of America.

Preface

Although there is now a large literature on the theory of credit rationing, there is no consensus on an appropriate definition of that concept. Most economists would probably agree that credit rationing occurs when in some sense the demand for credit exceeds the amount supplied. But the demand for credit cannot be determined without specifying the relevant price, and as two recent surveys suggest [4] [8, Ch. 2], it is not always obvious how this should be done.

This study examines and contrasts two concepts of credit rationing. The first concept takes the relevant price of credit to be the explicit interest rate on the loan and defines the demand for credit as the amount an individual borrower would like to receive at that rate. Accordingly, rationing is said to occur whenever a customer receives a smaller loan than he would desire at the interest rate charged by the bank. Under the alternative definition, the price of credit consists of the complete set of loan terms confronting a class of borrowers with given characteristics, while the demand for credit equals the total number of loan which members of the class would like to receive at those terms. Thus, in this case rationing occurs whenever the total quantity of loans demanded by the class at those terms exceeds the total quantity supplied by banks.

If lenders were for some reason slow to adjust loan rates to changes in the cost or supply of loanable funds, rationing in one or both of these two senses might well occur as a temporary disequilibrium phenomenon. It is also well recognized that a ceiling on loan rates or a regulatory constraint on lenders' freedom to charge different rates to borrowers of different risk could lead to the rationing of credit. The present study demonstrates that the two types of rationing defined above may also be observed in equilibrium situations and in the absence of government-imposed constraints on the setting of loan rates. In particular, equilibrium rationing may occur in the first sense if there is competition among lenders and a risk of default which increases with the size of the loan, and may occur in the second sense if there exists a moral hazard problem resulting from the lender's inability to monitor all relevant characteristics of the borrower's investment project. The study also addresses certain unanswered questions about the impact of a loan rate ceiling on the volume and distribution of bank credit.

Before examining these results in greater detail, it is important to articulate the reasons for studying credit rationing in the first place:

(1) Economists find it paradoxical that sellers would fail to raise prices when the demand for a good exceeds the amount supplied. The primary motivation for most theoretical studies of equilibrium credit rationing has been the desire to resolve this paradox, i.e. to demonstrate that there are plausible circumstances in which it would be rational for lenders to behave in such a seemingly perverse manner.

(2) Since the price system is known to allocate resources efficiently under certain ideal conditions, the question naturally arises whether the nonprice allocation of credit has any adverse implications for economic efficiency--either by introducing some new distortion or by increasing the welfare loss from an already existing market imper-

fection.

(3) The interest in credit rationing in the U.S. originated with the debate over the "availability doctrine" in the early 1950's. The central idea underlying this doctrine was that monetary policy could be used to restrain aggregate demand without causing significant increases in interest rates, even if firms' demand for investment were highly insensitive to the cost of borrowing, as was widely believed to be the case. In particular, it was argued that a restrictive monetary policy would cause banks to reduce the availability of credit and to ration funds among borrowers rather than raise interest rates on loans. The original proponents of the availability doctrine were trying to establish that the Federal Reserve could abandon its policy of pegging the Treasury bill rate and control private spending without generating a sharp increase in interest rates on government securities. But independently of this issue, monetary economists have shown great interest in credit rationing over the years as a third "channel of influence" of monetary policy, in addition to the conventional cost-of-credit effect on investment and wealth effect on consumption [5].

Unfortunately, most recent contributions to the theory of equilibrium rationing appear to have lost sight of the original reason for interest in the subject, and consequently fail to even consider whether the type of rationing explained has the kind of implication for monetary policy that proponents of the availability doctrine had in mind. It is also unusual to find any careful discussion of the efficiency implications of the type of rationing which is being considered. Although most of the present study is devoted to explaining how the two types of rationing defined earlier may occur, I have also attempted to spell out the implications of the two types of rationing for the efficiency of resource allocation and the effectiveness of monetary policy. Indeed, a major theme is that the second type of equilibrium rationing has the kind of implications for these questions that one would expect rationing to have, while the first does not.

At the time this study was undertaken, the first definition of rationing had already been employed by a number of authors and appeared to enjoy widespread acceptance. At first glance, it seems natural to view the interest rate on a loan as the price the borrower pays and the price the lender receives for each dollar of credit granted, so it is not surprising that the definition should have become popular. The second type of rationing has not received so much attention in the literature, but is appealing for at least two reasons. First, the case to which it refers is exactly analagous to involuntary unemployment in labor markets--i.e. to the situation in which some individuals are unable to obtain a job even though they would be willing to work at the same wage and at the same hours as other individuals who are currently employed and have identical skills. Whether this kind of phenomenon occurs in credit markets or in labor markets, there can be little disagreement that it involves an excess of demand over supply.

The other attraction of the second definition is that it captures in extreme form a practice which is claimed to pervade both credit and insurance markets, but which has not been adequately explained in either context. This is the practice of rejecting applicants who appear relatively uncreditworthy or accident prone, instead of accomodating these individuals at an appropriately higher price. As described by one source, in normal times

> lenders inquire about the applicant's credit rating and then state the terms of the loan. But when funds are in short supply, the lender will first determine whether the applicant is entitled to credit on the basis of his past relationship with the lender. If the applicant is not, he will probably be turned down with no discussion of what rates would be charged and whether the applicant would be willing to pay those rates. [1,pp. 26-27]

Similarly, when consumer credit institutions compute a composite score indicating an applicant's overall creditworthiness, they do not charge the lowest-scoring applicants a higher interest rate but instead establish a cutoff point, rejecting the poorer risks outright. Although the present study is not directly concerned with insurance markets, it is well documented that automobile insurers behave in essentially the same way, using certain types of information (e.g. age, territory, sex) to establish rating categories but using other information (e.g. occupation, personality traits) to make an accept-or-reject decision within each category [15,Ch. 2]. Although such behavior can always be explained by social pressures or regulatory constraints on rate-setting, one suspects that there is more involved.

Now, when credit rationing occurs in the second sense, those individuals who are denied credit are by definition indistinguishable from other individuals who succeed in obtaining loans. Strictly speaking, and in contrast to the practice just described, this means that the lender's accept-or-reject decision will be random, based in effect on a flip of the coin. However, if it is possible for credit rationing to occur in this extreme form, a fortiori it must also be possible for a loan applicant to be rejected even though he is only marginally worse than the least creditworthy applicant accepted by the lender, and even though he would be willing to pay some discrete amount more to receive a loan at the same terms as that marginal customer. Thus, any theory wich succeeds in explaining rationing in the strong sense of the second definition will also help account for the failure of lenders to quote prices to applicants who fall just below the cutoff point.

With this background, I will now attempt to give the reader an overview of the study, point out some recent related work by other authors, and indicate how I have extended some of the results in the last chapter in subsequent research.

Chapter I focuses on the first type of rationing. The principal point made in this chapter is that bank credit is likely to have the features of a nonhomogeneous or differentiated good, in which case the borrower will generally fail to receive the amount of credit that would maximize his expected profits at the prevailing loan rate. If there were no risk of default and if lending costs for a particular class of borrowers were proportional to the amount loaned, a bank's total expected profits from the class would depend only on the interest rate charged and the total amount loaned. In this case bank credit could be treated as a homogeneous good, and each borrower would be observed in competitive equilibrium to receive that size loan which he desired at the prevailing interest rate for his class.

However, if there is a risk of default and if diminishing marginal returns to investment cause this risk to increase with the size of the loan, the bank's expected revenues from a loan will fail to increase in proportion with loan size given any interest rate. Furthermore, there is reason to believe that a significant portion of a bank's administrative costs will depend on the number of loans granted, rather than the amount of funds loaned. For both reasons, the bank's expected profits will depend not just on the interest rate and the volume of credit extended to each class, but on the interest rate, the number of loans, and the size of each loan. This suggests that bank loans be viewed as a special kind of nonhomogeneous or differentiated good, with loan size interpreted as a "characteristic" of the loan in the same sense that horsepower is a characteristic of automobiles or floor space a characteristic of houses. The analogy between loans and other differentiated goods has also been noted by Baltensperger [3][4] and by Barro [2].

In Chapter I it is shown that this nonhomogeneity property will result in each borrower failing to receive that size loan which would maximize his expected profits at the interest rate charged by the bank. In particular, the existence of default risk and diminishing marginal returns to investment will tend to produce a competitive equilibrium in which each borrower receives a smaller loan than he would desire at the interest rate charged, while the dependence of administrative costs on the quantity of loans rather than the volume of credit will lead to an equilibrium in which each borrower receives a larger loan than would be optimal for him at the quoted rate.

Although the failure of the borrower to receive that amount of credit he desires appears to represent an imbalance of supply and demand, this results from the specification of the contractual loan rate as the relevant price of credit. An alternative approach, suggested by the analogy with other nonhomogeneous goods, is to think of the borrower as confronting a price schedule which indicates for each loan size the loan rate at which the lender is just able to break even on an additional loan. When the borrower's demand for credit is redefined as the amount he would like to borrow given this schedule, demand will again be observed to equal supply in equilibrium, a point which has also been recognized by Baltensperger and Barro.

Given this perspective, it should not be surprising that credit rationing in the first sense need have no adverse implications for economic efficiency: in the equilibrium described in Chapter I each borrower will undertake that size investment which maximizes the excess of the expected project outcome over the opportunity cost of the funds loaned, whether or not the amount of credit he receives is that which he would desire at the contractual loan rate. Chapter I also makes clear that if the first type of rationing does occur in equilibrium, it will have no tendency to enhance the effectivess of monetary policy.

The possibility that a firm may receive a lesser or greater amount than it would desire at the prevailing rate does, however, have two other interesting implications. First, a restrictive monetary policy will tend to produce a smaller increase in the contractual loan rate--though not in the expected interest cost--if credit is being rationed in the initial equilibrium. As a result, changes in observed loan rates may provide a poor indicator of monetary tightness. The second implication concerns the impact of an interest rate ceiling on the market for bank loans, a question which is considered in detail in Chapter II.

Most discussions of loan rate ceilings treat the market for bank loans just like the market for any other homogeneous good: it is assumed that the aggregate demand for credit varies inversely with the loan rate, that the aggregate supply of deposits increases with the deposit rate, and that a bank earns profits on each dollar loaned equal to the loan rate minus the deposit rate (with suitable adjustments for risk premia, reserve requirements, or administrative costs which are proportional to the size of the loan). This approach leads to the conclusion that a ceiling on the loan rate will cause total lending and the deposit rate to both fall, but it provides no indication how that reduced supply of credit will be distributed among borrowers.

Chapter II explains how an interest rate ceiling will affect the loan market when bank credit instead has the features of a nonhomogeneous good. Both the aggregate and distributive effects of a ceiling are shown to depend on the relative importance of default risk and of those administrative costs which vary with the quantity of loans rather than the volume of credit. If there exist a risk of default and diminishing marginal returns to investment but administrative costs do not depend on the quantity of loans, the imposition of a ceiling will cause a decrease in the size of each loan and in total lending. Also, all firms will continue to receive credit in the new equilibrium, unless the ceiling is so low that banks are compelled to shut down completely. However, if administrative costs depend in large part on the quantity of loans, and if the regulatory authorities do not allow banks to evade the ceiling by charging borrowers special fees to pay for these costs, total lending may increase as a result of the ceiling. Furthermore, it need no longer be the case that all firms within a given class receive credit. If the ceiling lies below a critical level, some firms will continue to receive credit while other, identical firms are denied loans altogether; thus, rationing of the second type will occur.

The last result merits some explanation because it suggests the conditions that must be met if the second type of rationing is to occur in unrestricted markets. In the situation analyzed in the first chapter, a bank's expected revenues from a loan increase with the interest rate on the loan until default becomes certain. It is because of this property that an equilibrium cannot occur in which some firms are able to obtain loans while other, identical firms which would strictly prefer to receive credit at the same terms are rejected: any firm without credit would be willing to pay a slightly higher interest rate than banks were currently charging to obtain a loan, and banks would be happy to make loans at that higher interest rate since their expected profits would be increased.

When there is a ceiling on the loan rate, a firm which has not received credit and which would be willing to pay a higher interest rate to obtain a loan will be prevented from doing so by the ceiling. However, if a bank could earn higher expected profits by charging the same interest rate and reducing the size of the loan, a firm will still be able to obtain credit by offering to take a somewhat smaller loan than banks are currently granting. Thus, an interest rate ceiling will not lead to rationing of the second type unless there is also some indivisibility in the lending process which establishes a minimum loan size below which banks are unable to break even. Such an indivisibility will exist if the cost to the bank of administering an additional loan is independent of the size of the loan, as assumed in Chapter II, or if the marginal returns to investment are at first increasing and then decreasing, i.e. if there is lumpiness in the investment project itself.

In the last chapter of this study it is shown that moral hazard may perform essentially the same role as a ceiling on the loan rate in inducing the second type of rationing. A number of authors, beginning with Fama and Miller [6,pp. 179-180], have observed that a borrower who enjoys limited liability will have an incentive to increase the riskiness of his investment project: because a fixed amount is due at the end of the period, the borrower receives all of the gain from exceptionally high outcomes, but because he enjoys limited liability, he suffers none of the losses from exceptionally low outcomes. As a result, he will benefit at the expense of the lender if he can alter the characteristics of his investment project in such a way as to increase the probability of both very low and very high outcomes. In fact, as Jensen and Meckling [9] and Galai and Masulis [7] have both observed, the borrower may well prefer a project with greater risk to one with a higher expected outcome.

In some cases the lender may find it possible to specify all relevant characteristics of the borrower's investment project in the loan contract and enforce such agreements by monitoring the borrower's behavior. However, if this cannot be done, the lender will obviously want to take into account the effect that the terms of a loan will have on the borrower's project choice. In Chapter III it is assumed that the borrower can alter the characteristics of the project in a way which increases the probability of both very low and very high outcomes, but that after some point he can achieve further increases in risk only at a sacrifice in total expected income from the project. In these circumstances, a borrower who is interested in maximizing expected profits will generally refrain from choosing the riskiest project possible. However, an increase in the interest rate on the loan will affect his project choice in much the same way that an increase in insurance coverage will influence a policyholder's level of care in avoiding illness or accident. In particular, because the borrower will be less vulnerable to low outcomes, he will be more willing to gambe on high outcomes, even if this entails a reduction in the total expected outcome of the project.

The change in project characteristics caused by an increase in the loan rate will have an adverse indirect effect on the lender's expected revenues which may be sufficiently strong to offset the favorable direct effect of an increase in the amount due. If this is the case, if there also exists some indivisibility which makes it impossible for the lender to earn higher expected profits by decreasing the size of the loan, and if firms' owners have sufficiently few resources of their own that they are still better off borrowing at the prevailing terms than going it alone, credit rationing of the second type may occur. Just as the effects of a loan rate ceiling on the distribution of credit can be compared to the effects of a minimum wage on employments, so can the phenomenon described here be related to labor market theories such as the "efficiency wage" model, which attributes unemployment in less developed countries to employers' unwillingness to hire a worker at a low wage because the level of consumption he could afford would be so low as to significantly affect his productivity [12][16].

Chapter III establishes general conditions under which increases in the loan rate will lead the borrower to increase the risk of his project, explains how this can lead to the second type of rationing in the extreme case in which the size of each investment project is fixed, and employs a specific example involving putty-clay investment to show that this type of rationing can also occur if project size is variable but banks' administrative costs of lending are to some extent independent of the size of the loan. If such rationing does occur, a restrictive monetary policy will have no effect on the equilibrium loan terms for the rationed class but will cause banks to make even fewer loans. Thus, as claimed by the availability doctrine, monetary policy may have a significant impact on investment even if firms' demand for investment is relatively insensitive to changes in the expected cost of borrowing. In addition, the failure of some firms to receive credit may involve an inefficient allocation of resources, in the sense that the total expected return to investment could be increased by distributing the same volume of credit more evenly among potential borrowers. As noted above, these are two implications which the first type of rationing does not have.

Since completing this study, I have come to realize that the type of moral hazard examined in Chapter III is but one member of a broader class of loan market imperfections which share certain important properties. When any one of these imperfections is present, an increase in the interest rate on a loan will cause the joint expected return to borrower and lender to fall, and will have an adverse indirect effect on the lender's expected revenues which may outweigh the favorable direct effect of the increase in the total amount due.

One such imperfection arises from the fact that the lender may have to incur liquidation, collection and recovery costs if the outcome of the investment project is insufficient to repay the loan and the borrower is forced to default. As observed by Miller in his early paper on credit rationing [11] and more recently by Barro [2], an increase in the loan rate raises the probability of default and increases the expected value of these bankruptcy costs. Thus, given any loan size, increases in the loan rate will reduce the total expected return to the project and after some point may cause the lender's expected income to fall.

A second type of loan market imperfection with similar properties was first noted by Myers [13], and arises when the outcome of the investment project depends both on some "state of nature" which is realized at a later date and on the amount of additional resources that the firm's owners or managers are willing to contribute to the firm after that state is realized but before the loan becomes due. In Myers' treatment, these resources consist of new capital required to exercise "investment options" that would otherwise expire. Another possibility, however, is that the firm is owned and managed by a few individuals who can vary the amount of effort they expend on behalf of the firm or the amount of perquisites they consume, without detection by the lender.

Since the owners of the firm receive only that part of the project outcome which remains after repaying the loan, they will either contribute the same amount of new resources as if they received the entire project outcome and repay the loan in full, or they will contribute no new resources and default. Since the owners will choose the latter course whenever the amount left over after paying back the loan would be less than the opportunity cost of the new resources, an increase in the total amount due on the loan makes it more likely that they will default and that a reduction in the potential value of the firm's assets will occur. Thus, as before, increases in the loan rate will cause the joint expected return to borrower and lender to fall and may even fail to increase the expected revenues of the lender. This phenomenon involves a moral hazard problem, but of a different kind than considered in Chapter III. The analogy in this case is not to the insurance policyholder's disincentive to exercise care in avoiding accident or illness, but rather to his incentive to order excessive medical treatment or repairs for property damage if the accident or illness occurs, because he pays only part of the cost. Indeed, the individual whose insurance policy contains a deductible but no coinsurance will make the same type of all-or-nothing choice when he experiences an accident: either he will not make a claim and obtain the same amount of treatment he would if he had to pay the full cost himself, or he will make a claim and obtain as much treatment as he desires at a zero price [14]. A reduction in the size of the deductible will thus have the same effect on this decision as an increase in the loan rate will have on the owners' decision to contribute new resources to the firm in the event that the state of nature is unfavorable.

In recent work I have shown that these three imperfections--the incentive for the borrower to choose a relatively risky project, the existence of bankruptcy costs, and the disincentive for owners to contribute new resources when default is imminent--can all be modelled in the same way and will have identical implications for the volume and distribution of credit and the efficiency of resource allocation. One such implication is that credit may be rationed, as explained in Chapter III. Another is that firms which are relatively unaffected by the three imperfections or which have relatively large amounts of collateral to offer will tend to receive the greatest amounts of credit, even if no firm is denied a loan. Finally, when one of the imperfections is present, it will generally be possible to increase the total social expected return to lending above that which prevails in the market equilibrium, by reducing the rate of interest, increasing the size of each loan, and if credit is rationed in the second sense, granting a larger number of loans. These and other aspects of the three imperfections are explored in detail in [10].

Each of the three imperfections involves a deadweight loss, compared to the situation in which the owners of the investment opportunity are able to finance the project entirely out of their own wealth. In many instances the loss in question could be avoided or reduced if the firm used some other means than fixed payment debt to raise funds. Suppose for example that both the owners of the firm and the lender were risk-neutral and that the former promised the latter a percentage of the project outcome rather than a fixed amount at the end of the period. Then in the situation described in Chapter III, it would always be in the interest of the owners to choose that project with the highest expected outcome, and the conflict of interest between the two parties would not arise.

One reason that borrowers and lenders may nevertheless continue to rely on fixed-payment debt is that other methods of financing also involve deadweight losses. For instance, as Jensen and Meckling have observed [9], issuing equity to an outside party will encourage the owner-manager of a firm to continually exert less effort and consume greater perquisites than would be jointly optimal, because he will receive only a fraction of the marginal return to his effort and pay for only a fraction of the cost of his perquisites. Jensen and Meckling neglected to point out that fixed-payment debt could have exactly the same effect by reducing the owner-manager's share of the marginal expected return to his effort or of the marginal expected cost of his perquisites. However, there is good reason to believe that debt will have a smaller distortionary impact than outside equity on those decisions which must be made by the owner-manager before he knows what the outcome of the project will be.

Debt may also be preferred to outside equity if effort, consumption of perquisites, and related aspects of managerial behavior can be verified by the outside party, but only at some cost. Suppose for example that the outside party can by incurring this cost detect and recover any resources which have been diverted by the owner-manager to his own uses during the period. If a debt contract is used to finance the investment, and if the owner-manager believes that the lender will exercise his right to take over the firm's assets in the event of default, this monitoring and recovery cost will have to be incurred only in those states of nature in which the true project outcome is insufficient to repay the loan. With an equity or profit-sharing contract, however, the owner-manager will always have an incentive to understate the profits from the venture, so the monitoring cost will have to be incurred in all states for the outside party to be sure that he is not a victim of "creative accounting" or outright fraud.

Since each possible method of financing investment is likely to have adverse incentive effects of some kind, it is unlikely that one method will always dominate the others. Also, the fact of the matter is that in many countries such as the U.S., depository institutions are prohibited from purchasing equity and are required to invest only in assets which promise a fixed payment. In my view, this makes it worthwhile to study the behavior of the market for bank loans in the presence of imperfections such as moral hazard and bankruptcy costs, even if the adverse effects of those particular imperfections could be avoided by using some means other than fixed-payment debt to finance investment. This is the approach underlying Chapter III, which focuses on one aspect of loan market behavior, the distribution of credit among borrowers with identical characteristics. The alternative is to investigate in a systematic way the circumstances in which one type of contract will be preferred to another, in the sense of yielding a smaller total deadweight loss from all sources. Although this has not been attempted in the present study, it is worth pursuing.

New Haven
July 1979

References

[1] Anderson, Paul and Ostas, James, "Private Credit Rationing," New England Economic Review, May/June 1977

[2] Barro, Robert, "The Loan Market, Collateral, and Rates of Interest," Journal of Money, Credit, and Banking, November 1976, Volume 8

[3] Baltensperger, Ernst, "The Borrower-Lender Relationship, Competitive Equilibrium and the Theory of Hedonic Prices," American Economic Review, June 1976, Volume 66

[4] ________, "Credit Rationing: Issues and Questions," Journal of Money, Credit, and Banking, May 1978, Volume 10

[5] De Leeuw, Frank and Gramlich, Edward, "The Channels of Monetary Policy," Federal Reserve Bulletin, June 1969, Volume 55

[6] Fama, Eugene and Miller, Merton, The Theory of Finance (Hinsdale, Ill., Dryden Press, 1972)

[7] Galai, Dan and Masulis, Ronald, "The Option Pricing Model and the Risk Factor of Stock," Journal of Financial Economics, January/March 1976, Volume 3

[8] Jaffee, Dwight, Credit Rationing and the Commercial Loan Market (New York, John Wiley and Sons, 1971)

[9] Jensen, Michael and Meckling, William, "Theory of the Firm: Managerial Behavior, Agency Costs and Ownership Structure," Journal of Financial Economics, 1976, Volume 3

[10] Keeton, William, "Moral Hazard, Bankruptcy Costs and Credit Rationing in Competitive Loan Markets," unpublished paper, June 1979

[11] Miller, Merton, "Credit Risk and Credit Rationing: Further Comment," Quarterly Journal of Economics, August 1962, Volume 76

[12] Mirlees, James, "A Pure Theory of Underdeveloped Economies," in Reynolds, Lloyd (ed.), Agriculture in Economic Development (New Haven, Yale University Press, 1975)

[13] Myers, Stewart, "Determinants of Corporate Borrowing," Journal of Financial Economics, November 1977, Volume 5

[14] Pauly, Mark, "The Economics of Moral Hazard: Comment," American Economic Review, June 1968, Volume 58

[15] Stanford Research Institute, The Role of Risk Classifications in Property and Casualty Insurance, Supplement, (Menlo Park, Calif., Stanford Research Institute, 1976)

[16] Stiglitz, Joseph, "Alternative Theories of Wage Determination and Unemployment in L.D.C.'s: I. The Efficiency Wage Model," Cowles Foundation Discussion Paper No. 357, 1973

Abstract

Equilibrium Credit Rationing
by
William R. Keeton

Submitted to the Department of Economics in August, 1976 in partial fulfillment of the requirements for the degree of Doctor of Philosophy.

There are at least two senses in which banks can be said to "ration" credit to borrowers. According to the first definition, credit is rationed whenever a customer receives a loan of smaller size than he would desire at the interest rate quoted by the bank. The second definition, on the other hand, applies when the total number of loans demanded exceeds the total number of loans provided by banks, or more precisely, when some firms are able to obtain loans while other, identical firms are not. It has long been recognized that a ceiling on loan rates could lead to rationing in one or both of these senses. More recently, it has been suggested that the first type of rationing could occur if a monopolistic bank were required to charge a uniform loan rate to nonidentical customers. In Chapter I we give an alternative explanation of the first type of credit rationing which does not rely upon institutional constraints on the setting of loan rates and which does not assume monopoly power on the part of banks. It is shown that borrowers will generally fail to receive the amount of credit they desire at the prevailing loan rate whenever bank credit is a nonhomogeneous good. This condition will be met if (1) there exists a risk of default on each loan and marginal returns to investment are diminishing, or (2) the bank incurs costs of administration which depend on the number of loans that it makes rather than the volume of lending. The first factor tends to lead to a competitive equilibrium in which each borrower receives a smaller loan than he would desire at the quoted loan rate, and the second factor to an equilibrium in which each borrower receives a larger loan (and undertakes a larger investment project) than he would desire.

The particular type of rationing considered in Chapter I does not have certain implications which are often associated with credit rationing. For one thing, the existence of an excess demand for credit on the part of each borrower need have no tendency to enhance the effectiveness of monetary policy, as claimed by proponents of the availability doctrine. Also, the competitive equilibrium will allocate resources efficiently even though borrowers fail to receive the amount of credit they demand. The possibility that firms will not receive the amount of credit they demand at the equilibrium loan rate does, however, have important consequences for a different issue: the impact of interest rate ceilings on the market for bank loans. This question is considered in detail in Chapter II. Both the aggregate and distributive effects of a loan rate ceiling are seen to depend on the relative importance of default risk and administrative costs. If there exists a risk of default but no cost of administration, the imposition of a ceiling will cause a decrease in the size of each loan and in total lending. In the new equilibrium all firms will continue to receive credit, unless the ceiling is so low that banks are forced to shut down altogether. Introducing costs of administration which depend on the number of loans made by banks alters both these conclusions. In the presence of such costs, the possibility arises that the ceiling will lead to an increase in total lending. Furthermore, it need no longer be true that all firms receive credit in the postceiling equilibrium: if the ceiling lies below a critical level, credit will be rationed in the second sense defined above.

In Chapter III we show that credit rationing in the second sense can also occur in the absence of a ceiling on the loan rate, provided there is "moral hazard" in the lending process. This situation will arise if (1) the bank is unable to exercise direct control over certain characteristics of the borrower's investment project by specifying them in the loan contract; (2) by altering those characteristics the borrower can increase the riskiness of the project outcome, in the sense of shifting probability density from the center of the distribution to the tails; and (3) after some point further increases in risk can be achieved only at a sacrifice in the total expected income from the project. Under these conditions, increases in the loan rate will cause a borrower interested in maximizing expected profits to alter the characteristics of his investment project in such a way as to increase the risk of the project and reduce the total expected outcome. Such a change in project characteristics will tend to reduce the bank's expected revenues from a loan, and if this effect is sufficiently strong it may offset the increase in the total amount due from the borrower. If so, any firm which has not received a loan will find that it cannot obtain one by offering to pay a higher rate of interest than banks are currently charging. This possibility has two important implications. First, by affecting the number of firms which are able to obtain loans, an easing or tightening of monetary policy can have a significant impact on total lending and investment even if the size of individual investment projects is completely unresponsive to changes in the cost of borrowing. Second, if some firms are receiving credit in equilibrium while other firms with identical investment projects are not, the allocation of resources may be inefficient, in the sense that the net expected return from investment could be increased by distributing the same volume of credit more evenly among firms. As already noted, the first type of rationing, in which borrowers are able to obtain credit but receive smaller loans than they desire, has neither of these implications.

Thesis Supervisor: Peter A. Diamond
Title: Professor of Economics

Acknowledgements

I am indebted to the members of my thesis committee, Professors Peter Diamond and Stanley Fischer, for their criticisms, suggestions, and encouragement. Professor Richard Eckaus introduced me to the subject of credit rationing and stimulated my interest in it. For discussions on many of the issues considered in this thesis, I am grateful also to Dennis Carlton, Mark Kuperberg, and Evan Kwerel. Evan also read and commented upon substantial portions of the manuscript. Barbara Feldstein is responsible for the excellent typing job. Financial assistance was provided by the National Science Foundation and the Federal Deposit Insurance Corporation.

Cambridge
August 1976

LIST OF SYMBOLS

C	bank's total cost of administering loans
h	opportunity rate or deposit rate
L	loan size
L_T	total volume of lending by all banks
m	number of loans made by bank
M	total number of firms with investment projects
r	loan rate
S	total number of firms receiving credit
x	outcome of investment project
x_m	minimum possible value of x
x_M	maximum possible value of x
y	random variable on which outcome of investment project depends
γ	project characteristic
Ω	function relating h to total volume of lending
ψ	function relating x to random variable y
μ_R	bank's expected revenues from loan
u	borrower's expected profits from loan
μ_x	expected outcome of investment project
δ	bank's expected profits per loan, excluding administrative costs
π	bank's total expected profits
ϕ	bank's iso-profit locus
θ	borrower's iso-profit locus
z	total amount due on loan

TABLE OF CONTENTS

CHAPTER II. AN ANALYSIS OF LOAN RATE CEILINGS

CHAPTER III. MORAL HAZARD AND EQUILIBRIUM CREDIT RATIONING

CHAPTER I. COMPETITIVE MARKETS FOR NONHOMOGENEOUS GOODS: AN APPLICATION TO THE THEORY OF CREDIT RATIONING

Introduction

In general, there are at least two senses in which banks can be said to "ration" credit to borrowers. According to the first definition, credit is rationed whenever a customer receives a loan of smaller size than he would desire at the interest rate quoted by the bank. The second definition, on the other hand, applies when the total number of loans demanded exceeds the total number of loans provided by banks, or more precisely, when some firms are able to obtain loans while other, identical firms are not. The present chapter has two objectives: (1) to develop a model of a purely competitive market for bank loans, and (2) to demonstrate that the first type of credit rationing may occur in such a market. The approach taken here is closely related to Rosen's analysis of product differentiation under pure competition [4] and to the theory of spatial equilibrium: We shall argue that bank loans are nonhomogeneous goods and that competitive equilibrium in the loan market is determined in much that same way as in other markets for differentiated goods.

There has been a great deal of interest among economists in the circumstances, if any, in which banks would choose to ration credit.[1] It has long been recognized that a ceiling on loan rates could lead to rationing in one or both of the senses defined above. Recently a different kind of institutional constraint on the setting of loan rates has been suggested as a possible cause of the first type of rationing. It has been argued by Jaffee and Modigliani [3], and in a somewhat different context by Eckaus [1], that a monopolistic bank might choose to provide some of its customers with smaller loans than they desired if the bank were required by law or social convention to charge a uniform rate to nonidentical borrowers. In particular, the bank might ration that group of customers which would have been charged the highest interest rate had the bank been free to discriminate among borrowers.

In this chapter we will give an alternative explanation of the first type of credit rationing which does not rely upon institutional constraints on the setting of loan rates and which does not assume monopoly power on the part of banks. The principal condition is that bank credit be a nonhomogeneous good. This requires that a bank not be indifferent to the manner in which its credit is distributed among borrowers, even when those borrowers are identical. In the first section of the chapter we consider the implications of treating bank credit as a nonhomogeneous good, without attempting to explain what features of the lending process make it appropriate to do so. In the second section, we develop a model of the market for bank loans which explicitly incorporates some of those features -- most importantly, the existence of default risk -- and show that the properties of a competitive equilibrium are much the same as in the simpler model of the first section. In neither case, it should be noted, does the existence of rationing entail any inefficiency in the allocation of resources.

We begin in Section I. A. by considering a competitive market for a good with a single, measurable characteristic. It is assumed initially that all firms are identical and that all consumers are identical. Each consumer purchases only one unit of the good. His utility depends on the characteristic and on the price of the good. We define the implicit price of the characteristic as the price of the good divided by the amount of the characteristic, and derive a function indicating the amount of characteristic the consumer would demand if he could purchase it at a constant implicit price. This demand for the characteristic can also be interpreted as the "brand" of the good the consumer would select if he faced a price function for the good which was linear in the characteristic.

In equilibrium the terms offered by each firm will yield the same level of utility to a representative consumer, and each firm will have chosen the price, number of units produced, and characteristic of the good so as to maximize total profits given that level of utility. If a firm's costs depend only on the total amount of the characteristic contained in all units produced, the good can be treated as homogeneous. In this case the good will possess precisely that amount of the characteristic which the consumer demands at the equilibrium implicit price. However, if the firm's costs do not take this form -- e.g. if the cost of producing one unit of the good is a strictly convex function of the amount of the characteristic -- the good may possess less of the characteristic than the consumer would desire at the equilibrium implicit price. At the end of Section I. A. we show that these results are not affected if the assumption of identical consumers is relaxed.

In Section I. B. we apply the above framework to the case of bank loans. Each bank is assumed to have total revenues equal to the loan rate times the volume of lending, and total costs which depend both on the number of loans and on the size of each loan. In this case the size of a loan may be regarded as the characteristic and the loan rate as the implicit price of the characteristic. Thus, if a bank's costs are not simply a function of the total volume of funds loaned -- e.g. if the cost of making each loan is a strictly convex function of the size of the loan -- each customer may receive a smaller loan than he demands at the equilibrium loan rate. We shall observe, however, that credit will not be rationed in the alternative sense that some firms receive loans while other, identical firms receive no credit at all. Finally, it will be noted that the Jaffee-Modigliani-Eckaus explanation of credit rationing -- that a monopolistic bank is required to charge a uniform rate to nonidentical customers -- also requires that bank loans be nonhomogeneous.

The model described above is unsatisfactory in one important respect. It enables us to determine certain properties of the market equilibrium, once we know how a bank's costs of lending depend on the number and size of its loans. But it provides little guidance as to why those costs might take one form rather than another. In Section II we present an alternative model which yields more concrete results. The principal difference between this model and the first lies in the treatment of default risk: whereas the first model simply includes such risks in the bank's cost of lending, the second explicitly takes into account the existence of uncertainty in the lending process.

The main features of the model are described in Section II. A. Firms are assumed to have identical one-period investment projects which they can finance only by borrowing from banks. The outcome of an individual project is uncertain and for each possible "state of the world" will be an increasing, strictly concave function of the size of the investment. Since the firm has limited liability, a bank's revenues from a loan will equal the lesser of two amounts: the amount due on the loan (i.e. the principal and interest) and the total income generated by the project. The bank's costs include the opportunity cost of making loans -- e.g. the return foregone on alternative, riskless investments or the interest which must be paid to attract deposits. In addition the bank may incur certain administrative costs, or "costs of intermediation." Each bank seeks to maximize its total expected profits, while each borrower seeks to maximize the expected surplus of the income from the project over the principal and interest on the loan.

An equilibrium exists when no bank has an incentive to alter either the terms at which it grants loans or the number of firms to which it lends. In making this determination, the individual bank must take into account the relationship of its terms to those prevailing on the market. In particular, the bank cannot expect to retain its customers if it establishes terms less favorable to the borrower than those being offered by its competitors. The properties of such an equilibrium are discussed informally in Section II. B. and derived formally in Section II. C. An important feature of the equilibrium is that a borrower's demand for credit at the prevailing loan rate will not in general equal the size of the loan he receives. If the only cost to the bank of making a loan is the interest paid on deposits, each firm will receive less credit than it desires at the equilibrium loan rate -- i.e. the equilibrium will be characterized by the first type of rationing. However, if the bank must also incur certain administrative costs which depend only on the number of loans, the firm's demand for credit at the equilibrium loan rate may either exceed or fall short of the size of the loan it actually receives. In any event, credit will not be rationed in the second sense; that is, all firms will be able to obtain loans.

In Section II. D. we consider how the market equilibrium will be affected by monetary policy and by shifts in the risk or productivity of investment projects. Section II. E. relaxes the assumption that all projects are identical, and Section II. F. presents a specific example which illustrates the above results. Finally, in Section III, we summarize the major findings of the chapter.

I. The market for bank loans viewed as a market for a nonhomogeneous good

A. A model of a competitive market for a nonhomogeneous good

1. In this section we consider a competitive market for a particular kind of nonhomogeneous good. We assume that each consumer purchases one unit of the good and that the utility derived from the good depends on some measurable characteristic w. The good in question might be automobiles or houses and the characteristic some measure of size (e.g. the weight of the automobile or the floor space of the house).

It is assumed that all consumers are identical and that the utility of each individual is $U(y-p,w)$ where p is the price of the good and y is income. The utility function U is strictly quasi-concave and strictly increasing in both its arguments. Define p_w to equal p/w, the implicit price of the characteristic w. Then U can be expressed as a function $\mathcal{U}(p_w,w)$. Since U is strictly decreasing in p_w, there exists a function $\theta(w,U)$ such that $\mathcal{U}[\theta(w,U),w] = U$. The function $\theta(w,U)$ indicates that value of p_w such that a good of characteristic w selling at price $p = p_w w$ yields utility U. Given $\theta(w,U)$ we can trace out a family of iso-utility curves in p_w-w space, as in Figure 1. Since $\partial\mathcal{U}/\partial p_w < 0$, lower curves represent higher levels of utility for the consumer.

Let $D(p_w)$ be the value of w which maximizes $\mathcal{U}(p_w,w)$ given p_w, i.e. the value of w such that $\partial\mathcal{U}/\partial w = 0$. This value will be unique for each p_w, since the strict quasi-concavity of $U(y-p,w)$ implies $\partial^2\mathcal{U}/\partial w^2 < 0$.

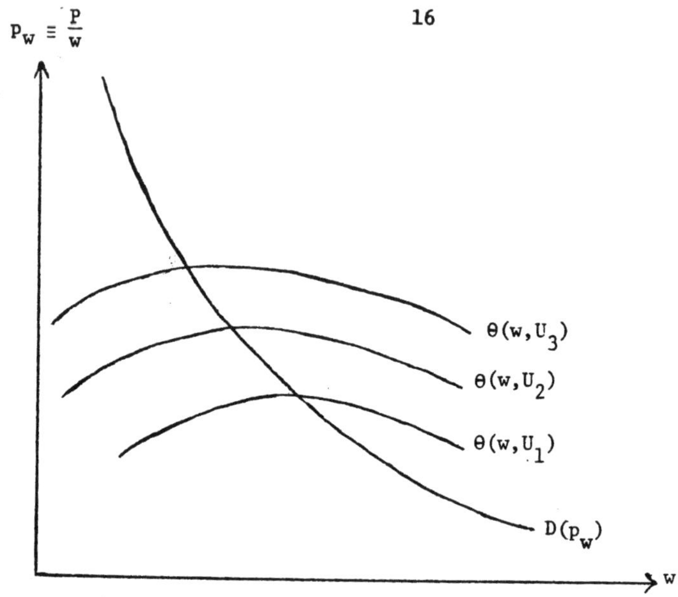

$U_1 > U_2 > U_3$

Figure 1

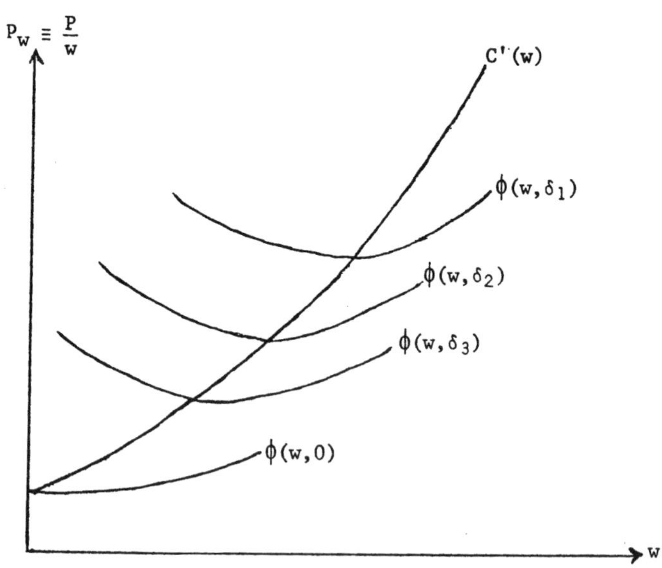

$\delta_1 > \delta_2 > \delta_3$

Figure 2

Also, $\frac{\partial\theta}{\partial w} = -\frac{\partial U/\partial w}{\partial U/\partial p_w} \gtrless 0$ as $w \lesseqgtr D(p_w)$: each iso-utility curve is positively sloped to the left of the point of intersection with the locus $D(p_w)$ and negatively sloped to the right of that point. For convenience we shall assume that the characteristic w is not an inferior good, so that $D'(p_w) < 0$.

It is assumed that all firms producing the good have the same cost function $C(m,w)$, where m is the number of units of the good produced.[2] Let us suppose first that $C(m,w) = mC(w)$ with $C(0) = 0$, $C' > 0$, and $C'' > 0$. Then the profits of the firm are $\pi = mp - mC(w) = m[p_w w - C(w)]$. Define δ to equal $p_w w - C(w)$, the firm's profits from each unit of the good produced. It is clear that δ can be expressed as a function of p_w and w and that $\frac{\partial\delta(p_w,w)}{\partial p_w} > 0$. It follows that a function $\phi(w,\delta)$ can be defined such that $\delta[\phi(w,\delta),w] = \delta$; $\phi(w,\delta)$ indicates that value of p_w for which $p_w w - C(w) = \delta$. Given this function, it is possible to draw a family of curves in p_w-w space along which profits per unit δ are constant (see Figure 2). It is easily verified that each such iso-profit curve is downward sloping before the point of intersection with the marginal cost curve $C'(w)$ and upward sloping beyond that point, and that higher curves correspond to higher values of δ. Also, the zero iso-profit curve $\phi(w,0)$ has positive slope throughout.

We may now consider the conditions for market equilibrium. Since consumers are identical, equilibrium can exist only if all combinations of p and w offered by firms yield the same level of utility $\bar{U}$ for a representative consumer. If this condition were not met, those firms offering less favorable terms would lose all their customers. Now, at a given level of U, each firm will clearly choose that combination of p and w (or equivalently, of p_w and w) which maximizes its profits δ from each unit of the good produced; that is, each firm will choose that point on the consumer iso-utility curve $\theta(w,U)$ at which $\delta(p_w,w)$ is maximized. But total profits of the firm are homogeneous of degree one in the number of units produced, i.e. $\pi = m\delta(p_w,w)$. Thus if $\underset{w}{\text{Max}}\ \delta[\theta(w,U),w]$ is positive at a given U, each firm will have an incentive to offer slightly more favorable terms to customers in order to capture the entire market. It follows that equilibrium can exist only if p_w and w are such that $0 = \underset{p_w,w}{\text{Max}}\ \delta(p_w,w)$ subject to $p_w = \theta[w,\mathcal{U}(p_w,w)]$: in equilibrium each firm will have chosen a point (p_w^*,w^*) on the zero iso-profit curve $\phi(w,0)$ at which the consumer's utility $U = \mathcal{U}(p_w,w)$ is maximized (see Figure 3).

It is not difficult to see that in equilibrium the good will possess less of the characteristic w than would maximize the consumer's utility at the implicit price p_w, i.e. that $w^* < D(p_w^*)$. For $\mathcal{U}(p_w,w)$ to attain a maximum along $\phi(w,0)$ at (p_w^*,w^*), it is necessary that $\frac{d\mathcal{U}[\phi(w,0),w]}{dw} = \frac{\partial \mathcal{U}}{\partial p_w}\phi_w(w,0) + \frac{\partial \mathcal{U}}{\partial w} = 0$ at that point. But since $\partial \mathcal{U}/\partial p_w < 0$ and $\phi_w(w,0) > 0$, this implies $\partial \mathcal{U}/\partial w > 0$ and thus $w^* < D(p_w^*)$.

2. We have assumed above that the good can be produced with constant returns to scale, in the sense that costs are homogeneous of degree one in the number of units. As a result, competition among firms will drive profits to zero even in the absence of free entry. Let us now suppose that some portion of the firm's cost of production depends only on the total number of units produced, and that marginal costs are

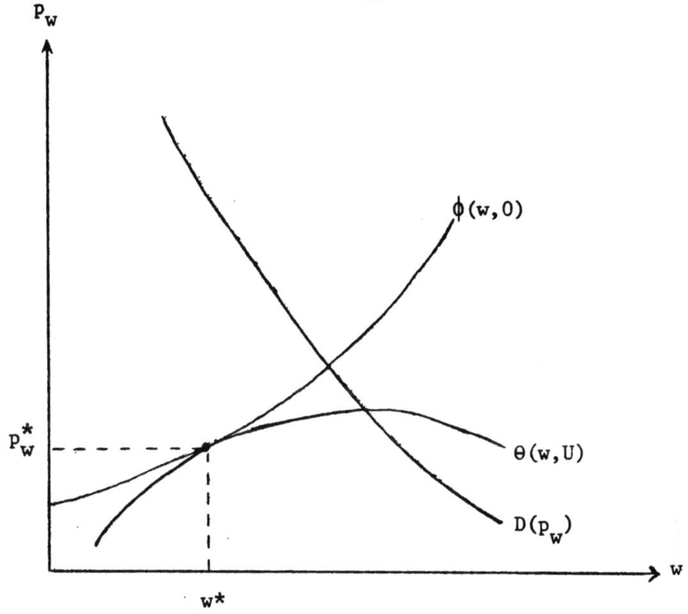

Figure 3

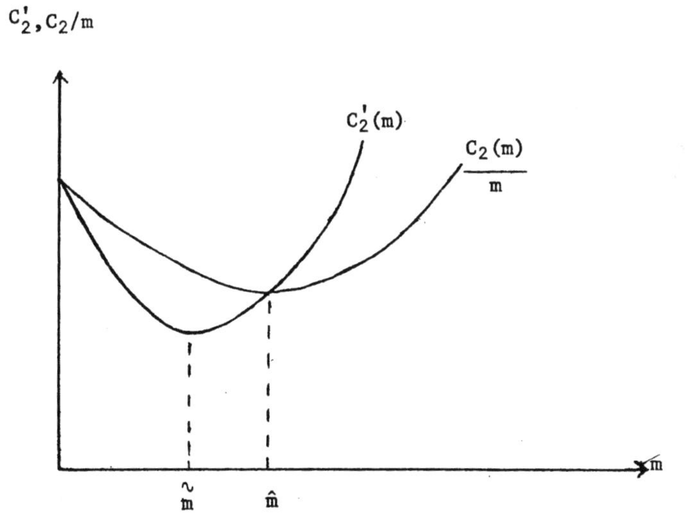

Figure 4

strictly increasing after some point. In contrast to the case analyzed above, the equilibrium size of the firm will be determinate. Also, if entry to the industry is restricted, competition among firms will not force profits to zero. We shall see, however, that whether or not free entry exists, the good may in equilibrium possess less of the characteristic w than would maximize the consumer's utility at the equilibrium value of p_w.

Let all firms have the cost function $C(m,w) = mC_1(w) + C_2(m)$. We treat m as perfectly divisible and assume $C_1' > 0$, $C_1'' > 0$, $C_2' > 0$, $C_2'' < 0$ for $m < \tilde{m}$, and $C_2'' > 0$ for $m > \tilde{m}$. As shown in Figure 4, the average cost curve $\frac{C_2(m)}{m}$ will be U-shaped, attaining a minimum at a value of m greater than $\tilde{m}$.

To begin with, we suppose that the number of firms in the industry is fixed and equal to N. It is assumed that N is sufficiently large that each firm behaves as a perfect competitor. In particular, each firm believes that it can sell as many units of the good as it wants if it chooses a combination of p and w which is no less favorable to the consumer than the combinations of p and w being offered by other firms. As before, the terms offered by different firms in equilibrium must leave consumers equally well off -- i.e. the various combinations of p and w chosen by firms must yield the same level of utility U for a representative consumer. In assuming perfect competition we suppose that each firm chooses p, w, and m so as to maximize its total profits at the prevailing level of U. The equilibrium U is then determined by the requirement that mN, the total supply of the good, equal M, the number of consumers.

In the case in which $C(m,w) = mC(w)$, the firm's total profits were homogeneous of degree one in the number of units produced. Thus, as long as profits per unit were positive the firm would have an incentive to offer slightly more favorable terms in order to attract more customers. However, with increasing marginal costs of producing units of the good (i.e. $C_2''(m) > 0$), the firm's total profits will attain a maximum at some finite number of units given any p and w. Thus, in the equilibrium defined in the previous paragraph, no firm would have an incentive to offer a more favorable combination of p and w even if its profits per unit were positive.

Total profits of the firm are $\pi = m[p_w w - C_1(w)] - C_2(m) = m\delta - C_2(m)$, where as before $p_w = p/w$ and $\delta = p - C_1(w)$. Let $\hat{m}$ be value of m at which the average cost $\frac{C_2(m)}{m}$ attains a minimum. Then given δ the optimal number of units for the firm to produce will be zero if $\delta < \frac{C_2(\hat{m})}{\hat{m}}$, since in this case $m\delta < C_2(m)$ for all positive m. If on the other hand δ exceeds $\frac{C_2(\hat{m})}{\hat{m}}$, the firm will choose that $m > \hat{m}$ for which $\delta = C_2'(m)$. Since $C_2''(m) > 0$ for all $m > \tilde{m}$, the first-order condition $\delta = C_2'(m)$ determines a function $m(\delta)$ with $dm/d\delta > 0$. Thus, $\pi = m(\delta)\delta - C_2[m(\delta)]$ and $d\pi/d\delta = m + (\delta - C_2')\, dm/d\delta = m > 0$: the firm's total profits are strictly increasing in δ for all $\delta > \frac{C_2(\hat{m})}{\hat{m}}$.

Since $\partial\delta/\partial p_w > 0$ and $d\pi/d\delta > 0$ for $\delta > \frac{C_2(\hat{m})}{\hat{m}}$, there will exist a function $\lambda(w,\pi)$ such that $p_w = \lambda(w,\pi)$ and $m = m[\delta(p_w,w)]$ imply $m\delta(p_w,w) - C_2(m) = \pi$. The function $\lambda(w,\pi)$ indicates that value of p_w such that the firm's total profits equal π when it chooses m optimally given p_w

and w. Given this function, it is possible to trace out a family of iso-profit curves in p_w-w space. Since π is a strictly increasing function of δ, this family of curves will coincide with the family of iso-profit curves $\phi(w,\delta)$ derived earlier. That is, the level of total profits will be constant along each iso-profit curve $\phi(w,\delta)$ and higher curves will represent higher values of π.

At a given level of consumer utility, the firm will choose that combination of p, w, and m (or equivalently, of p_w, w, and m) which maximizes total profits. In other words, the firm will choose that point on the iso-utility curve $\theta(w,U)$ at which π attains a maximum. It follows that the equilibrium combination of p_w and w will lie on the contract curve, i.e. at a point of tangency between an iso-profit curve and an iso-utility curve.

It is easily seen that the contract curve must lie between the schedules $C_1'(w)$ and $D(p_w)$ as shown in Figure 5. As we move up the curve, U falls and π and δ rise. Since $dm/d\delta > 0$ for $\pi > 0$, the quantity of the good supplied by each firm therefore increases monotonically above the point of intersection with the zero iso-profit curve $\lambda(w,0)$. Equilibrium exists at that point on the contract curve at which $m = M/N$, i.e. at the point at which the total supply of the good equals the number of consumers in the market.[3] It is clear that this point need not lie on the schedule $D(p_w)$. In equilibrium the good may possess either more or less of the characteristic w than would maximize the consumer's utility at the implicit price p_w. In particular, if the ratio M/N of consumers to firms is sufficiently small, $D(p_w)$

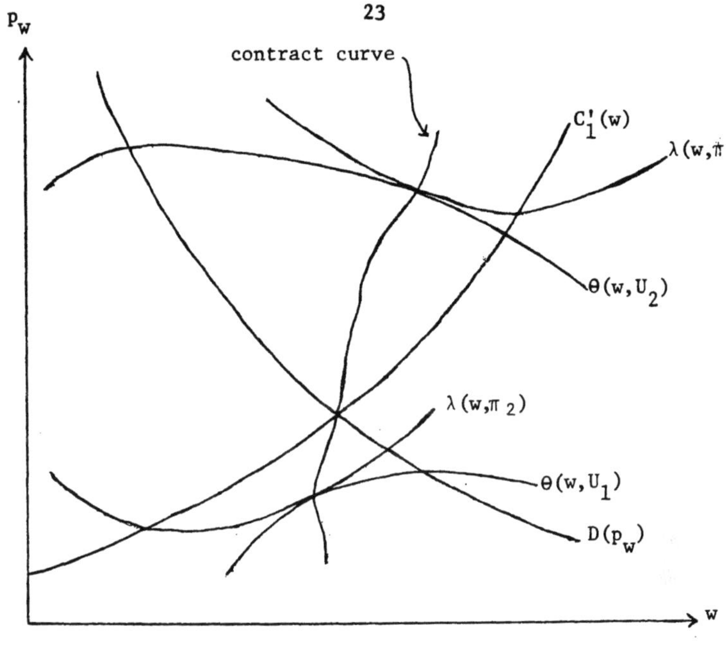

$U_1 > U_2$, $\pi_1 > \pi_2$

Figure 5

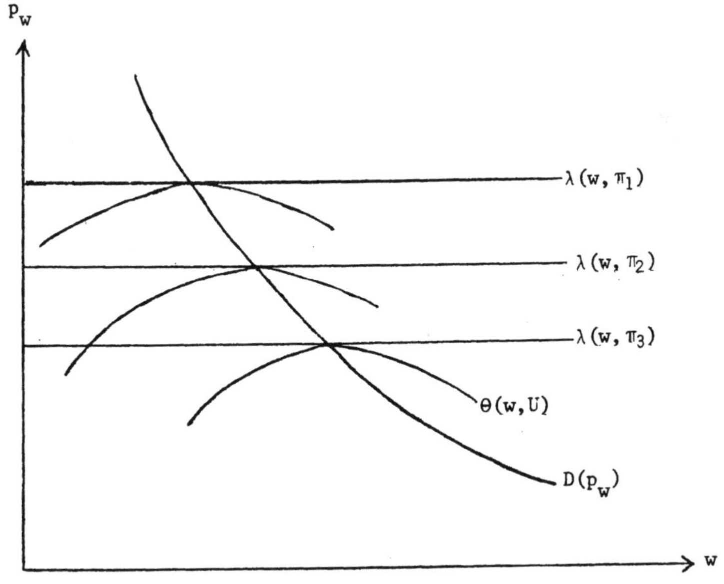

$\pi_1 > \pi_2 > \pi_3$

Figure 6

will exceed w.

Up to this point we have assumed that the number of firms in the industry is fixed. As a result, firms may earn positive profits in equilibrium. With free entry, however, firms will enter the industry until profits are driven to zero: a long-run equilibrium can exist only at that point on the contract curve at which $\pi = m\delta - C_2(m) = 0$. Each firm will operate at the minimum point on the average cost curve $\frac{C_2(m)}{m}$, producing $\hat{m}$ units of the good. The number of firms in the industry will thus equal $M/\hat{m}$. Furthermore, since the zero-profit point on the contract curve may lie above or below the point of intersection of the schedules $D(p_w)$ and $C_1'(w)$, w need not equal $D(p_w)$ in equilibrium. If the minimum average cost $\frac{C_2(\hat{m})}{\hat{m}}$ is sufficiently low, the equilibrium values of w and p_w will be such that $w < D(p_w)$, i.e. the good will possess less of the characteristic w than would maximize the consumer's utility at the implicit price p_w.

3. We now consider the case in which the good can be treated as homogeneous. Suppose that costs are a function only of the total amount of the characteristic w contained in all units produced by the firm. In particular, let the cost function of the firm be $C(m,w) = C(mw)$, with $C' > 0$, $C'' < 0$ for $mw < mw$, and $C'' > 0$ for $mw > mw$. For each p_w there will clearly exist a value of mw which maximizes $\pi = p_w mw - C(mw)$. Let $S(p_w)$ be that value. Then given any p_w and w, the firm's optimal m will be $S(p_w)/w$ which implies $\pi = p_w S(p_w) - C[S(p_w)]$. It follows that each iso-profit curve will be a horizontal line in p_w-w

space, with higher lines representing higher levels of total profits (see Figure 6).

It is clear that in this case the contract curve will coincide with the demand schedule $D(p_w)$. Now at any p_w and w, the firm will supply $S(p_w)/w$ units of the good. Thus, since $D'(p_w) < 0$ and $S'(p_w) > 0$, the number of units of the good supplied by the firm increases as we move up the demand curve. If the number of firms in the industry is fixed at N, the equilibrium combination of p_w and w will be found at that point on the demand curve at which $m = M/N$. If on the other hand entry is not restricted, equilibrium will occur at the zero-profit point on the demand curve, with all firms operating at minimum average cost $\frac{C(mw)}{mw}$. In either event, of course, $w = D(p_w)$ in equilibrium: the good possesses exactly that amount of the characteristic which maximizes the consumer's utility at the implicit price p_w.

In more general terms, a good can be treated as homogeneous whenever $\frac{\partial\pi(p_w,w)}{\partial w} = 0$ for all p_w and w, where π is the variable that the firm seeks to maximize and $\pi(p_w,w)$ is the value of π when m is chosen optimally given p_w and w.[4] When this condition is met, the iso-profit or iso-utility curves of the firm in p_w-w space will be horizontal, implying that the equilibrium point must lie on the demand schedule $D(p_w)$.

4. To conclude this section, let us relax the assumption that all consumers are identical. Following Rosen [4], we may suppose that tastes can be characterized by a parameter α and that the distribution of consumers over α is given by a continuous function $G(\alpha)$ with $0 \leq G(\alpha) \leq 1$.

Consider first the case in which $C(m,w) = mC(w)$ with $C' > 0$ and $C'' > 0$. Equilibrium requires that all combinations of p_w and w offered to members of a particular class of consumers yield the same level of utility $U_\alpha = U(p_w,w;\alpha)$. At any given value of U_α, a firm will offer that combination of p_w and w which maximizes profits per unit δ. But since total profits of the firm are homogeneous of degree one in the number of units produced, competition among firms will ensure that δ equals zero in equilibrium. It follows that the combination of p_w and w offered to class α in equilibrium must be a point of tangency between the zero iso-profit curve $\phi(w,0)$ and an iso-utility curve $\theta(w,U_\alpha)$. The set of all equilibrium combinations will consist of a segment of the curve $\phi(w,0)$. Furthermore, $D(p_w)$ will exceed w for each class of consumers.

Suppose alternatively that $C(m,w) = mC_1(w) + C_2(m)$, with $C_2' > 0$ and $C_2'' > 0$ for $m > \tilde{m}$. In equilibrium $\delta(p_w,w) = p_w w - C_1(w)$ must be the same for all classes of consumers. If this were not the case, firms would want to sell their entire output to that class of consumers for which $\delta(p_w,w)$ was highest. All equilibrium combinations of p_w and w will yield the same δ and therefore lie on the same iso-profit curve $\lambda(w,\pi)$. If entry is restricted, the equilibrium value of π will be that for which $mN = M$. In the absence of barriers to entry, equilibrium requires $\pi = 0$ and thus $\delta = \text{Min}\ \frac{C_2(m)}{m}$. In either case, the set of all equilibrium points will consist of a segment of the iso-profit curve $\lambda(w,\pi)$; each equilibrium point will be a point of tangency between the iso-profit curve and the iso-utility curve of a particular class of consumers.[5] It is easily seen that $D(p_w) \gtreqless w$ in equilibrium. Also, $D(p_w) > w$ may hold for some classes of consumers while $D(p_w) = w$ or $D(p_w) < w$ holds for others.

Finally, consider the case in which $C(m,w) = C(mw)$. As before, all equilibrium combinations of p_w and w must lie on the same iso-profit curve $\lambda(w,\pi)$. Also each equilibrium point will be a point of tangency between the iso-profit curve and the iso-utility curve $\theta(w,U_\alpha)$ of a particular class of consumers. We have seen, however, that the iso-profit curves have zero slope when $C(m,w) = C(mw)$. Thus, in equilibrium p_w will be the same for all consumers and $w = D(p_w)$ will hold for each class.

B. Implications for the theory of credit rationing

The phenomenon of credit rationing may be analyzed in terms of the model developed in the previous section. Let us suppose that there are M identical customers seeking bank loans, and that each customer can take out only one loan. In this section we shall not attempt to explain how the utility U of the customer depends on the terms of the loan. It is assumed, however, that there exists a function $\theta(L,U)$ which indicates the loan rate r at which the customer's utility from a loan of size L equals U. We assume also that the customer's iso-utility curves in r-L space exhibit the same properties as the iso-utility curves derived in Section I. A. Thus, a downward sloping demand curve D(r) can be defined indicating the customer's optimal loan size given r. Iso-utility curves are positively sloped to the left of that curve and negatively sloped to the right, and lower curves represent higher levels of utility for the customer.

Let the costs to the bank of making loans be C(m,L), where m is the number of loans and L the size of each loan, and assume that the bank's revenues from each loan are rL. Total profits are then $\pi = mrL - C(m,L)$. It should now be clear that bank loans are a special case of the nonhomogeneous good analyzed in Section I. A.; the size of the loan L corresponds to the characteristic w while the loan rate r corresponds to the implicit price p_w. Thus, if $C(m,L) = mC(L)$, with $C' > 0$ and $C'' > 0$, $L < D(r)$ in equilibrium: credit will be rationed, in the sense that each customer receives a smaller loan than would maximize his utility at the equilibrium loan rate. If on the other hand $C(m,L) = mC_1(L)$

$+ C_2(m)$, with marginal costs $C_2'(m)$ strictly increasing beyond some point, $L \gtreqless D(r)$ in equilibrium. With entry to the industry restricted, the customer's demand for credit will be more likely to exceed the size of the loan the larger is the ratio of banks to customers. In the absence of barriers to entry, $D(r) > L$ will be more likely to occur the smaller the minimum value of the average cost $\frac{C_2(m)}{m}$. Finally, if loan costs are a function only of the total volume of funds loaned-- i.e. if $C(m,L) = C(mL)$ -- the equilibrium loan size will always equal the customer's demand for credit. In any event, credit will not be rationed in the second sense that the total number of loans demanded exceeds the number of loans provided by banks, i.e. that some customers receive loans while other, identical customers receive no credit at all.

Jaffee and Modigliani and Eckaus pointed out that a bank might ration credit in the first sense if it exercised monopoly power and were required to charge a uniform rate to all its customers. Suppose, for example, that a monopolistic bank faces two nonidentical customers with demand schedules $D_1(r_1)$ and $D_2(r_2)$ respectively, and that the bank's loan costs are $C = C_1(L_1) + C_2(L_2)$. If required to charge the same rate to both customers, the bank will choose some loan rate r^* such that $r_1^* \leq r^* \leq r_2^*$, where r_1^* and r_2^* are the rates it would charge the two customers if it were free to discriminate between them. In this case it is entirely possible that the bank will maximize its profits by choosing an r^*, L_1^*, and L_2^* such that $D_1(r^*) = L_1^*$ and $D_2(r^*) > L_2^*$. It is interesting to note, however, that this explanation of credit rationing does not hold if the bank's loan costs depend only on the total volume of credit, i.e. if $C = C(L_1 + L_2)$. If loan costs are of this nature, the bank will behave exactly like a monopolist which produces a homogeneous good and is unable to discriminate among its customers, i.e. it will operate on its aggregate demand schedule. We thus see that the existence of credit rationing in the first sense depends in a crucial way on the nonhomogeneity of loans. Previous contributions to the literature on credit rationing do not seem to have recognized this point, stressing instead such factors as the existence of monopoly power on the part of banks or the presence of institutional constraints on the setting of loan rates.

Although the model discussed in this section provides some insights into the phenomenon of credit rationing, it is unsatisfactory in several important respects:

(1) No justification has been given for assuming that a borrower's utility depends on r and L in the same way that a consumer's utility depends on p_w and w. Why, for example, should there exist an optimal loan size which varies with the loan rate charged by the bank?

(2) It is not clear why each customer would borrow from only one bank, as we have assumed.

(3) No attempt has been made to explain the nature of the bank's loan costs. It is thus unclear why the marginal costs of lending would increase with the size of the loan. One possibility is that the cost of making a loan includes a "risk premium" associated with the possibility of default and that the size of the premium is a nonlinear function of the size of the loan. However, if the existence of uncertainty

is to be acknowledged, it should be modelled explicitly rather than subsumed under the concept of a risk premium.

(4) The model is not easily extended to deal with the case in which borrowers are not identical. When we relaxed the assumption of identical consumers at the end of Section I. A., we assumed that the firm's cost of production did not depend on the class of consumer that purchased the good. But if borrowers differ, it is unlikely that loan costs will be the same for one class of customers as for another: the costs of making a loan will be related in some way to the characteristics of the borrower.

In Section II we shall examine a more sophisticated model which is not subject to these difficulties. The major attraction of this model is that is explicitly takes into account the existence of uncertainty in the loan process. It will be seen that when default is possible and marginal returns to investment are diminishing, bank loans cannot be treated as homogeneous commodities. As a result, in competitive equilibrium the customer's demand for credit will generally not equal the size of the loan he receives.

II. The market for bank loans in the presence of uncertainty

A. General description of the model

Let us suppose that there are M identical firms seeking to finance one-period investment projects. We assume that firms can finance investment only by borrowing from banks, i.e. that firms cannot raise funds by issuing equity. The outcome x of an individual project is nonnegative and may be interpreted as the end-of-period value of the firm. This outcome is uncertain. In particular, it has a cumulative distribution function F(x,L), where L is the volume of bank credit obtained by the firm.

A bank receives the full principal and interest on a loan only if the outcome of the borrower's investment project is sufficiently high to repay the debt. When this is not the case, i.e. when the borrower defaults, the bank receives the entire outcome of the project. Its revenues from a loan may therefore be expressed as $R = \min\{x, (1+r)L\}$, where L is the size of the loan and r is the interest rate charged on the loan. For the moment we shall suppose that each firm can take out only one loan.[6] A bank's expected revenues from a loan are then

$$
\begin{aligned}
\mu_R(r,L) &= \int_{x_m}^{z} xF_x(x,L)\,dx + z\int_{z}^{x_M} F_x(x,L)\,dx \\
&= z - \int_{x_m}^{z} F(x,L)\,dx
\end{aligned}
\tag{1}
$$

where z is equal to (1+r)L, the principal and interest on the loan; x_M

is the maximum possible outcome of the customer's investment project; and x_m is the minimum possible outcome of the project. The borrower's profits from the investment project are simply x-R, the surplus of the project outcome over the debt repayment to the bank. Its expected profits are thus

$$(2) \quad u(r,L) = \int_{z}^{x_M} (x-z)F_x(x,L)dx$$

Finally, the total expected outcome of the project, μ_x, is equal to the sum of the bank's expected revenues μ_R and the borrower's expected profits u, or

$$(3) \quad \mu_x(L) = \int_{x_m}^{x_M} xF_x(x,L)dx$$

We will assume that the project outcome takes the particular form $x = \psi(L,y)$, where y is a random variable or "state of the world" whose probability distribution does not depend on L and the function ψ satisfies

$$\psi \geq 0, \; \psi_y > 0, \; \psi_L > 0, \; \psi_{LL} < 0,$$

$$\psi(L,y_{min}) \leq L$$

The restrictions $\psi_L > 0$ and $\psi_{LL} < 0$ imply that the marginal returns to investment will be positive but diminishing; that is, the project outcome corresponding to each state of the world will increase with the size of the project but at a decreasing rate. Also, the restriction $\psi(L,y_{min}) \leq L$ ensures that $x_m < z$, i.e. that there exists a risk of default on each loan.

It is shown in the Appendix that the above restrictions on ψ imply that

$$\frac{d\mu_x}{dL} > 0, \frac{d^2\mu_x}{dL^2} < 0$$

and that

$$\frac{\partial\mu_R}{\partial L} > 0, \frac{\partial^2\mu_R}{\partial L^2} < 0, \left.\frac{\partial\mu_R}{\partial L}\right|_{z \text{ const.}} > 0$$

for all r and $L > 0$. As shown in Figure 7, the bank's expected revenues μ_R are an increasing, strictly concave function of the size of the loan. As the size of the loan is increased at a given value of r, the amount due to the bank (the principal and interest on the loan) rises at a constant rate. However, because the investment project is subject to diminishing returns, an increase in loan size will also cause (1) a rise in the probability of default, and (2) a less than proportionate increase in the expected value of the collateral on the loan (the amount the bank receives in the event of default). It is the latter two effects which cause the bank's expected revenues from the loan to increase at a diminishing rate.

In making a loan of size L, the bank incurs an opportunity cost $(1+h)L$. The opportunity rate h may be interpreted as the rate of return which the bank could earn on some alternative riskless investment, or as the rate of interest which it must pay on deposits. Each bank takes h as given; however, we will allow for the possibility that the rate varies with the total volume of lending by banks. There may also exist certain administrative costs $C(m)$ which depend on the total number of loans m made by the bank.[7] When such administrative costs do exist, it will be assumed that marginal costs $C'(m)$ are at first strictly decreasing and then strictly increasing, so that the average cost function $\frac{C(m)}{m}$ is U-shaped.

Each bank seeks to maximize the expected value of its total profits from lending. Expected profits from an individual loan, excluding administrative costs, are

$$\delta(r,L,h) = \mu_R(r,L) - (1+h)L$$ [8]

Since $\partial^2\mu_R/\partial L^2 < 0$, there will exist a function $Q(r,h)$ indicating for each r and h the value of L that maximizes $\delta(r,L,h)$. Following Jaffee and Modigliani, we shall refer to the locus $Q(r,h)$ as the bank's "offer curve."

The bank's total expected profits from m identical loans may be expressed as

$$\pi(r,L,m,h) = m\delta(r,L,h) - C(m)$$

For any combination of r, L, and h such that $\delta(r,L,h) \geq \text{Min}\ \frac{C(m)}{m}$, the bank's total expected profits will be maximized by choosing m so that $C'(m) = \delta$. This condition determines a function $m(\delta)$ which indicates the bank's optimal number of loans given δ; of course, in the absence of administrative costs, the bank's optimal number of loans will be infinite for all positive values of δ.

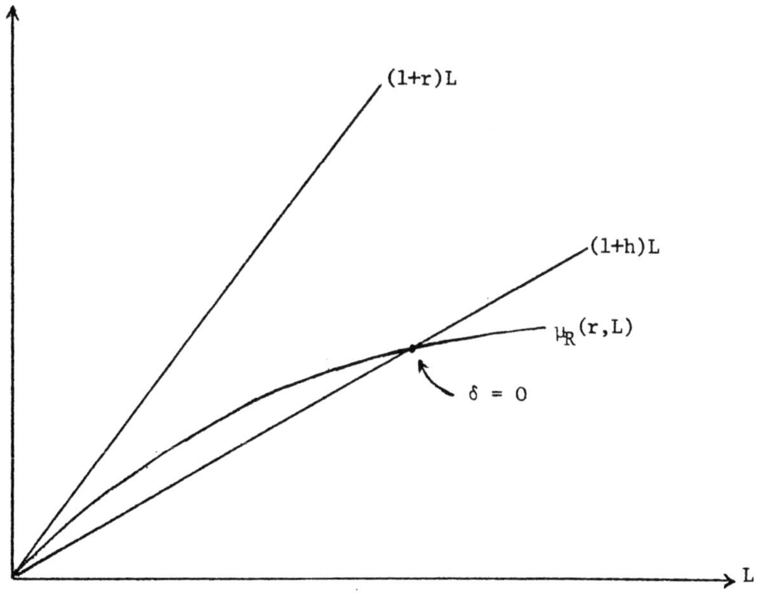

Figure 7

Let us define $\hat{r}(L)$ to be that loan rate above which default becomes certain, i.e. the value of r at which the principal and interest z is just equal to the maximum possible project outcome x_M. At this loan rate, $\mu_R(r,L) = \mu_x(L)$: the bank's expected revenues from the loan are equal to the total expected outcome of the project. Now, from the expression for the bank's expected revenues in (1), it is easily verified that

$$\frac{\partial \mu_R}{\partial r} = L[1 - F(z)] > 0 \text{ for } r < \hat{r}(L)$$

$$= 0 \qquad \text{" } r \geq \hat{r}(L)$$

Thus, for values of L and δ such that $L > 0$ and $0 \leq \delta < \mu_x(L) - (1+h)L$, a function $\phi(L,h,\delta)$ can be defined indicating the loan rate the bank must charge if its expected profits per loan are to equal δ. Given this function, it is possible to trace out a family of "iso-profit" curves in r-L space, as in Figure 8. Along each such curve expected profits per loan δ will be constant; if administrative costs are non-zero, the maximum value of the bank's total expected profits, $\underset{m}{\text{Max}}\ \pi(r,L,m,h)$, will also be constant.

Since $\frac{\partial \delta}{\partial r} > 0$, higher iso-profit curves will represent higher levels of δ (and also of π, if there are administrative costs). Furthermore, since $\partial^2\mu_R/\partial L^2 < 0$ implies $\partial\delta/\partial L \lesseqgtr 0$ as $L \gtreqless Q(r,h)$, $\phi_L = -\frac{\partial\delta/\partial L}{\partial\delta/\partial r} \gtreqless 0$ as $L \gtreqless Q(r,h)$: each iso-profit curve will be negatively sloped to the left of the point of intersection with the offer curve Q(r,h) and positively sloped to the right of that point. Of particular interest to us will be the bank's zero iso-profit curve $\phi(L,h,0)$. That this curve must be upward sloping throughout can easily be seen from Figure 7: Given any loan rate, the bank's expected profits per loan will equal zero at the point of intersection of the curve $\mu_R(r,L)$ and the ray $(1+h)L$. At this point any increase in loan size will raise the opportunity cost of the loan by more than the bank's expected revenues. Thus, for expected profits δ to remain equal to zero, the increase in L must be accompanied by an increase in r.

Firms also seek to maximize their expected profits. As we have seen, a borrower's expected profits from a loan are $u(r,L) = E[x-r]$. From the expression for u in equation (2) it is easily seen that $u(r,L) = 0$ at loan rate $\hat{r}(L)$ and that

$$\frac{\partial u}{\partial r} = -L[1 - F(z)] < 0 \text{ for } r < \hat{r}(L)$$

$$= 0 \qquad \text{"} \quad r \geq \hat{r}(L)$$

It follows that for all L and u such that $0 < u \leq \mu_x(L)$, a function $\theta(L,u)$ can be defined indicating the interest rate at which the customer's expected profits from a loan of size L equal u. Given this function, we can again trace out a family of iso-profit curves in r-L space, with higher curves representing lower levels of expected profits for the firm (see Figure 9).

If a firm does not take out a loan, its expected end-of-period value will be $\mu_x(0)$. Thus, it will be willing to borrow at terms r and L only if $u(r,L) \geq \mu_x(0)$. Since $\partial u/\partial r < 0$ for $r < \hat{r}(L)$ and $u = 0$ for $r \geq \hat{r}(L)$, there exists for each loan size L a loan rate r at which the borrower is just indifferent to receiving the loan; we shall refer to

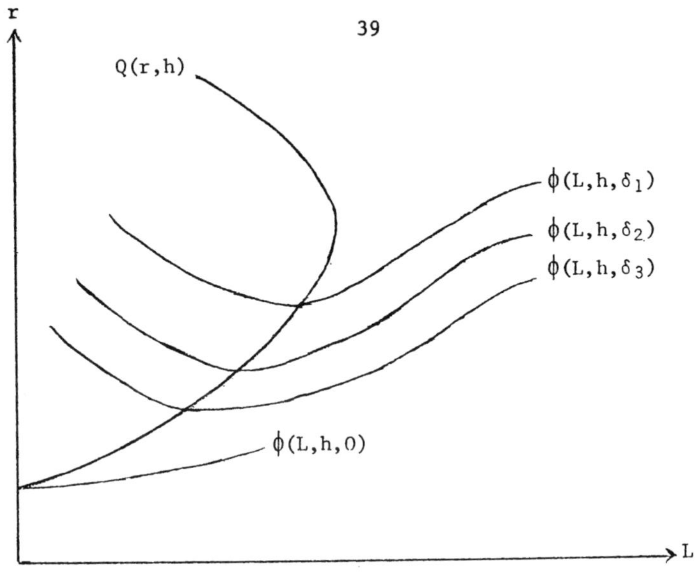

$\delta_1 > \delta_2 > \delta_3$

Figure 8

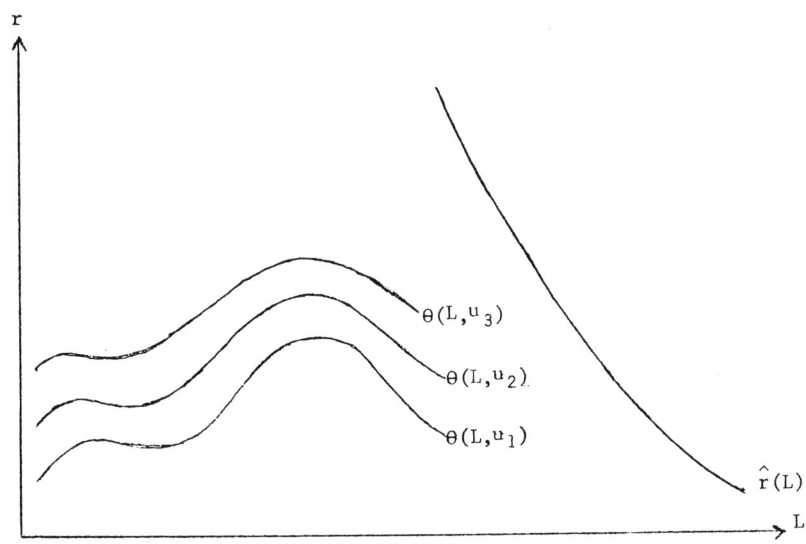

$u_1 > u_2 > u_3$

Figure 9

this value of r as the borrower's reservation loan rate. If the firm's end-of-period value is certain to equal zero in the absence of any investment, i.e. if $\mu_x(0) = 0$, the reservation loan rate is simply $\hat{r}(L)$, the rate at which default becomes certain. However, if the firm owns assets which can have positive value at the end of the period even in the absence of any investment, $\mu_x(0)$ will exceed zero; in this event, the reservation loan rate will be $\theta(L,\mu_x(0)) < \hat{r}(L)$.

Provided $\lim_{L\to\infty} \psi_L \leq 1$, the borrower's expected profits u(r,L) must attain a maximum at a finite value of L, given any loan rate.[9] If u is a strictly concave function of L, this value will also be unique -- i.e. it will be possible to define a demand curve D(r) which gives the customer's optimal value of L for each r. In this event each iso-profit curve $\theta(L,u)$ will be increasing to the left of the point of intersection with D(r) and decreasing to the right of that point. It should be noted, however, that our assumptions do not ensure $\partial^2u/\partial L^2 < 0$.

B. Equilibrium in the market for bank loans: an informal discussion

Since firms are identical, the terms offered by each bank in equilibrium must yield the same level of expected profits u for a representative customer. Also, for an equilibrium to exist no bank can have an incentive to alter either the terms at which it grants loans or the number of firms to which it lends. Of course, in making this determination, the individual bank must take into account the relationship of its terms to those prevailing in the market. In particular, we assume that a bank will expect to lose all its customers if it establishes terms less favorable to the borrower (i.e. terms yielding a lower level of u) than those being offered by its competitors.

If the expected profits of a bank did not depend on the manner in which credit was distributed among customers, given the loan rate and the total volume of lending, the above definition of a competitive equilibrium would be equivalent to the one usually given for homogeneous goods. That is, each bank could be considered to take the loan rate as given in determining its supply of credit, and equilibrium would occur at that loan rate at which the total supply of credit by all banks just equalled the total demand for credit on the part of firms with investment projects. In this equilibrium, each firm would receive exactly the amount of credit it desired at the prevailing loan rate; if this did not happen, an individual bank would always be able to alter the terms and the total number of its loans in such a way as to increase its own expected profits without reducing those of each of its customers.

The reason this description of the market equilibrium does not apply in our case is that the expected profits of the bank do depend in an important way on how total lending is distributed among customers. This is true even though borrowers are identical, i.e. even though the outcome of each borrower's investment project has the same probability distribution. The simplest case is that in which the administrative costs of lending are negligible, so that the only cost incurred by the bank in making a loan is the opportunity cost (1+h)L. The bank's total costs will in this case depend only on the total volume of its lending and not on the manner in which credit is distributed among borrowers. However, as long as there is a risk of default and as long as each investment project is subject to decreasing returns to scale, the same will not be true of the bank's total expected revenues.

We observed in the previous section that the bank's expected revenues from a loan, μ_R, will be an increasing strictly concave function of the size of the loan, given the loan rate. Clearly, then, the bank's total expected revenues will depend not just on the total volume of its lending but also on the distribution of credit. In particular, if the number of customers is increased and the size of each loan reduced by just enough to maintain lending at the original level, the total expected revenues of the bank must always increase.[10] The immediate implication, in the case in which the administrative costs of making loans are negligible, is that each borrower must receive a smaller loan than he desires in the competitive equilibrium. If this were not the case -- e.g. if borrowers received exactly as much credit as they desired at the interest rate charged -- a bank would always be able to increase its own expected profits, without reducing those of each of its customers, by granting a larger number of loans of somewhat smaller size and charging a slightly lower rate of interest.

We are now in a position to see that each borrower may receive either a smaller or a larger loan than he desires when there exist costs of administering loans. As we noted above, when the only cost incurred by the bank in making a loan is the opportunity cost $(1+h)L$, total costs will depend only on the total volume of credit and not on its distribution among customers. But this will clearly not be true when there are also costs of administration which increase with the total number of loans. In this case any increase in the number of customers and accompanying reduction in loan size which leaves total lending unchanged must raise the bank's total costs. If this effect is sufficiently strong, it will outweigh the favorable effect of such a change in the distribution of lending on the bank's total expected revenues. On balance, then, an increase in the number of customers and a reduction in the size of each loan by just enough to maintain lending at its original level may reduce the bank's total expected profits. Therefore, in contrast to the case of zero administrative costs, the equilibrium may be one in which customers receive larger loans and undertake larger investment projects than they would desire at the prevailing loan rate.

There is an alternative interpretation of the competitive equilibrium which provides some insight into the role of default risk and makes clear the sense in which credit may be rationed to borrowers. Let us suppose once again that the only cost incurred by the bank is the opportunity cost of lending. Let us also define the bank's expected rate of return on a loan as $\rho \equiv \frac{\mu_R(r,L)}{L} - 1$. For an equilibrium to exist, no bank can have an incentive to expand or contract the number of its loans. In the present case, this requires that banks earn zero expected profits on each loan and therefore that the expected rate of return on a loan, ρ, just equal the opportunity rate, h. At this expected rate of return the bank will of course be indifferent as to the size of the loan, i.e. its supply of credit will be infinitely elastic (see Figure 10).

Now, for each value of ρ, there will exist a unique loan size maximizing the borrower's expected profits $u = \mu_x - \mu_R = \mu_x(L) - (1+\rho)L$. This allows us to specify the borrower's demand for credit as a decreasing function $D(\rho)$ of the bank's expected rate of return. As shown in Figure 10, equilibrium must occur at the intersection of the supply and demand curves, just as it does in the usual case of a homogeneous good. Each borrower will receive exactly that amount of credit which he desires at the equilibrium expected rate of return $\rho = h$. That is, if the size of the loan were either increased or decreased and the loan rate adjusted so as to keep the expected rate of return ρ constant, the borrower would find himself worse off. However, at the loan rate actually charged in equilibrium, it is not difficult to see that the borrower would be better off with a larger loan: From Figure 7 it is clear that increasing the size of the loan while holding the rate of interest constant reduces ρ. At any point on the borrower's demand curve $D(\rho)$,

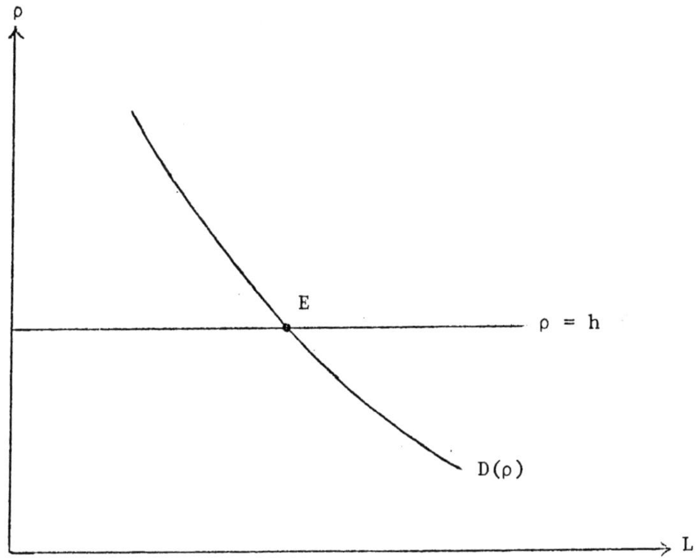

Figure 10

the effect of the two changes -- the increase in loan size and the decline in the expected rate of return to the bank -- must be to raise the expected profits of the borrower, provided the increase in loan size is sufficiently small. Thus, credit rationing can be said to occur if the borrower's demand is defined in terms of the loan rate r, but not if it is defined in terms of the expected rate of return to the bank, ρ. Of course, in the absence of default risk, the expected rate of return to the bank and the rate of interest charged on the loan will be identical. This implies that credit can be rationed in equilibrium only if projects have uncertain outcomes.

In this section we have established that each firm must receive a smaller loan than it desires if there are no costs of administration; we have also indicated why the opposite condition might hold if those costs are significant and if they increase with the total number of loans made by the bank. We now give a formal derivation of the competitive equilibrium for these two cases. This will enable us to describe the market equilibrium in greater detail and also to evaluate the impact of monetary policy on total lending and investment and the level of interest rates.

C. Equilibrium in the market for bank loans: a formal derivation

In equilibrium banks will charge the same loan rate and grant loans of the same size to all customers. Let N be the number of banks and m_i the number of loans supplied by the ith bank. Then the equilibrium values of r, L, N, h, and $\{m_i\}$ must satisfy the following conditions:

(E.1) $\sum_{1}^{N} m_i \leq M$

(E.2) $u(r,L) \geq \mu_x(0)$ and $\sum_{1}^{N} m_i < M$ only if $u(r,L) = \mu_x(0)$

(E.3) $\nexists$ an r', L', and m' such that $\pi(r',L',m',h) >$ $\pi(r,L,m_i,h)$ and $u(r',L') \geq u(r,L)$

(E.4) $h = \Omega(\sum_{1}^{N} m_i L)$

(E.5a) $N = \bar{N}$ (restricted entry)

(E.5b) $\pi(r,L,m_i,h) = 0$ (free entry)

Condition (E.1) expresses the obvious constraint that the total number of loans supplied by banks cannot exceed the number of firms with investment projects. Condition (E.2) states that some firms will fail to receive credit in equilibrium only if those firms which do receive loans are earning expected profits $\mu_x(0)$--i.e. only if the prevailing loan terms are such that a firm is just indifferent to borrowing. If this were not the case, any firm which had been unable to obtain a loan would be willing to pay a somewhat higher loan rate to obtain one, and any bank would be happy to make a loan at that higher loan rate since its expected profits $\hat{\delta}$ would be greater.[11]

Condition (E.3) ensures that no bank will have an incentive to alter either the terms at which it grants loans or the number of firms to which it lends. Since the bank's total expected profits can be expressed as a function of δ and m alone, with $\partial\pi/\partial\delta > 0$, the condition has two parts:

(a) $\nexists$ an r' and L' such that $\delta(r',L',h) > \delta(r,L,h)$ and $u(r',L') \geq u(r,L)$

(b) $\nexists$ an m' such that $\pi(\delta,m') > \pi(\delta,m_i)$

If (a) holds, any change in r and L will either fail to increase expected profits per loan or cause the bank to lose all its customers. If (b) holds, the bank will be unable to increase total expected profits by changing its supply of loans.

The remaining equilibrium conditions are straightforward. Condition (E.4) gives the relationship between the total volume of credit, $\sum_1^N m_i L$, and the opportunity rate h. We assume $\Omega' \geq 0$; in the extreme case in which h is constant, $\Omega' \equiv 0$. To ensure an equilibrium will exist, we also require $1 + \Omega(0) < \lim_{L\to 0} \frac{d\mu_x}{dL}$ and $1 + \Omega(\infty) > \lim_{L\to\infty} \frac{d\mu_x}{dL}$. Condition (E.5a) states that the number of banks will be fixed at $\bar{N}$ if entry to the industry is restricted. If entry to the industry is unrestricted, the equilibrium number of banks must be treated as endogenous; in this event the zero-profit condition (E.5b) will apply.

Conditions (E.1)-(E.5) determine a unique competitive equilibrium in the market for bank loans. We will describe this equilibrium first for the case in which administrative costs C(m) are zero, and then for the case in which those costs are nonzero. We shall see that in the first case each borrower must receive a smaller loan than he desires at the interest rate charged by the bank; in the second case, however, the borrower may receive either a smaller or larger loan than he desires.

1. The case of zero administrative costs

When administrative costs C(m) are negligible, a bank's total expected profits are proportional to the number of loans that it makes; that is, $\pi(r,L,m,h) = m\delta(r,L,h)$. Equilibrium condition (E.3) therefore requires that banks earn zero expected profits per loan; if δ were positive a bank would wish to expand its loans, and if δ were negative a bank would wish to contract them. Condition (E.3) also requires that the equilibrium loan size maximize $\delta(r,L,h) + u(r,L) = \mu_x(L) - (1+h)L$, given the opportunity rate h; only when this condition is satisfied will the individual bank be unable to alter the terms r and L in such a way as to increase its expected profits per loan δ without losing customers to competing banks.

From the requirement that δ equal zero and that L maximize $\mu_x(L) - (1+h)L$, and from the assumption $1 + \Omega(0) < \lim_{L\to 0} \frac{d\mu_x}{dL}$, it is easily seen that the borrower's expected profits u(r,L) must exceed $\mu_x(0)$ in equilibrium.[12] But in this case condition (E.2) requires that all M firms receive credit. Defining $\mathcal{L}(h)$ to be the value of L which maximizes the expression $\mu_x(L) - (1+h)L$, we can then determine the equilibrium opportunity rate h* as the solution to the equation $h = \Omega(M\mathcal{L}(h))$. Since $\frac{d^2\mu_x}{dL^2} < 0$ implies $d\mathcal{L}/dh < 0$ and since $\Omega' \geq 0$, this solution will be unique; its existence follows from the boundary conditions on Ω. The equilibrium loan size will be $\mathcal{L}(h^*)$ and the equilibrium loan rate the value of r at which $\delta(r,\mathcal{L}(h^*),h^*) = 0$.

In terms of Figure 11, equilibrium occurs at the point of tangency of the bank's zero iso-profit curve $\phi(L,h^*,0)$ with a customer iso-profit curve $\theta(L,u)$. Since the bank's zero iso-profit locus is positively sloped throughout, this implies $\partial u/\partial L > 0$ and $\partial\delta/\partial L < 0$. Each bank will "ration" credit to its customers, in the sense of providing them with smaller loans than they would desire at the quoted interest rate. This result may be stated more formally as follows:

Proposition. Suppose that administrative costs C(m) are zero, and let r* and L* be the equilibrium values of r and L. Then (1) $u(r^*,L) < u(r^*,L^*)$ for all $L < L^*$; and (2) there exists an $L > L^*$ such that $u(r^*,L) > u(r^*,L^*)$.

Proof: (1) Suppose that there exists an $L_1 < L^*$ such that $u(r^*,L_1) \geq u(r^*,L^*)$. Then since $\partial u/\partial r < 0$ and $\phi_L(L,h^*,0) > 0$, $u[\phi(L_1,h^*,0),L_1] > u(r^*,L_1) \geq u(r^*,L^*)$. This is a contradiction, since $L^* = \mathcal{L}(h^*)$ and $r^* = \phi(L^*,h^*,0)$ imply $u(r^*,L^*) > u[\phi(L,h^*,0),L]$ for all $L \neq L^*$.

(2) Since $u[\phi(L,h^*,0),L]$ attains a maximum at L*, $\frac{\partial u}{\partial L} + \frac{\partial u}{\partial r}\phi_L(L,h^*,0) = 0$ at that point. But $\partial u/\partial r < 0$ and $\phi_L(L,h^*,0) > 0$. Thus, $\partial u/\partial L > 0$ at $L = L^*$ and $r = r^*$.

It will be noted that the above proposition does not require that the customer demand curve $D(r)$ be defined at $r = r^*$, i.e. that $u(r^*,L)$ attain a maximum at a unique value of L. Also, it should be emphasized that although the size of each loan in equilibrium will be smaller than desired by the customer at the quoted loan rate, the total supply of loans will equal the total demand (i.e. M, the number of firms).[13]

Up to this point we have assumed for convenience that each firm can take out only one loan. It is not difficult to show that this assumption is unnecessary if the bank making the first loan always has priority over the firm's assets in the event of default. In particular, in the equilibrium described above no bank will have an incentive to make a loan to a customer who has already borrowed from another bank. To see this, let $\tilde{\delta}_1(r_1,L_1,L_2,h)$ be a bank's expected profits from a loan of size L_1 at rate r_1 to a customer who takes out a second loan of size L_2 from another bank; let $\tilde{\delta}_2(r_1,L_1,r_2,L_2,h)$ be a bank's expected profits from a loan of size L_2 at rate r_2 to a customer who has already received a loan of size L_1 at rate r_1 from another bank; and let $\tilde{u}(r_1,L_1,r_2,L_2)$ be a customer's total expected profits from two loans. In addition, define $\bar{L} = L_1 + L_2$ and $\bar{r} = \frac{L_1}{\bar{L}} r_1 + \frac{L_2}{\bar{L}} r_2$. Then it is easily verified that

$$\delta(\bar{r},\bar{L},h) = \tilde{\delta}_1(r_1,L_1,L_2,h) + \tilde{\delta}_2(r_1,L_1,r_2,L_2,h)$$

(4)

$$u(\bar{r},\bar{L}) = \tilde{u}(r_1,L_1,r_2,L_2)$$

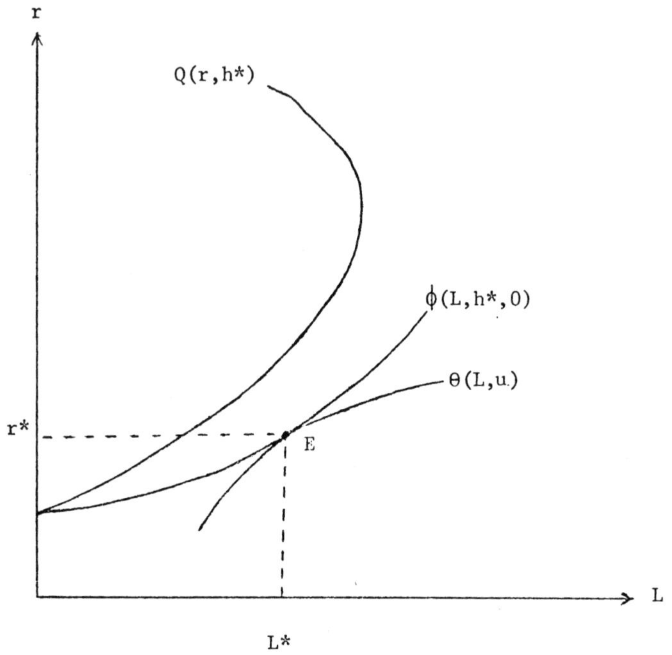

Figure 11

Also, $\left.\frac{\partial \mu_R}{\partial L}\right|_{z \text{ const.}} > 0$ implies that $\tilde{\delta}_1(r_1,L_1,L_2,h) > \delta(r_1,L_1,h)$ for any $L_2 > 0$.

Consider now the equilibrium loan rate r* and loan size L* determined above under the assumption that each firm can borrow from only one bank. Suppose that there eixst an r_2 and L_2 such that when a firm takes out a loan from a second bank at those terms neither the firm nor the second bank is worse off, i.e. $\tilde{u}(r^*,L^*,r_2,L_2) \geq u(r^*,L^*)$ and $\tilde{\delta}_2(r^*,L^*,r_2,L_2,h) \geq 0$. Then from (4) and $\tilde{\delta}_1(r^*,L^*,L_2,h) > \delta(r^*,L^*,h)$, it follows that $\delta(\bar{r},\bar{L},h) > \delta(r^*,L^*,h)$ and $u(\bar{r},\bar{L}) \geq u(r^*,L^*)$. However, this means that r* and L* cannot satisfy equilibrium condition (E.3), which is a contradiction. Thus, if a firm has borrowed L* at rate r* from one bank, there will exist no incentive for another bank to give a second loan to that firm.

2. The case of nonzero administrative costs

To begin with, let us consider the short-run case in which the number of banks is fixed and equal to $\bar{N}$ (restricted entry). We noted earlier that for a given level of expected profits per loan δ, a bank's optimal supply of loans would be $m(\delta)$, the value of m which maximizes its total expected profits $\pi = m\delta - C(m)$. Equilibrium condition (E.3) therefore implies $m_i = m(\delta(r,L,h))$ for all i. Also, as in the case of zero administrative costs, condition (E.3) requires that the equilibrium loan size be $\mathcal{L}(h)$, the value of L that maximizes $\delta(r,L,h) + u(r,L) = \mu_x(L) - (1+h)L$.

Let us define $\delta(m)$ to be the level of expected profits per loan δ

at which an individual bank will wish to supply exactly m loans, i.e. the value of δ for which $m(\delta) = m$. Also, as before, let h* be the solution to the equation $h = \Omega(ML(h))$. It then follows from equilibrium condition (E.2) that all M firms must receive credit as long as $\delta(M/\bar{N}) \leq \underset{L}{\text{Max}}\ \mu_x(L) - (1+h^*)L - \mu_x(0)$.[14] This determines the equilibrium level of expected profits per loan as $\delta(M/\bar{N})$, the value of δ at which the total supply of loans by all banks is just equal to the total number of firms with investment projects. The equilibrium opportunity rate will be h*, the equilibrium loan size $L(h^*)$, and the equilibrium loan rate the value of r for which $\delta(r,L(h^*),h^*) = \delta(M/\bar{N})$.

If $\delta(M/\bar{N}) > \text{Min}\ \frac{C(m)}{m}$, each bank will earn positive total expected profits π in the equilibrium described above. Thus, if entry is unrestricted, new banks will enter the industry until total expected profits are driven to zero. In long-run equilibrium each bank will be of smaller size and will operate at the minimum point on the average cost curve $\frac{C(m)}{m}$; since all M firms must continue to receive credit, this determines the total number of banks as $N = M/\hat{m}$, where $\hat{m}$ is the number of loans at which $\frac{C(m)}{m}$ attains a minimum. The equilibrium opportunity rate will remain equal to h* and the equilibrium loan size will still be $L(h^*)$; however, the equilibrium loan rate will have been reduced to that value of r at which $\delta(r,L(h^*),h^*) = \text{Min}\ \frac{C(m)}{m}$.

The determination of the equilibrium loan terms is illustrated in Figures 12a and 12b. We define δ^* to be the value of expected profits per loan in equilibrium; this is equal to $\delta(M/\bar{N})$ in the case of restricted entry and $\text{Min}\ \frac{C(m)}{m}$ in the case of free entry. The equilib-

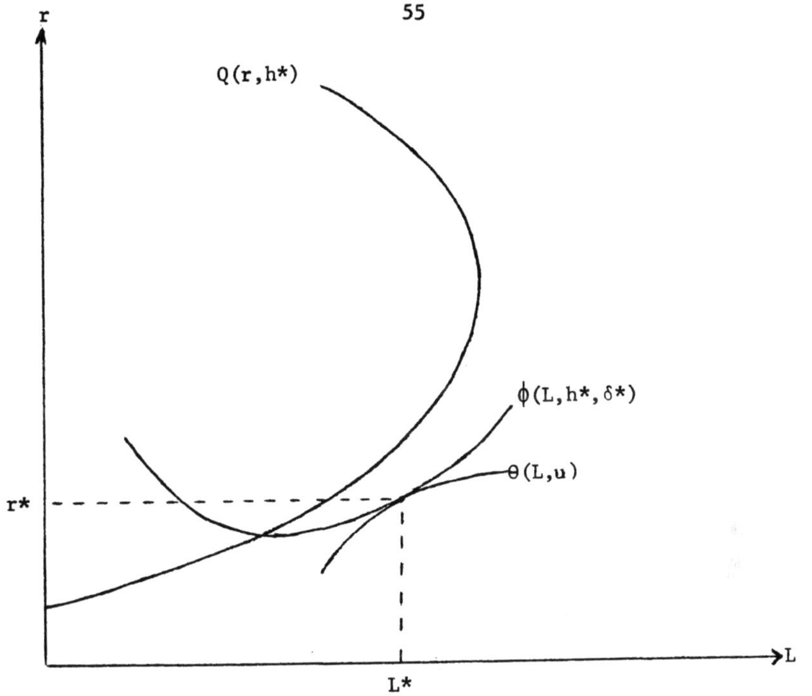

Figure 12a

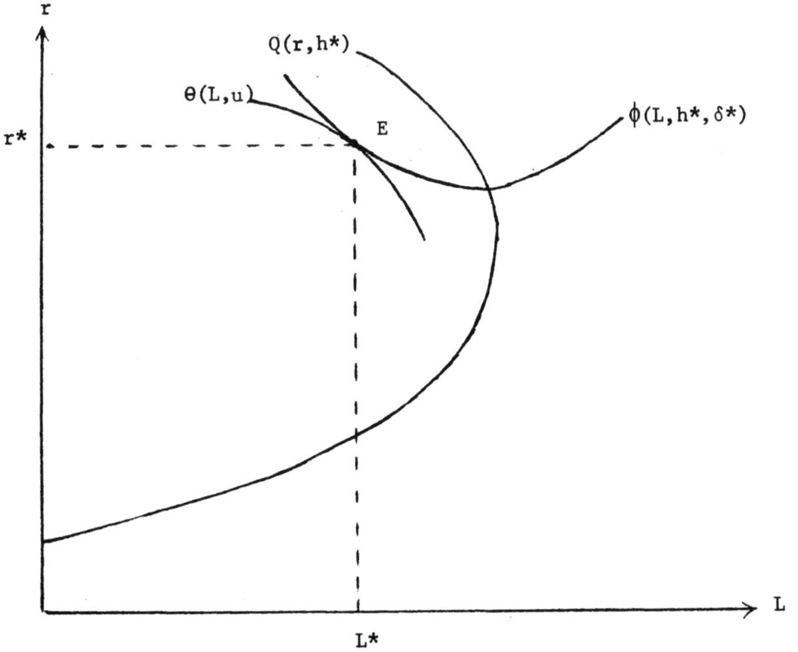

Figure 12b

rium point will lie on the bank iso-profit curve $\phi(L,h^*,\delta^*)$, at the point of tangency with a firm iso-profit curve $\theta(L,u)$. Since $\delta^* > 0$, the bank iso-profit curve may have either positive or negative slope at that point. If the minimum average administrative cost is relatively small (case of free entry) or if the ratio of firms to banks is low (case of restricted entry), ϕ_L will be positive in equilibrium. As we noted in the previous section, this implies $\partial u/\partial L > 0$ and $\partial \delta/\partial L < 0$; firms would prefer to receive larger loans at the equilibrium loan rate and banks would prefer to make smaller loans at that rate.[15] But if ϕ_L is negative at the equilibrium point, the exact opposite condition will exist; firms will receive more credit than they desire at the quoted loan rate ($\partial u/\partial L < 0$) and banks will make smaller loans than are optimal at that rate ($\partial \delta/\partial L > 0$). Only by accident will a customer receive in equilibrium that size loan which maximizes his expected profits at the equilibrium loan rate.

Equilibrium was determined above under the assumption that each firm could take out only one loan. However, if the bank making the first loan always has priority over the firm's assets, this assumption is unnecessary. By the same argument used in the previous section, it can be shown that in equilibrium no bank will have an incentive to make a loan to a customer who has already borrowed from another bank.

D. Comparative statics

The properties of the market equilibrium were described in detail in the preceding section. We now consider how this equilibrium will be affected by two types of disturbances--first, shifts in monetary policy, and second, changes in the risk or productivity of investment projects.

1. Monetary policy may be viewed as affecting the market for bank loans through shifts in the function Ω, which indicates the opportunity rate h corresponding to each volume of total lending L_T. A restrictive monetary policy, for example, will tend to reduce the relative attractiveness of bank deposits to wealth-holders. As a result, banks will have to pay a higher rate of interest to attract a given total volume of deposits--i.e. the function Ω will shift upward. Conversely, an expansionary monetary policy may be represented by a downward shift in Ω. This approach is of course a partial equilibrium one, in that it ignores the impact of bank lending on real income and prices and thus indirectly on wealth-holders' demands for assets or on the productivity of investment.

In the previous section we saw that the equilibrium value of h must satisfy the equation $h = \Omega(M\mathcal{L}(h))$, where $\mathcal{L}(h)$ is a negatively sloped function indicating the size of each loan that would be granted in equilibrium if the opportunity rate were h. Thus, in terms of Figure 13, the equilibrium opportunity rate and equilibrium volume of total lending are jointly determined by the intersection of the curves

$L_T = M\mathit{l}(h)$ and $h = \Omega(L_T)$. A restrictive monetary policy which shifts the function Ω upward for all values of L_T will raise the equilibrium opportunity rate h, decrease the equilibrium loan size $\mathit{l}(h)$, and reduce the total volume of lending $L_T = M\mathit{l}(h)$. By contrast, an expansionary policy which shifts Ω downward for all L_T will lead to a decline in the opportunity rate, an increase in loan size, and a rise in total lending.

The impact of monetary policy on the equilibrium loan rate is more complex. Consider, for example, an upward shift in Ω. As we have just seen, such a shift will lead to an increase in the opportunity rate h. In the new equilibrium banks must continue to earn the same expected profits per loan δ^*. Thus, if loan size remained unchanged, the increase in h would have to be accompanied by an increase in the loan rate, since $\partial\delta/\partial h < 0$ and $\partial\delta/\partial r > 0$. However, the increase in h will also lead to a reduction in the equilibrium loan size $\mathit{l}(h)$. If in the initial equilibrium firms are receiving larger loans than they desire ($\partial u/\partial L < 0$) and banks making smaller loans than they prefer ($\partial\delta/\partial L > 0$), this reduction in the equilibrium loan size will tend to decrease the bank's expected profits per loan, reinforcing the negative effect on δ of the increase in h. In this case, then, the equilibrium loan rate must clearly rise. But if firms are initially receiving smaller loans than they desire ($\partial u/\partial L > 0$) and banks making larger loans than they prefer ($\partial\delta/\partial L < 0$), the decrease in the equilibrium loan size will tend to <u>raise</u> δ. It is easily established that this indirect effect may be sufficiently strong to offset the direct

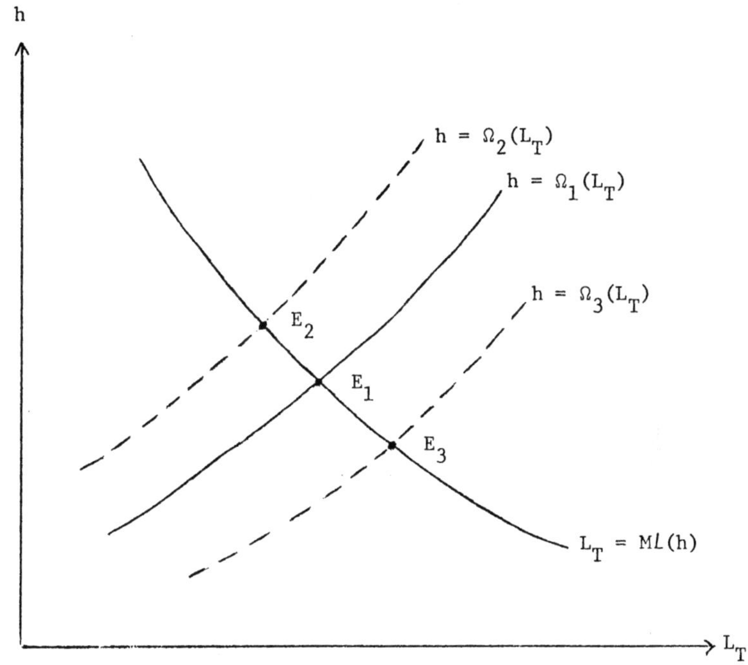

Figure 13

effect on δ of an increase in h. When this is the case, a restrictive monetary policy will cause the equilibrium opportunity rate to rise but the equilibrium loan rate to fall.[16]

Although the impact of monetary policy on the equilibrium loan rate will depend in an important way on whether banks are rationing credit in the initial equilibrium, in the sense of providing each customer with a smaller loan than he would desire, this is not true of the impact on total lending and investment. We have seen that borrowers will always receive smaller loans than they would desire if administrative costs C(m) are zero but that they may receive loans as large or larger than they would desire if the cost of administering each loan is high. The equilibrium opportunity rate and the equilibrium volume of total lending, however, are independent of the level of administrative costs. Thus, the effect of monetary policy on the two variables will not depend on whether administrative costs are sufficiently low that credit is rationed in the initial equilibrium.

A similar conclusion emerges when we consider the effect of monetary policy on the extent to which banks ration credit to their customers. The traditional view, espoused by proponents of the availability doctrine, is that a tightening of monetary policy will increase the degree of credit rationing and an easing of monetary policy reduce it. In this way, it has been argued, monetary policy can have a significant impact on total lending and investment even when each firm's demand for investment is highly interest-rate inelastic. In the particular example presented in Section II.F. below, however, we shall see that an increase in the opportunity rate h actually reduces the amount of rationing, as measured by the excess demand for credit in equilibrium, $D(r^*) - L^*$. Thus, the existence of that variety of credit rationing in which each borrower receives a smaller loan than he desires need have no tendency to enhance the effectiveness of monetary policy.

2. Changes in $F(x,L)$, the probability distribution of the outcome of a representative investment project, will also have an impact on the market for bank loans. Consider first the case in which each project undergoes an identical "mean-preserving" increase in risk, in the sense used by Rothschild and Stiglitz [5]. In this case the expected project outcome μ_x will be the same for each value of L, but the new cumulative distribution function F_2 will have more weight in the tails than the original distribution F_1. More precisely, F_1 and F_2 will satisfy the integral conditions

$$\int [F_2(x,L) - F_1(x,L)]dx = 0$$

$$\int_{x \leq x'} [F_2(x,L) - F_1(x,L)]dx \geq 0 \text{ for all } x'$$

Now, we have seen that at any value of h, the equilibrium loan size $L(h)$ will be that value of L that maximizes the total expected profits of borrower and lender, $\mu_x(L) - (1+h)L$. Since the increase in the riskiness of F is assumed not to affect the mean outcome μ_x, it follows that the equilibrium loan size, the equilibrium opportunity rate, and the equilibrium volume of total lending must remain unchanged. The increase in risk will, however, tend to reduce the expected revenues of the bank, as can easily be seen from the second integral condition and the expression for μ_R in equation (1). Since banks must continue to earn the same level of expected profits δ^* in equilibrium, this means that the equilibrium loan rate will have to rise.

If the shift in F does change the expected outcome of each project, the impact on the market equilibrium will not be so simple. Suppose, for example, that the project outcome $\psi(L,y)$ corresponding to each "state of the world" y is increased by a constant proportion. For any given loan size L, the expected outcome μ_x will then also increase by that proportion. In terms of Figure 13, this will shift the curve $ML(h)$ outward, increasing both the equilibrium opportunity rate and the equilibrium loan size. The effect on the equilibrium loan rate may, however, be ambiguous. At given values of h and L, the increase in the productivity of each project will tend to raise the bank's expected revenues and thus reduce the loan rate r at which expected profits per loan are equal to δ^*; but if banks are initially making loans of larger than optimal size (i.e. if $\partial\delta/\partial L < 0$ in equilibrium, as in the case of zero administrative costs), the increase in the equilibrium loan size will work in the opposite direction, tending to raise the equilibrium loan rate.[17]

In this section we have considered how shifts in the probability distribution of each investment project would affect equilibrium in the market for bank loans, given that all projects are identical. We now take up a closely related question--how will equilibrium in the market for bank loans be determined when projects are not identical but differ in the probability distributions of their outcomes?

E. Allowing for differences among investment projects

To relax the assumption that borrowing firms are identical, let us now suppose that the probability distribution of the investment project can be characterized by a parameter α which differs among firms. Although different loan terms will be offered to each class of firms, expected profits per loan δ must be the same for all borrowers in equilibrium. If δ were higher for one class of customers than for another, banks with relatively unprofitable customers would have an incentive to offer slightly more favorable terms to the highly profitable customers in order to lure them away from other banks. Given that δ will be the same for all classes of customers, it should be clear that its equilibrium value δ^* will be determined as in Section II.C.

The equilibrium loan size for a particular class of firms will be $\mathcal{L}(h;\alpha)$, the value of L which maximizes $\mu_x(L;\alpha) - (1+h)L$. The equilibrium loan rate for that class of customers will be the value of r for which $\delta(r,\mathcal{L}(h;\alpha),h;\alpha) = \delta^*$. If investment projects differ only in riskiness and not in total expected outcome--i.e. if increases in α reflect mean-preserving increases in the riskiness of the distribution $F(x,L;\alpha)$--all classes of borrowers will receive loans of the same size in equilibrium and the riskier borrowers will be charged higher loan rates. However, if projects differ in productivity, the equilibrium loan size will generally not be the same for each class of borrowers. Furthermore, in this case the least productive borrowers, those for whom a bank cannot earn expected profits per loan δ^* even if it charges the borrower's reservation loan rate, will fail to receive credit. The marginal class of borrowers will be that for which $\max_L \mu_x(L;\alpha) - (1+h)L - \mu_x(0;\alpha) = \delta^*$. Since the expression on the left is decreasing in h, monetary policy may in this case affect not only the size of each loan granted in equilibrium but also the number of firms receiving credit.

As in the case of identical firms, credit may be rationed in equilibrium in the sense that $D(r^*) > L^*$. If there are no costs of administering loans, all customers will be rationed. In the case of nonzero administrative costs, however, it is possible that some customers will be rationed while other are not.

F. An example

In this concluding section we shall examine a simple example which illustrates the results obtained above. We suppose that the outcome x of each customer's investment project is $\psi(L,y) = aL^{\alpha}y$, where $a > 0$, $\alpha < 1$, and y is a random variable distributed uniformly over the interval (0,1). In this case

$$(5)\quad \begin{aligned} \delta(r,L,h) &= (1+r)L \int_{\hat{y}}^{1} dy + aL^{\alpha} \int_{0}^{\hat{y}} y\,dy - (1+h)L \\ u(r,L) &= \int_{\hat{y}}^{1} [aL^{\alpha}y - (1+r)L]dy \end{aligned}$$

where $\hat{y} = \frac{1+r}{aL^{\alpha-1}}$.

The value of L that maximizes $\mu_x(L) - (1+h)L = aL^{\alpha}/2 - (1+h)L$ is

$$(6)\quad L(h) = \left[\frac{a\alpha}{2(1+h)}\right]^{\frac{1}{1-\alpha}}$$

The bank's offer curve is derived by setting the partial derivative $\partial\delta/\partial L$ equal to zero. This yields

$$\begin{aligned} Q(r,h) &= \left[\frac{2a(r-h)}{(2-\alpha)(1+r)^2}\right]^{\frac{1}{1-\alpha}} && \text{for } r \leq 2(1+h)/\alpha - 1 \\ &= L(h) && \text{" } r > 2(1+h)/\alpha - 1 \end{aligned}$$

Since $\psi_{LL} = -a\alpha(1-\alpha)L^{\alpha-2}y < 0$, the second order condition $\partial^2\delta/\partial L^2 < 0$ is satisfied. It is easily shown that $\partial Q/\partial r > 0$ for $r < 1+2h$ and

$\partial Q/\partial r < 0$ for $1+2h < r < 2(1+h)/\alpha - 1$. Thus, the offer curve bends backward at $r = 1+2h$ and becomes vertical at $r = 2(1+h)/\alpha - 1$ (see Figure 14).

The maximum possible outcome of the customer's investment project is aL^{α}. Let $\hat{L}(r)$ be that value of L such that $(1+r)L = aL^{\alpha}$. Then

$$\hat{L}(r) = \left(\frac{1+r}{a}\right)^{-\frac{1}{1-\alpha}}$$

and $u(r,L) = 0$ for $L \geq \hat{L}(r)$. Although $\partial^2 u/\partial L^2 \gtrless 0$, it is also possible to define a demand curve D(r) in this example. By partially differentiating the expression for u(r,L) in (5) we obtain

$$\frac{\partial u}{\partial L} = \frac{1}{2}\left(1 - \frac{1+r}{aL^{\alpha-1}}\right)\left[a\alpha L^{\alpha-1} - (1+r)(2-\alpha)\right] \quad \text{for } L < \hat{L}(r)$$

Let D(r) be the value of L such that $\partial u/\partial L = 0$, i.e.

$$D(r) = \left[\frac{2-\alpha}{a\alpha}(1+r)\right]^{-\frac{1}{1-\alpha}}$$

It is then easily verified that $\partial u/\partial L > 0$ for $L < D(r)$ and $\partial u/\partial L < 0$ for $D(r) < L < \hat{L}(r)$: given r, the customer's expected profits attain a unique maximum at $L = D(r)$. The demand curve is downward sloping and approaches the vertical axis as r goes to infinity.

In Section II.C. we distinguished among three cases: (1) zero administrative costs; (2) nonzero costs of administering loans and restricted entry to the banking industry; and (3) nonzero costs of administering loans and free entry. In all three cases, the equilib-

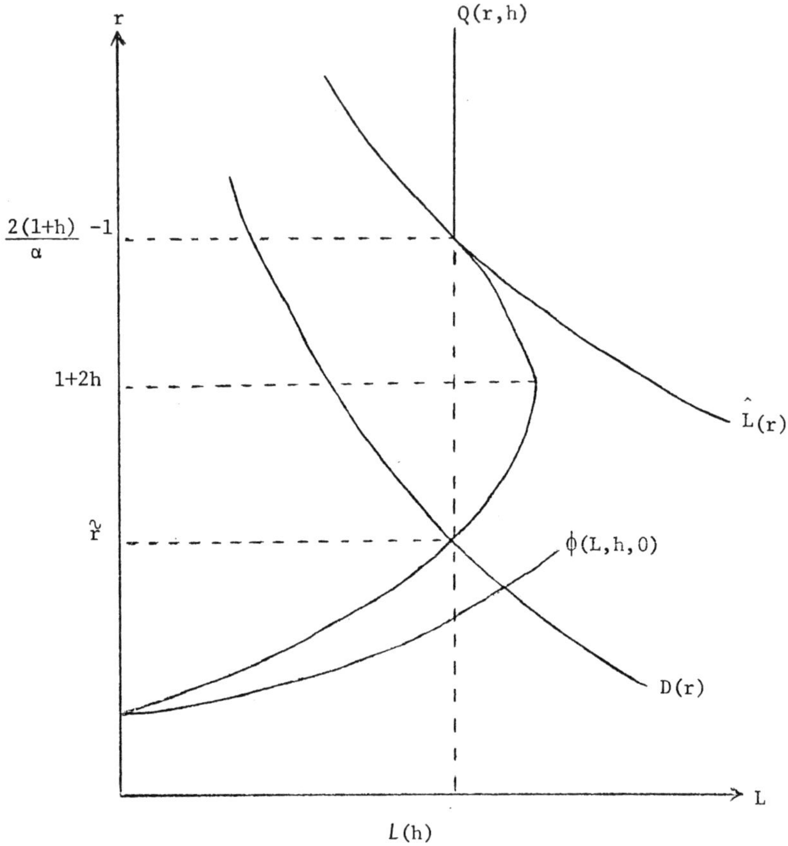

Figure 14

rium loan size is $L^* = \mathit{L}(h)$, the value of L that maximizes $\mu_x(L) - (1+h)L$. The equilibrium value of δ will, however, differ in the three cases. In particular, δ^* equals zero in case (1), $\delta(M/\bar{N})$ in case (2), and Min $\frac{C(m)}{m}$ in case (3). The equilibrium loan rate in each case will be that value of r for which $\delta(r,L^*,h) = \delta^*$. For $\delta^* < \mu_x(L^*) - (1+h)L^* = (\frac{a\alpha}{2})^{\frac{1}{1-\alpha}} (1+h)^{-\frac{\alpha}{1-\alpha}} \frac{1-\alpha}{\alpha}$ this can be shown to imply

$$(7)\quad 1 + r^* = \frac{2(1+h)}{\alpha} [1 - (1-\alpha A)^{\frac{1}{2}}]$$

where $A = 1 + (\frac{a\alpha}{2})^{-\frac{1}{1-\alpha}} (1+h)^{\frac{\alpha}{1-\alpha}} \delta^*$.

In the case of zero administrative costs, it is easily verified that $D(r^*) > L^*$; credit is rationed in the sense that the customer receives a smaller loan than he demands at the equilibrium loan rate. Furthermore, since $\delta^* = 0$ implies $A = 1$, $1+r^*$ is directly proportional to the average opportunity cost $1+h$. It is also interesting to note that $D(r^*) - L^*$, the customer's excess demand for credit in equilibrium, decreases as the opportunity rate h rises. In this sense a restrictive monetary policy will decrease the degree to which banks ration credit.

If costs of administration C(m) are nonzero, $D(r^*) \gtreqless L^*$ as $r^* \lesseqgtr \tilde{r}$, where $\tilde{r}$ is the loan rate at which $D(r) = Q(r,h) = L^*$, i.e. the rate at which the customer's demand curve and the bank's offer curve intersect. It can be shown in our example that

$$\delta(\tilde{r},L^*) = B(1+h)^{-\frac{\alpha}{1-\alpha}}$$

where

$$B = \left(\frac{a}{2}\right)^{\frac{1}{1-\alpha}} \alpha^{\frac{2-\alpha}{1-\alpha}} \frac{1-\alpha}{(2-\alpha)^2}$$

Thus, $\partial\delta/\partial r > 0$ implies that $D(r^*) \gtreqless L^*$ as $\delta^* \lesseqgtr B(1+h)^{-\frac{\alpha}{1-\alpha}}$. It will be noted that credit is more likely to be "rationed" the lower is the opportunity rate h. If the opportunity rate is sufficiently low that credit rationing does occur, the excess demand $D(r^*) - L^*$ will increase as h is reduced further. From (7) it also follows that $dr^*/dh > 0$: as in the case of zero administrative costs, the equilibrium loan rate and the opportunity rate move in the same direction.

The model is readily extended to allow for differences among customer's investment projects. We may suppose, for example, that projects differ only by the parameter a and that there exists some continuous distribution of firms over a. The equilibrium loan size and the equilibrium loan rate for each class of borrowers will then be given by equations (6) and (7). These two equations define a locus $r^*(L)$ of equilibrium points, with each point corresponding to a distinct class of borrowers. It is easily seen from equation (6) that $\partial L^*/\partial a > 0$--i.e. the higher the productivity of a customer's investment project, the larger will be the loan he receives in equilibrium. Also, equation (7) implies that r^* is independent of a if $\delta^* = 0$ and decreasing in a if $\delta^* > 0$. In the latter case, the locus of equilibrium points $r^*(L)$ will be downward sloping and higher-productivity customers will be charged lower loan rates.

If administrative costs are zero, $D(r^*)$ will exceed L^* for all customers. However, with nonzero costs of administration, it is possible that $D(r) > L$ will hold for some classes of customers while $D(r) < L$ holds for others. Since $\partial B/\partial a > 0$, there will in this case exist a critical value of a such that $D(r) > L$ for customers with higher productivity and $D(r) < L$ for customers with lower productivity.

III. Conclusions

In this chapter we have seen that the type of credit rationing in which each borrower receives a smaller loan than he desires can arise in a competitive market for bank loans in the absence of any institutional constraints on the setting of loan rates. Borrowers will generally fail to receive the amount of credit they would desire at the prevailing loan rate if bank credit is a nonhomogeneous good--i.e. if the bank is not indifferent to the manner in which its credit is distributed among borrowers, even when those borrowers are identical. This condition will be met if (1) there exists a risk of default on each loan and marginal returns to investment are diminishing, or (2) the bank incurs costs of administration which depend on the number of loans rather than the volume of lending. The first factor tends to lead to a competitive equilibrium in which each borrower receives a <u>smaller</u> loan than he would desire at the quoted loan rate, and the second factor to an equilibrium in which each borrower receives a <u>larger</u> loan (i.e. undertakes a larger investment project) than he would desire.

The particular type of credit rationing we have been concerned with in this chapter does not have certain implications which are often associated with that phenomenon. We have seen, for example, that the existence of an excess demand for credit on the part of each borrower at the equilibrium loan rate need have no tendency to enhance the effectiveness of monetary policy, as claimed by proponents of the availability doctrine; indeed, the degree of credit rationing, as measured by total excess demand, may vary inversely with the tightness of monetary conditions. It is also not difficult to show that the equilibrium we have described will allocate resources efficiently even though borrowers fail to receive the amount of credit they demand. More precisely, the equilibrium volume of lending and investment and the equilibrium distribution of credit among firms will maximize the excess of total expected income from investment over total social cost (the opportunity cost of employing funds in investment plus the costs of administering loans).[18] As we shall see in Chapter III, the implications of the second type of credit rationing for the effectiveness of monetary policy and the efficiency of resource allocation are more in accord with conventional notions.

The first type of credit rationing does have important consequences for the response of loan rates to shifts in monetary policy or to changes in the productivity of investment. A restrictive monetary policy will raise the opportunity rate (i.e. the deposit rate or the rate of return on an alternative, riskless investment). This increase in the opportunity rate will tend to reduce each bank's expected profits per loan and as a result put upward pressure on the loan rate. As we have seen, however, an increase in the opportunity rate will also lead banks to make loans of smaller size. If in the initial equilibrium borrowers were receiving smaller loans than they desired at the prevailing loan rate, banks must have been making larger loans than they preferred at that rate. As a result, the reduction in loan size will tend to <u>increase</u> expected profits per loan, putting downward pressure on the loan rate. This second effect will moderate any increase in the loan rate produced by the first effect and may even offset it entirely; in the latter case, the restrictive monetary policy will cause an increase in the deposit rate but a reduction in the loan rate. For the same reasons, the existence of the first type of rationing makes it possible that an increase in the productivity of investment will lead to a rise in the loan rate even when the opportunity rate is constant, an event that could not occur if borrowers always received as much credit as they desired.

The possibility that firms will not receive the amount of credit they demand at the equilibrium loan rate also has important implications for a different issue: the impact of interest rate ceilings on the market for bank loans. This question is considered in detail in the next chapter. By allowing for default risk and costs of administration in the manner indicated in Section II, we will see that the aggregate effects of a loan rate ceiling may be quite different from those suggested by the conventional model of a competitive credit market. We will also find that our model provides answers to questions about the distributive effects of a ceiling on which the conventional model can shed no light whatsoever.

Appendix

In this appendix we prove several propositions about the case in which $x = \psi(L,y)$, where y is a nonnegative random variable distributed as g(y) and ψ satisfies the following conditions:

$$\psi \geq 0,\ \psi_y > 0,\ \psi_L > 0,\ \psi_{LL} < 0$$

$$\psi(L,y_{min}) \leq L$$

<u>Proposition 1.</u> $\frac{d\mu_x}{dL} > 0,\ \frac{d^2\mu_x}{dL^2} < 0$

Proof: $\mu_x(L) = \int_{y_{min}}^{y_{max}} \psi(L,y)g(y)dy$ implies

$$\frac{d\mu_x}{dL} = \int_{y_{min}}^{y_{max}} \psi_L(L,y)g(y)dy > 0$$

and

$$\frac{d^2\mu_x}{dL^2} = \int_{y_{min}}^{y_{max}} \psi_{LL}(L,y)g(y)dy < 0$$

<u>Proposition 2.</u> $\left.\frac{\partial\mu_R}{\partial L}\right|_{z\ \text{const.}} > 0$ for all r and $L > 0$.

Proof: Let $\hat{y}(r,L)$ be that value of y for which $\psi(L,y) = z \equiv (1+r)L$. Then

$$\text{(A.1)} \qquad \mu_R = \int_{y_{min}}^{\hat{y}} \psi(L,y)g(y)dy + z \int_{\hat{y}}^{y_{max}} g(y)dy$$

which implies

$$\left.\frac{\partial\mu_R}{\partial L}\right|_{z\ const.} = \int_{y_{min}}^{\hat{y}} \psi_L(L,y)g(y)dy$$

The assumption $\psi(L,y_{min}) \leq L$ ensures that $\hat{y}(r,L) > y_{min}$ for all r and $L > 0$. Since $\psi_L(L,y) > 0$, it follows that $\left.\frac{\partial\mu_R}{\partial L}\right|_{z\ const.} > 0$ for positive r and L.

Proposition 3. $\frac{\partial\mu_R}{\partial L} > 0$ and $\frac{\partial^2\mu_R}{\partial L^2} < 0$ for all r and $L > 0$.

Proof: Differentiating (A.1) we obtain

$$\frac{\partial\mu_R}{\partial L} = (1+r) \int_{\hat{y}}^{y_{max}} g(y)dy + \int_{y_{min}}^{\hat{y}} \psi_L(L,y)g(y)dy > 0$$

and

$$\text{(A.2)} \qquad \frac{\partial^2\mu_R}{\partial L^2} = [\psi_L(L,\hat{y}) - \frac{\psi(L,\hat{y})}{L}]g(\hat{y}) \frac{\partial\hat{y}}{\partial L} + \int_{y_{min}}^{\hat{y}} \psi_{LL}(L,y)g(y)dy$$

Now by partially differentiating the equation $\psi(L,\hat{y}) = z$ with respect to L we obtain

$$\psi_L(L,\hat{y}) + \psi_y(L,\hat{y}) \frac{\partial \hat{y}}{\partial L} = 1 + r = \frac{\psi(L,\hat{y})}{L}$$

or

$$\frac{\partial \hat{y}}{\partial L} = \frac{1}{\psi_y(L,\hat{y})} [\frac{\psi(L,\hat{y})}{L} - \psi_L(L,\hat{y})]$$

We have already seen that $\hat{y}(r,L) > y_{min}$ for all r and $L > 0$. Thus (A.2) implies $\frac{\partial^2 \mu_R}{\partial L^2} < 0$ for positive r and L.

Footnotes

1 For a survey of the earlier literature on the theory of credit rationing, see Jaffee [2].

2 In writing the cost function in this form we have implicitly assumed that each firm can sell only one "brand," i.e. that all units of the good produced by the firm have the same characteristic w. This assumption is made to simplify the exposition. In each case examined below, we would obtain the same equilibrium solution if the firm were allowed to produce more than one brand. Thus, the firm's costs could be expressed as $\Sigma\, m_i C(w_i)$ rather than $mC(w)$, or as $\Sigma\, m_i C_1(w_i) + C_2(\Sigma\, m_i)$ rather than $mC_1(w) + C_2(m)$.

3 If π did not attain a unique maximum along each iso-utility curve, i.e. if there were multiple tangencies, the equilibrium values of U and π would be determined in the same manner. In this case, however, the equilibrium combination of p_w and w might not be unique.

4 If $\pi = m\delta(p_w, w)$, the optimal value of m is of course infinite for all p_w and w such that $\delta(p_w, w) > 0$. In this case, the good can be treated as homogeneous if $\delta(p_w, w) = 0$ always implies $\delta_w = 0$.

5 An equivalent approach, followed by Rosen, would be to derive an equilibrium price function $p(w)$ or $p_w(w)$. Firms would be assumed

to take the function $p_w(w)$ as given and choose w and m so as to maximize $\pi = m\delta(p_w(w),w) - C_2(m)$. Consumers would also take $p_w(w)$ as given, choosing w so as to maximize $U(y-wp_w(w),w)$. For equilibrium to exist, the total number of units of the good supplied by firms at each point on the function $p_w(w)$ would have to equal the number of consumers wishing to buy the good at that combination of p_w and w. Although this approach leads to the same result in the present case, it cannot be applied when all firms are identical and all consumers are identical. In the latter case only one combination of p_w and w will be offered in equilibrium, so that the equilibrium price function $p_w(w)$ degenerates to a single point. As a result, the equilibrium solution will be indeterminate.

6 We shall see later that this assumption is unnecessary if the bank making the first loan always has priority over the firm's assets in the event of default.

7 If the bank also incurs an administrative cost equal to a constant proportion of the size of the loan, we can simply redefine the opportunity cost (1+h)L to include that cost. For an argument that a bank's administrative costs will depend primarily on the number of its loans rather than the volume of credit, see [6].

8 Henceforth we shall refer to δ as the bank's expected profits per loan. It should be remembered, however, that δ is calculated

gross of administrative costs.

9 The restrictions $\psi \geq 0$, $\psi_L < 0$, and $\psi_{LL} < 0$ imply that $\frac{\psi(L,y)}{L}$ is a strictly decreasing function of L. Also, $\lim_{L\to\infty} \psi_L \leq 1$ implies $\lim_{L\to\infty} \frac{\psi(L,y)}{L} < 1+r$ for all y and $r > 0$. But $u(r,L) > 0$ if $x_M = \psi(L,y_{max}) > (1+r)L$ and $u(r,L) = 0$ if $x_M = \psi(L,y_{max}) \leq (1+r)L$. Thus, for each loan rate there will exist a finite value of L, say $\hat{L}$, such that $u(r,L) > 0$ for $0 < L < \hat{L}$ and $u(r,L) = 0$ for $L \geq \hat{L}$.

10 The effect on total expected profits π of a marginal reduction in loan size L and an accompanying increase in the number of loans m just sufficient to maintain total lending at a constant level $\overline{mL}$ is

$$-\overline{mL}\,\frac{\partial}{\partial L}\,\frac{\mu_R(r,L)}{L} = m\left(\frac{\mu_R}{L} - \frac{\partial \mu_R}{\partial L}\right)$$

Since $\mu_R(r,0) = 0$ and $\partial^2\mu_R/\partial L^2 < 0$, this expression is positive.

11 This is so because $u(r,L) > \mu_x(0) \geq 0$ implies $r < \hat{r}(L)$ and thus $\partial\delta/\partial r = \partial\mu_R/\partial r > 0$.

12 In equilibrium $u(r,L) = \underset{L}{\text{Max}}\ \mu_x(L) - (1+h)L$. Thus, $u(r,L) = \mu_x(0)$ implies $L = 0$. But then $h = \Omega(0)$. Since $1 + \Omega(0) < \lim_{L\to 0} \frac{d\mu_x}{dL}$, this implies $\underset{L}{\text{Max}}\ \mu_x(L) - (1+h)L > \mu_x(0)$, which is a contradiction.

13 If we relax the assumption that there exists a risk of default on loans of all size, it need no longer always be the case that credit is rationed in equilibrium. Suppose, for example, that each firm has collateral with a certain end-of-period value $B > 0$, so that the outcome of the investment project is $x = B + \psi(L,y)$. In this case the probability of default will be zero for any loan of sufficiently small size that $x_m \equiv B + \psi(L,y_{min}) \geq (1+r)L$. In terms of Figure 11, the bank's zero iso-profit curve will contain a horizontal segment at $r = h$ and will be upward sloping thereafter. The equilibrium loan size will be that value of L which maximizes $\delta + u = \mu_x(L) - (1+h)L$ and will therefore be independent of B. But the loan size at which default becomes possible will be an increasing function of B, given any loan rate. Thus, the likelihood that credit will be rationed--i.e. that equilibrium will occur at a point on the positively sloped segment of the bank's zero iso-profit curve--will be greater the lower the value of the firm's collateral.

14 Let S be the total number of loans granted and let h_s be the solution to the equation $h = \Omega(S\mathcal{L}(h))$. Suppose that $S < M$ in equilibrium. Then (E.2) implies $u(r,L) = \mu_x(0)$; (E.3) implies $\delta < \delta(M/\bar{N})$; and (E.3) and (E.4) imply $h = h_s \leq h^*$. Since $u(r,L) + \delta(r,L,h)$ must equal $\underset{L}{\text{Max}}\ \mu_x(L) - (1+h)L$ in equilibrium, and since the latter expression is decreasing in h, it follows that

$$\underset{L}{\text{Max}}\ \mu_x(L) - (1+h^*)L - \mu_x(0)$$

$$\leq \underset{L}{\text{Max}}\ \mu_x(L) - (1+h_s)L - \mu_x(0) < \delta(M/\bar{N})$$

Thus, $S < M$ cannot hold in equilibrium if $\delta(M/\bar{N}) \leq \underset{L}{\text{Max}}\ \mu_x(L) - (1+h^*)L - \mu_x(0)$.

If $\delta(M/\bar{N}) > \underset{L}{\text{Max}}\ \mu_x(L) - (1+h^*)L - \mu_x(0)$, the equilibrium opportunity rate will lie below h*. Each customer will be charged his reservation loan rate, and some firms will not borrow at all.

15 In the event that a demand curve D(r) can be defined such that $\partial u/\partial L \gtreqless 0$ as $L \lesseqgtr D(r)$, D(r) will exceed L in equilibrium if and only if $\partial u/\partial L > 0$. In the more general case, however, the possibility exists that the customer's expected profits will attain a maximum at some smaller L even if $\partial u/\partial L > 0$ in equilibrium. We shall nevertheless say that the first type of rationing occurs whenever the latter condition holds.

16 At a given loan rate, the net effect of an increase in h on δ will be $\frac{\partial\delta}{\partial L}\frac{d\mathcal{L}}{dh} - L$. To see that this expression can be positive, suppose that the project outcome is $\psi(L)y = (aL^{\alpha} + bL)y$, where $\alpha < 1$, $b \leq 2$, and y is distributed uniformly over the interval (0,1). Then $\delta(r,L,h) = 0$ can be shown to imply

$$\frac{\partial\delta}{\partial L}\frac{d\mathcal{L}}{dh} - L = L\ \{\frac{(\psi' - \frac{\psi}{L})\hat{y}^2}{L\psi''} - 1\} = \frac{L}{\alpha}\ (\hat{y} - \alpha^{\frac{1}{2}})(\hat{y} + \alpha^{\frac{1}{2}})$$

where $\hat{y}(r,L)$ is the value of y for which $\psi(L)y = (1+r)L$. Also, $L = \mathcal{L}(h)$ and $\delta(r,L,h) = 0$ can be shown to imply $\hat{y} = 1 - (1-A)^{\frac{1}{2}}$, where $A = \frac{L\psi'}{\psi}$. But given a, α, and b, we can choose h so that $L(h) = 1$. Since $L = 1$ implies $1 - A = \frac{(1-\alpha)a}{a+b}$, $\frac{\partial\delta}{\partial L}\frac{dL}{dh} - L > 0$ will hold in this case for any values of the parameters a, α, and b such that $\hat{y} - \alpha^{\frac{1}{2}} = 1 - [\frac{(1-\alpha)a}{a+b}]^{\frac{1}{2}} - \alpha^{\frac{1}{2}} > 0$; an example in which this condition is satisfied is the case of $\alpha = 1/8$, $b = 2$, and $a = 4/5$.

17 To see that the second effect may dominate, suppose that $\psi(L,y) = t\psi(L)y$. The equilibrium loan size can then be expressed as a function $L(h,t)$ with $\partial L/\partial t = -\psi'/t\psi''$. If $\delta(r,L,h,t) = 0$, the net effect of an increase in t on δ, given h and r, will be

$$\frac{d\delta}{dt} = \frac{\partial\delta}{\partial t} + \frac{\partial\delta}{\partial L}\frac{\partial L}{\partial t} = \{\psi - \frac{\psi'}{\psi''}(\psi' - \frac{\psi}{L})\} \int_{y_{min}}^{\hat{y}} yg(y)dy$$

where $t\psi(L)\hat{y} = (1+r)L$. It is easily verified that the expression in brackets can be negative, e.g. if $\psi(L) = aL^{\alpha} + bL$ with $\alpha < 1$. When $\Omega' > 0$, the increase in t will lead to a rise in the equilibrium value of h, and this also will tend to reduce δ.

18 The total expected income from investment, net of administrative costs, may be defined as

$$W = \sum_{1}^{S}\{\mu_x(L_i) - \mu_x(0)\} - \sum_{1}^{N} C(m_j)$$

where $S \equiv \sum_{1}^{N} m_j$, the total number of loans made by all banks.
If there is free entry to the banking industry, the equilibrium values of L, m, and N will maximize W subject to the constraints

$\sum_{1}^{N} m_j \leq M$ and $\sum_{1}^{S} L_i = L_T$, where L_T is the volume of lending by all banks; thus the equilibrium distribution of credit among firms and the equilibrium allocation of loans among banks will be optimal. Under the optimal allocation of credit, however, it must be true that $\frac{dW^*}{dL_T} = \frac{d\mu_x}{dL}$, where W^* is the maximized value of W given L_T. Since the equilibrium loan size always satisfies $\frac{d\mu_x}{dL} = 1+h$, this means that the volume of total lending L_T will also be optimal, provided the opportunity rate h reflects the marginal social opportunity cost of employing resources in investment.

References

[1] Eckaus, Richard S., "Monopoly Power, Credit Rationing, and the Variegation of Financial Structures" in Organization of American States, Documents and Summary of Discussions: Third Annual Meeting of Capital Markets Development Program (Washington, D.C., General Secretariat, Organization of American States, 1974)

[2] Jaffee, Dwight M., Credit Rationing and the Commercial Loan Market (New York, John Wiley and Sons, 1971)

[3] _______________ and Modigliani, Franco, "A Theory and Test of Credit Rationing," American Economic Review, December, 1969

[4] Rosen, Sherwin, "Hedonic Prices and Implicit Market: Product Differentiation in Pure Competition," Journal of Political Economy, January-February, 1974

[5] Rothschild, Michael and Stiglitz, Joseph E., "Increasing Risk: I, A Definition," Journal of Economic Theory, September, 1970

[6] Smith, Paul F., Economics of Financial Institutions and Markets (Homewood, Ill., Richard D. Irwin, Inc., 1971)

CHAPTER II. AN ANALYSIS OF LOAN RATE CEILINGS

Introduction and Summary

The purpose of this chapter is to determine the effects of imposing a ceiling on the interest rate banks can charge for loans. Although most of the chapter is devoted to this problem, the analytical framework which we develop will be found readily applicable to a closely related question--that of the short-term impact of monetary policy when loan rates are sticky. In both instances we shall assume that the market for bank loans is competitive.

The imposition of a ceiling on the loan rate will in general have both aggregate and distributive effects. These effects may be classified under the following headings:

(1) The change in the total volume of credit and investment.

(2) The impact on the distribution of bank credit among borrowers.

(3) The effects of the action on the welfare of banks, borrowers, and depositors.

In (1), our interest is in the macroeconomic repercussions of the policy action. The second heading is concerned with the manner in which changes in total credit are distributed among potential borrowers. In particular, will all firms be able to obtain loans after the action has been undertaken? Or is it possible that some firms will receive credit while other, identical firms do not? The answers to these questions will have a bearing not only on the distribution of income among potential borrowers but also on the overall efficiency of resource allocation. The final area of interest relates to the effects of the policy action on the welfare of each of the different groups involved--banks, borrowers, and depositors. Of primary concern here is whether one group (e.g. borrowers) will be favored at the expense of another (e.g. depositors).

The conventional or "naive" model of the market for bank credit posits an aggregate demand for credit which is inversely related to the loan rate and an aggregate supply of deposits which is an increasing function of the rate of interest paid on deposits. The bank's rate of profit is simply the difference between the loan rate and the deposit rate. A clear implication of the model is that the imposition of a loan rate ceiling will lead to a decline in total lending and in the rate of interest paid to depositors. Unfortunately, however, the naive model can provide no additional information. The aggregate demand for credit at the new loan rate must exceed the amount supplied by banks, but there is no way of knowing how the excess demand will be distributed among borrowers. Also, although depositors will clearly be worse off, it is not possible to determine if borrowers as a group will benefit from the action--or, in other terms, whether the reduction in the loan rate will compensate for the decline in the amount of credit received and the change, if any, in its distribution.

Thus, the conventional model can shed little light on the distributive effects of a loan rate ceiling. To remedy this deficiency, and to provide a sounder theoretical framework for analyzing the aggregate effects as well, we shall employ the more sophisticated model described in detail in Section II of Chapter I. The distinguishing feature of this model is that it explicitly takes into account the risk of default on bank loans. In addition, the model allows for the possibility that administrative costs will depend on the number of loans that a bank makes rather than the volume of its lending.[1]

An important feature of the competitive equilibrium in this model is that the customer's demand for credit will not in general equal the size of the loan he receives. If the only cost to the bank of making a loan is the interest paid on deposits, each firm will receive less credit than it desires at the equilibrium loan rate. However, if the bank must also incur certain administrative costs which depend only on the number of loans, the firm's demand for credit may either exceed or fall short of the size of the loan it actually receives in equilibrium. In any event, whenever a firm would prefer to receive a larger volume of credit at the equilibrium loan rate, the bank would prefer to make a smaller loan at that rate--and vice versa.

The fact that the equilibrium loan size may be either larger or smaller than the bank's optimal loan size has important implications for the impact of a loan rate ceiling on the volume of lending. This is most easily seen when the supply of deposits to the banking industry is infinitely elastic and the deposit rate exogenous. If the ceiling is not prohibitively low, equilibrium will require that banks continue to earn the same expected profits per loan (i.e. the same excess of expected revenues over implicit interest payments to depositors) as they did before the ceiling. However, the reduction in the loan rate brought about by the imposition of the ceiling will by itself tend to reduce expected profits per loan. Thus, if expected profits per loan are to remain the same, the equilibrium loan size must change. If in the initial equilibrium banks are making larger loans than they desire, the adverse effect of the reduction in the loan rate can be offset only by a decrease in the size of each loan. But, if banks are initially making smaller loans than they prefer, as will be the case if administrative costs are high, the reduction in the loan rate can be compensated only by an increase in loan size. One of our major findings is that this relationship continues to hold when the deposit rate is endogenous, i.e. when the supply of deposits to the banking industry is less than perfectly elastic.

The effect of a loan rate ceiling on the distribution of credit among borrowers also depends on the significance of administrative costs. The reason all firms must receive credit in the absence of a ceiling is that the bank's expected revenues from a loan are an increasing function of the loan rate. Firms which failed to receive credit would always be willing to pay a slightly higher interest rate than banks were currently charging, and banks would always have an incentive to make loans at that higher rate of interest. When there is a ceiling on the loan rate, matters are not quite so simple. Obviously firms which have been unable to obtain credit cannot offer to pay a higher interest rate than banks are currently charging, if the loan rate is already at the ceiling. However, as long as the loans which are being granted are not of optimal size for the bank, any firm which has failed to receive credit should be able to obtain it by offering to accept a loan of different size at the same interest rate. If there is a risk of default on each loan but no cost of administration, this condition will always be satisfied; any loan made in the new equilibrium will be larger than the bank would prefer and as a result, all firms will be able to obtain credit. If costs of administration are nonzero, however, it is possible that banks will make loans in the postceiling equilibrium which are of optimal size at the ceiling rate; in this case, we shall see, there exists a critical level of the ceiling above which all firms receive loans and below which some are denied credit.

We begin, in Section I, by considering the effects of a ceiling on the loan rate in the conventional model of a competitive credit market. We also examine the implications of the model for monetary policy when loan rates are slow to adjust to equilibrium levels. The more sophisticated model used in the remainder of the chapter is summarized in Section II and applied in Section III to the analysis of a loan rate ceiling. In Section III.A. we indicate how the conditions for a competitive equilibrium in the market for bank loans must be modified to take account of the ceiling. These conditions are then used to determine the postceiling equilibrium--first in Section III.B. for the case in which the deposit rate or opportunity rate is exogenous and then in Section III.C. for the case in which the deposit rate is an increasing function of the total volume of bank deposits. At the end of Section III we demonstrate that the results of the conventional model can be obtained as a special limiting case. In Section IV we employ the model to evaluate the short-term impact of changes in underlying monetary conditions. Finally, in Section V, we summarize the major conclusions of the chapter.

A final question of terminology must be resolved before we proceed. As we noted in Chapter I, there are at least two senses in which credit can be said to be "rationed." First, an individual borrower may receive a smaller loan than he desires at the quoted loan rate. Secondly, some firms may receive loans while other, identical firms do not. Henceforth we shall refer to the first phenomenon as Type I credit rationing and to the second as Type II credit rationing.

I. The naive theory of loan rate ceilings

In this section we consider the effects of a ceiling on the loan rate in the conventional model of a competitive credit market. In the simplest form of this model, it is assumed that the bank's costs are the interest payments which it must make to depositors and that its revenues are the interest payments received from borrowers. It is further assumed in this extreme version of the model that loan revenues are certain and that no reserves need to be held. The bank's profits are thus $\pi = (r-h) \sum_{1}^{m} L_i$, where r is the loan rate, h is the rate of interest paid on deposits, L_i is the size of the loan made to the bank's i^{th} customer, and m is the number of customers of the bank.

The total supply of funds to the banking industry is assumed to be an increasing function S(h) of the interest rate paid on deposits. Also, aggregate demand for credit is assumed to be a decreasing function D(r) of the loan rate. Individual banks behave as perfect competitors. Since a bank's profits are proportional to the total volume of its deposits, there will exist an incentive to bid for additional deposits and increase lending as long as $h < r$. Furthermore, if $h \leq r$ and $S(h) < D(r)$, banks will presumably try to increase their profits by accepting additional deposits and making loans to those borrowers whose demand for credit is unsatisfied. Thus, in terms of Figure 1, equilibrium must occur at E, with $h = r$ and $S(h) = D(r)$.

Suppose now that a ceiling of $\bar{r}$ is imposed on the loan rate. As before, competition among banks for deposits will ensure that $h = r$ in equilibrium. Also, as long as $r < \bar{r}$, banks will be able to increase their profits by making loans to unsatisfied borrowers at a higher rate of interest. Equilibrium will thus occur at E' in Figure 1, with $h = r = \bar{r}$ and $D(r) > S(h)$. Banks will be obliged to ration credit, either by granting customers smaller loans than they would desire or by refusing to lend to certain borrowers. It is sometimes assumed that the bank's administrative costs and default losses can be represented as a constant proportion α of its volume of lending (e.g. [4]). In this case the loan rate will exceed the deposit rate by the margin α, but the effects of a ceiling will be the same.

Although the imposition of the ceiling will cause lending to fall, there is no way of determining from the model how that reduction will be distributed among borrowers. Those customers fortunate enough to receive credit may be better off as a result of the loan rate ceiling, but firms which are unable to obtain loans will certainly be worse off. It is apparently a widespread view among economists that interest rate ceilings will harm the majority of borrowers ([2], [3]).

The simple model described above has been employed not only to analyze the effects of interest rate ceilings, but also to determine the impact of changes in underlying credit conditions when interest rates charged by banks are sticky. In [5], for example, Tucker considers the effect of a restrictive monetary policy under the assumption that the loan rate moves toward the new equilibrium level only with a lag. He argues that banks will ration credit as long as the loan rate remains below the new equilibrium level, and that as a result monetary contraction will reduce lending and investment even in the short run. In terms of Figure 2, the restrictive policy shifts the loan supply

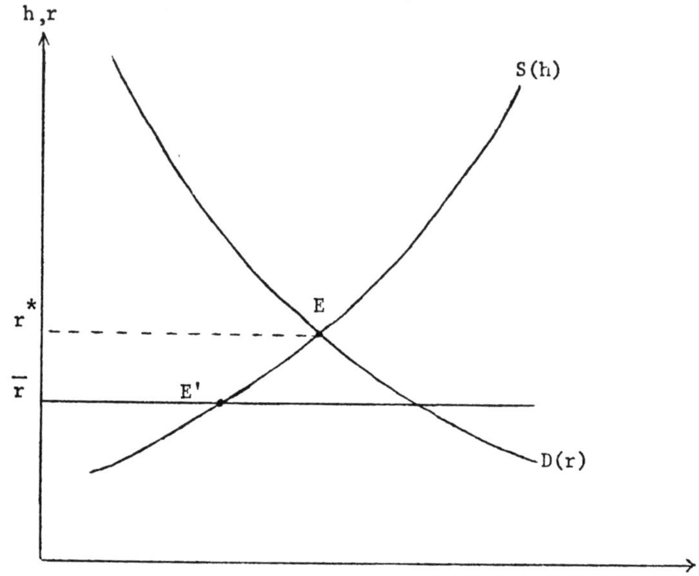

Figure 1

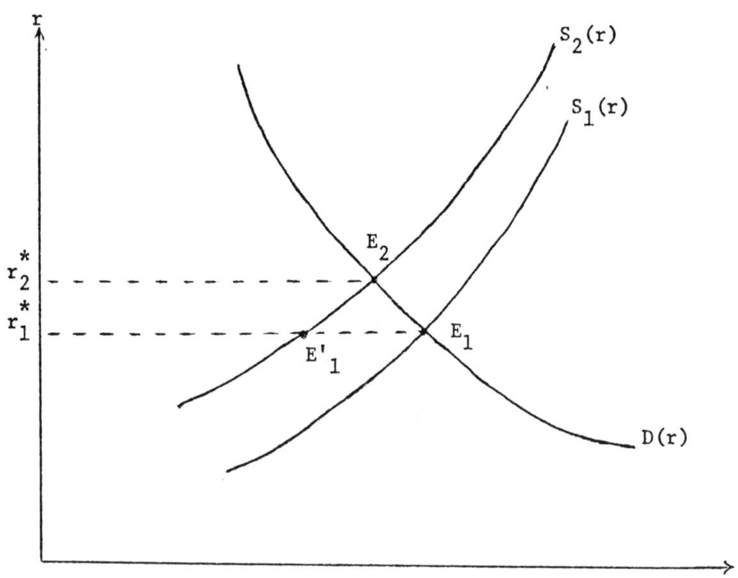

Figure 2

schedule from $S_1(r)$ to $S_2(r)$. At first banks reduce the volume of lending from $S_1(r_1^*)$ to $S_2(r_1^*)$. As the loan rate is gradually increased to r_2^*, the amount of lending increases until the excess demand for credit is eliminated.

Two important conclusions can be drawn from this analysis. The first is that monetary policy may be effective even if the investment demand function is highly inelastic with respect to interest rates. In the extreme case in which investment can be financed only by bank credit and demand is perfectly inelastic, a tightening of monetary conditions can have no long-run effect on investment. But if the loan rate is slow to adjust, firms will be forced to curtail their investment plans in the short run by their inability to obtain funds. Proponents of the so-called "availability doctrine" argue that this effect is sufficiently important to justify the use of monetary policy in controlling aggregate demand.

A second implication, with which Tucker's paper is primarily concerned, is that lags in interest rate adjustment may actually increase the speed of response of output and employment to monetary policy. Suppose that output adjusts only gradually to changes in product demand, but that the rate of adjustment depends on the amount of excess supply or excess demand for the product. Suppose further that investment must be financed primarily by bank loans. As we have seen, a tightening of monetary conditions will cause a greater decline in lending if the loan rate remains fixed than if it adjusts immediately to the new equilibrium level. But since the demand for investment goods is constrained by the availability of bank credit, the initial excess supply in the product market must also be greater with an interest rate lag than without one. Interest rate inflexibility will therefore tend to increase the speed of response of output and employment to a restrictive monetary policy.

We have explained what the conventional model has to say about the effects of a ceiling on the loan rate and the impact of monetary policy when the loan rate is slow to adjust to its equilibrium level. In the remainder of this chapter we will employ the more sophisticated model described in Section II of Chapter I. By treating default risk and administrative costs in an explicit manner, this model will allow us to determine the distributive effects of a loan rate ceiling; in addition, we will find that the aggregate impact of a ceiling may be quite different than indicated above.

II. A summary of the model

We begin by giving a brief summary of the model and reviewing the properties of the competitive equilibrium in the absence of constraints on the loan rate.

As in Chapter I, we assume that there are M identical firms which can finance their investment projects only by borrowing from banks. We shall also continue to suppose that the outcome of an investment project is $x = \psi(L,y)$, where L is the volume of bank credit obtained by the firm, y is a random variable or "state of the world" with probability density function g(y), and the function ψ satisfies the restrictions listed on p. 33. The more important of these restrictions, it will be recalled, are that marginal returns to investment are diminishing ($\psi_{LL} < 0$) and that default is possible on loans of all sizes ($\psi(L,y_{min}) \leq L$). For convenience, we will also assume in this chapter that the end-of-period value of the firm is certain to be zero if the firm does not undertake any investment, i.e. that $\psi(0,y) = 0$. This implies $\mu_X(L) = 0$ at $L = 0$, where $\mu_X = E[x]$, the expected project outcome.

The bank's revenues from a loan of size L are $R = \min\{x,(1+r)L\}$. In making a loan the bank incurs an opportunity cost $(1+h)L$. Each bank is assumed to take the opportunity rate h as given; however, we allow for the possibility that this rate may be a function Ω of the total volume of lending by all banks. There may also exist certain administrative costs C(m) which depend on the total number of loans m made by the bank. When such costs do exist, it will be assumed that marginal costs $C'(m)$ are at first strictly decreasing and then strictly increasing, so that the average cost function $\frac{C(m)}{m}$ is U-shaped.

It is assumed that each firm can take out only one loan.[2] The expected revenues of the bank from a loan of size L at interest rate r are thus

$$\mu_R(r,L) = \int_{y_{min}}^{\hat{y}} \psi(L,y)g(y)dy + (1+r)L \int_{\hat{y}}^{y_{max}} g(y)dy$$

where $\hat{y}(r,L)$ is that value of y which satisfies $\psi(L,y) = (1+r)L$. Expected profits from the loan, excluding administrative costs, are

$$\delta(r,L,h) \equiv \mu_R(r,L) - (1+h)L$$ [3]

For each r and h there exists a unique loan size $Q(r,h)$ that maximizes $\delta(r,L,h)$; we refer to the locus $Q(r,h)$ as the bank's "offer curve." Given h and δ, we can also define an "iso-profit" curve $\phi(L,h,\delta)$ indicating the loan rate the bank must charge if its expected profits per loan are to equal δ.

Each bank seeks to maximize the expected value of its total profits. If r and L are the same for all customers, total expected profits of the bank are

$$\pi(r,L,m,h) \equiv m\delta(r,L,h) - C(m)$$

For any r, L, and h such that $\delta(r,L,h) \geq \text{Min} \frac{C(m)}{m}$, the bank will maximize π by choosing m so that $C'(m) = \delta$. This condition determines a positively sloped function $m(\delta)$ which indicates the bank's optimal number of loans given δ. We define $\delta(m)$ to be that value of δ at which $m(\delta) = m$.

Each firm attempts to maximize the expected value of the surplus x-R. The objective function of the firm is thus

$$u(r,L) \equiv E[x-R] = \int_{\hat{y}}^{y_{max}} [\psi(L,y) - (1+r)L]g(y)dy$$

The borrower's expected profits $u(r,L)$ will be positive if and only if $r < \hat{r}(L)$, where $\hat{r}(L)$ is the loan rate at which default becomes certain, i.e. the value of r such that $\hat{y}(r,L) = y_{max}$. For $u > 0$, we can define an iso-profit curve $\theta(L,u)$ indicating the loan rate at which the borrower's expected profits are just equal to u.

An equilibrium exists when no bank has an incentive to alter either the terms at which it grants loans or the number of firms to which it lends. If there are no constraints on the loan rate, equilibrium will be determined by conditions (E.1)-(E.5) of Chapter I. For convenience those conditions are repeated below:[4]

(E.1) $\sum_1^N m_i \leq M$

(E.2) $\sum_1^N m_i < M$ only if $u(r,L) = 0$

(E.3) $\nexists$ an r', L', and m' such that $\pi(r',L',m',h) > \pi(r,L,m_i,h)$ and $u(r',L') \geq u(r,L)$

(E.4) $h = \Omega(\sum_1^N m_i L)$

(E.5a) $N = \bar{N}$ (restricted entry)

(E.5b) $\pi(r,L,m_i,h) = 0$ (free entry)

Here m_i is the number of loans supplied by the ith bank and N is the number of banks. Since the bank's total expected profits can be expressed as a function of δ and m alone, with $\partial\pi/\partial\delta > 0$, condition (E.3) has two parts:

(a) $\nexists$ an r' and L' such that $\delta(r',L',h) > \delta(r,L,h)$ and $u(r',L') \geq u(r,L)$

(b) $\nexists$ an m' such that $\pi(\delta,m') > \pi(\delta,m_i)$

We will assume that $\text{Min}\,\frac{C(m)}{m} < \delta(M/\bar{N}) < \mu_X(L(h^*)) - (1+h^*)L(h^*)$, where $\bar{N}$ is the number of banks when entry is restricted, $L(h)$ is the value of L that maximizes $\mu_X(L) - (1+h)L$, and h* is the solution to the equation $h = \Omega(ML(h))$. As we saw in Chapter I, this implies that the bank's expected profits per loan in equilibrium are

$\delta^* = 0$ if there are no administrative costs

$= \delta(M/\bar{N})$ if there are administrative costs and the number of banks is fixed at $\bar{N}$

$= \text{Min}\,\frac{C(m)}{m}$ if there are administrative costs and entry is free

In each case all M firms must receive credit. The equilibrium opportunity rate will be h*, the equilibrium loan size $L^* = L(h^*)$, and the equilibrium loan rate that value r* at which $\delta(r,L^*,h^*) = \delta^*$.

As shown in Figures 3 and 4, equilibrium occurs at a point of tangency of the bank iso-profit curve $\phi(L,h^*,\delta^*)$ with a borrower iso-profit locus $\theta(L,u)$. If administrative costs are zero (Figure 3), the locus $\phi(L,h^*,\delta^*)$ will have positive slope throughout. This implies $\partial u/\partial L > 0$ and $\partial\delta/\partial L < 0$ in equilibrium: firms would prefer to receive larger loans at the equilibrium loan rate and banks would prefer to make smaller loans at that rate. When administrative costs are non-zero, however, the curve $\phi(L,h^*,\delta^*)$ may have either positive or negative slope. If Min $\frac{C(m)}{m}$ is relatively small (case of free entry) or the ratio $M/\bar{N}$ low (case of restricted entry), ϕ_L will be positive at the equilibrium point (Figure 4a). In this case, it will again be true that $\partial u/\partial L > 0$ and $\partial\delta/\partial L < 0$ in equilibrium. But if ϕ_L is negative at the equilibrium point (Figure 4b), the exact opposite condition will exist; firms will receive more credit and undertake larger investment projects than they desire at the equilibrium loan rate ($\partial u/\partial L < 0$) and banks will make smaller loans than are optimal at that rate ($\partial\delta/\delta L > 0$).

Having described the equilibrium that will prevail in the absence of any constraints, we may now consider the effects of imposing a ceiling $\bar{r}$ on the loan rate.

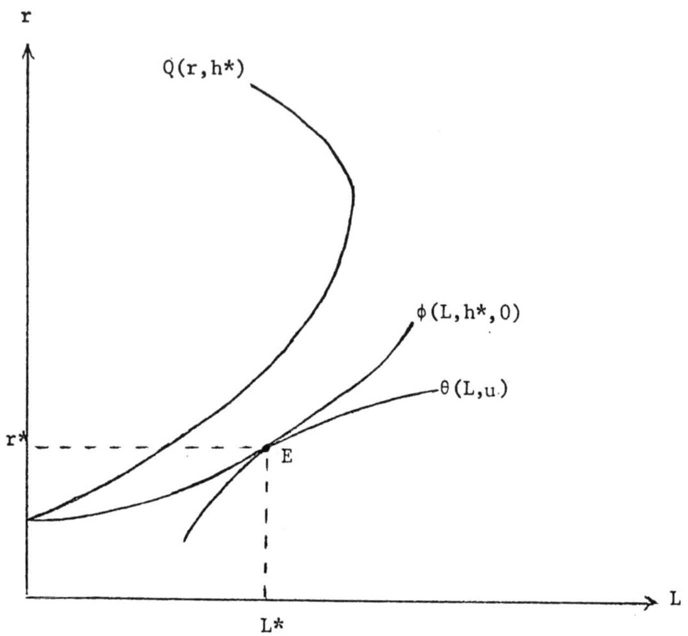

Figure 3

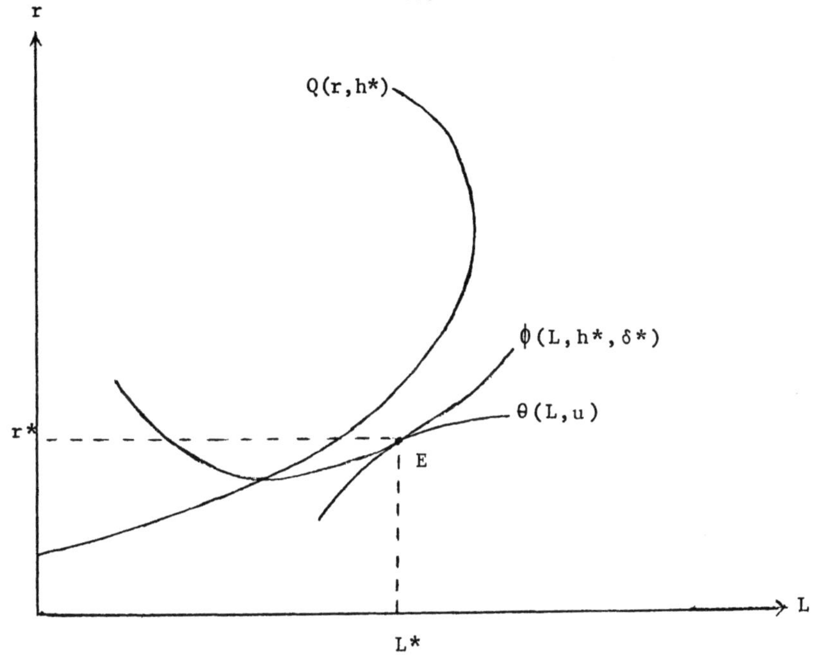

Figure 4a

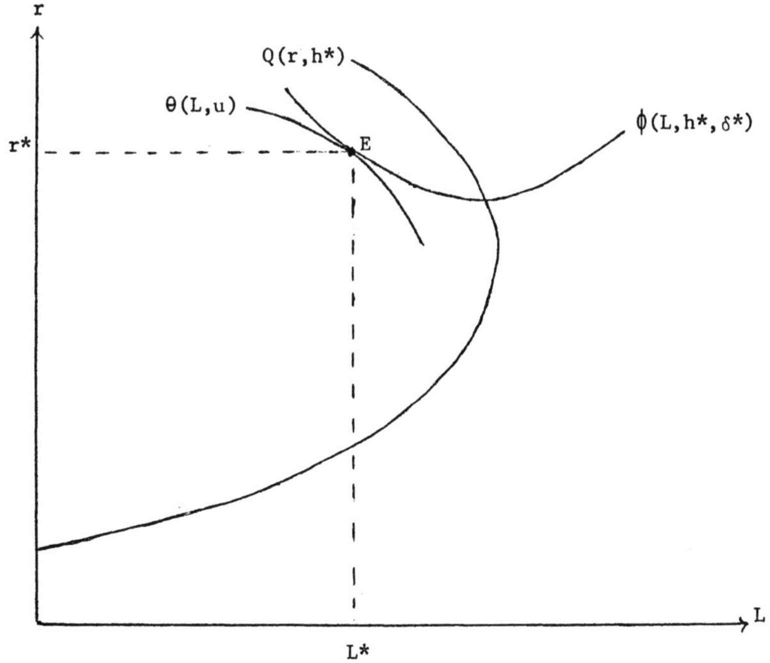

Figure 4b

III. The impact of a ceiling on the loan rate

A. Equilibrium conditions

Since firms are identical, banks will charge the same loan rate and grant loans of the same size to all customers.[5] Clearly the equilibrium values of r, L, N, h, and $\{m_i\}$ must satisfy conditions (E.1), (E.4), and (E.5) of the previous section. However, conditions (E.2) and (E.3) must be modified to take account of the ceiling on the loan rate. The new set of equilibrium conditions is

(E.1) $$\sum_1^N m_i \leq M$$

(E.2') $$\sum_1^N m_i < M \text{ only if } u(r,L) = 0 \text{ or } \delta(r,L,h) = \max_{r,L} \delta(r,L,h) \text{ subject to } r \leq \bar{r}$$

(E.3') $$\nexists \text{ an } r' \leq \bar{r},\ L',\text{ and } m' \text{ such that } \pi(r',L',m',h) > \pi(r,L,m_i,h) \text{ and } u(r',L') \geq u(r,L)$$

(E.4) $$h = \Omega(\sum_1^N m_i L)$$

(E.5a) $N = \bar{N}$ (restricted entry)

(E.5b) $\pi(r,L,m_i,h) = 0$ (free entry)

(E.6) $r \leq \bar{r}$

Condition (E.2') calls for some explanation. It allows for the possibility that some customers will fail to receive credit in equilibrium even if other firms are borrowing at terms that yield positive expected profits $u(r,L)$. In particular, if the prevailing loan rate and loan size maximize $\delta(r,L,h)$ subject to the constraint $r \leq \bar{r}$, and if each bank is supplying that number of loans which maximizes its total expected profits given δ, any firm which lacks credit will be unable to obtain it by offering to accept a loan at less favorable terms, i.e. at an r and L which yield lower expected profits u. Of course, this possibility could not arise in the absence of a ceiling on r, since $u(r,L) > 0$ implies $\partial\delta/\partial r > 0$.

By comparing the equilibrium determined by the above conditions to the equilibrium that would prevail without any constraint on r, we may evaluate the impact of a loan rate ceiling on the volume and distribution of bank credit. For purposes of exposition, we shall proceed by examining first the case in which Ω is simply a constant. We then take up the more interesting case in which h is endogenous.

B. h exogenous

When h is fixed, the initial equilibrium loan size can be expressed as $L^* = L(h)$ and the initial equilibrium loan rate as $r^* = \phi(L^*,h,\delta^*)$, where δ^*, it will be recalled, is the equilibrium value of expected profits per loan in the absence of any ceiling. The characteristics of the postceiling equilibrium will depend in a crucial way on the height of the ceiling. There are two possibilities which we must consider.

1. To begin with, we shall suppose that $\bar{r}$ lies below the initial equilibrium loan rate but above the level at which it is just possible for banks to earn expected profits per loan δ^*, i.e. above the minimum point on the bank iso-profit curve $\phi(L,h,\delta^*)$. We proceed by establishing that all firms must continue to receive credit in the new equilibrium and that banks must continue to earn the same expected profits per loan, δ^*, as in the absence of a ceiling. The latter condition is then employed with equilibrium condition (E.3'), which requires that no bank have an incentive to alter the terms of its loans, to determine the new equilibrium loan size.

The first step in the argument is to note that $\delta(r,L,h)$ can never exceed δ^* in the new equilibrium, regardless of the level of the ceiling: If there are no administrative costs, equilibrium condition (E.3') implies $\delta(r,L,h) = 0$. If there are administrative costs and entry is unrestricted, conditions (E.3') and (E.5b) require that $\delta(r,L,h) = \text{Min}\, \frac{C(m)}{m}$. Finally, if administrative costs are nonzero but entry is restricted, equilibrium conditions (E.1) and (E.3') imply $m(\delta)\bar{N} \leq M$ or $\delta(r,L,h) \leq \delta(M/\bar{N})$. Thus, $\delta = \delta^*$ in the first two cases and $\delta \leq \delta^*$ in the third.

Now suppose that some firms fail to receive loans after the ceiling is imposed, i.e. that $\sum_1^N m_i < M$. From condition (E.2') this implies either $u(r,L) = 0$ or $\delta(r,L,h) = \underset{r,L}{\text{Max}}\ \delta(r,L,h)$ subject to $r \leq \bar{r}$. The second possibility is ruled out because $\partial\delta/\partial r > 0$ and $\bar{r} > \underset{L}{\text{Min}}\ \phi(L,h,\delta^*)$ imply $\delta^* < \underset{r,L}{\text{Max}}\ \delta(r,L,h)$ subject to $r \leq \bar{r}$, which violates the condition $\delta(r,L,h) \leq \delta^*$ obtained above. Also, $r \leq \bar{r}$ and $u(r,L) = 0$ are easily seen to imply $L > L^* = L(h)$ [6] and thus $\partial\delta/\partial L = d\mu_X/dL - (1+h) < 0$. This would violate equilibrium condition (E.3'), since it would be possible to increase both $\delta(r,L,h)$ and $u(r,L)$ by holding r constant and decreasing L. Therefore, since neither of the two possibilities is consistent with equilibrium, $\sum_1^N m_i = M$.

We have already seen that the bank's expected profits per loan δ will be the same as in the absence of a loan rate ceiling, if there are no administrative costs or if entry is free. It is now clear that this must also be true if administrative costs are nonzero and entry is restricted, since $m_i = m(\delta)$ and $\sum_1^{\bar{N}} m_i = M$ imply $\delta = \delta(M/\bar{N})$. Thus, in all three cases $\delta(r,L,h) = \delta^*$, as we asserted to begin with.

From the above remarks and from equilibrium conditions (E.3') and (E.6), it follows that a particular combination of r and L will represent an equilibrium if and only if the following restrictions are satisfied:

(3.1) $\quad r \leq \bar{r}$

(3.2) $\quad \delta(r,L,h) = \delta^*$

(3.3) $\nexists$ an $r' \leq \bar{r}$ and L' such that $\delta(r',L',h) >$ $\delta(r,L,h)$ and $u(r',L') \geq u(r,L)$

The first two conditions imply that the equilibrium combination of r and L must lie on the bank iso-profit locus $\phi(L,h,\delta^*)$, at a point on or below the horizontal line $r = \bar{r}$. Thus, if a new equilibrium exists--i.e. if there exists a combination of r and L which satisfies (3.3) as well as (3.1) and (3.2)--the change in the equilibrium loan size will depend on the slope of the iso-profit curve at the initial equilibrium point. If $\phi_L(L^*,h,\delta^*) > 0$, as in Figure 5a, the size of each loan must be smaller in the new equilibrium; but if $\phi_L(L^*,h,\delta^*) < 0$, as in Figure 5b, the equilibrium loan size will increase as a result of the ceiling. The explanation is straightforward. In the first case, $\partial\delta/\delta L < 0$ in the initial equilibrium; thus, the bank's expected profits per loan must be lower at the same r and all higher values of L. Since r must be lower in the new equilibrium, and since $\partial\delta/\partial r > 0$, expected profits can remain equal to δ^* only if the size of each loan falls. In the second case, on the other hand, $\partial\delta/\partial L > 0$ before the imposition of the ceiling; thus, conditions (3.1) and (3.2) can be satisfied only if the size of each loan is greater in the new equilibrium.

It remains to show that a new equilibrium will exist and to determine its exact location. This is done in the following proposition:

<u>Proposition 1.</u> Let h be exogenous, and suppose that a ceiling of $\bar{r}$ is imposed on the loan rate, with $\min_L \phi(L,h,\delta^*) < \bar{r} < r^*$.

(a) If $\phi_L(L^*,h,\delta^*) > 0$, the new equilibrium will occur at loan

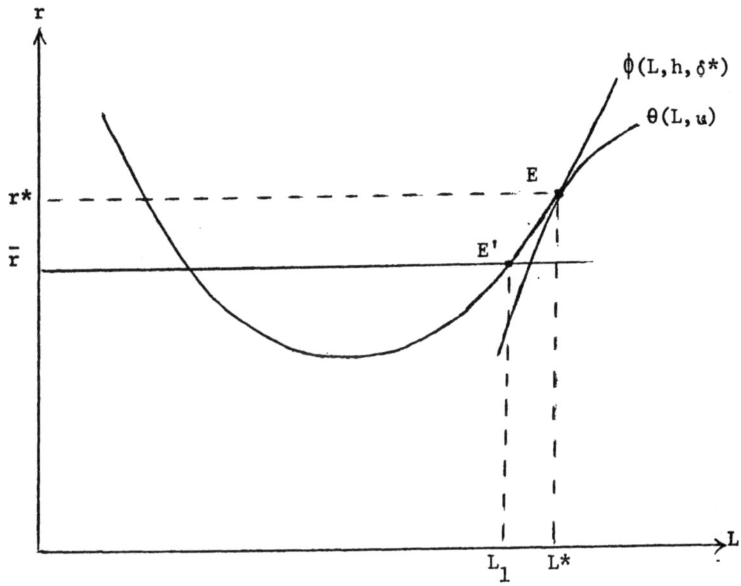

Case of $\phi_L(L^*,h,\delta^*) > 0$

Figure 5a

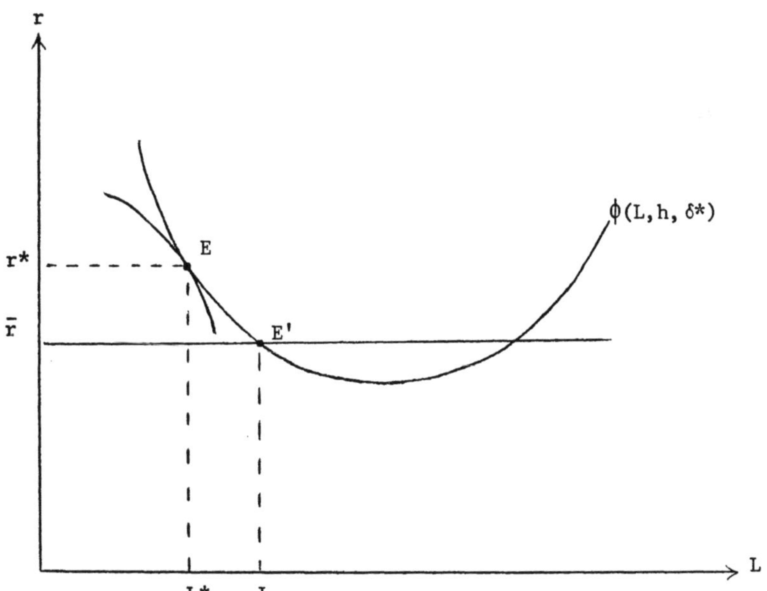

Case of $\phi_L(L^*,h,\delta^*) < 0$

Figure 5b

rate $\bar{r}$ and loan size $L_1 < L^*$, where L_1 is the maximum value of L such that $\phi(L,h,\delta^*) \leq \bar{r}$.

(b) If $\phi_L(L^*,h,\delta^*) < 0$, the new equilibrium will occur at loan rate $\bar{r}$ and loan size $L_2 > L^*$, where L_2 is the minimum value of L such that $\phi(L,h,\delta^*) \leq \bar{r}$.

Proof: (a) At $r = \bar{r}$ and $L = L_1$, conditions (3.1) and (3.2) are clearly satisfied. It remains to show that condition (3.3) is also satisfied. Note first that $\phi(L_1,h,\delta^*) = \bar{r} < r^* = \phi(L^*,h,\delta^*)$. From the assumption $\phi_L(L^*,h,\delta^*) > 0$, it then follows that $L_1 < L^*$. Now consider any $r' \leq \bar{r}$ and L' such that $\delta(r',L',h) > \delta^*$. Since $\delta_L(\bar{r},L_1,h) < 0$ and $\partial\delta/\partial r > 0$, $\delta(r,L,h) < \delta^*$ for any $r \leq \bar{r}$ and $L > L_1$. Thus, $L' < L_1 < L^*$ and $r' > \phi(L',h,\delta^*)$. However, $\mu_X(L) - (1+h)L$ is strictly increasing in L for all $L < L^*$. Since $u(r,L) = \mu_X(L) - (1+h)L - \delta(r,L,h)$ and $L_1 < L^*$, this implies $\frac{d}{dL} u[\phi(L,h,\delta^*),L] > 0$ for all $L < L_1$. From $L' < L_1$, $r' > \phi(L',h,\delta^*)$, and $\partial u/\partial r < 0$ it then follows that $u(r',L') < u(\bar{r},L_1)$. Thus, condition (3.3) is satisfied at $r = \bar{r}$ and $L = L_1$. It is easily seen that any other point satisfying conditions (3.1) and (3.2) must violate (3.3); the equilibrium is therefore unique.

(b) $\phi(L_2,h,\delta^*) < \phi(L^*,h,\delta^*)$ and $\phi_L(L^*,h,\delta^*) < 0$ imply $L_2 > L^*$. Consider any $r' \leq \bar{r}$ and L' such that $\delta(r',L',h) > \delta^*$. Since $\delta_L(\bar{r},L_2,h) > 0$ and $\partial\delta/\partial r > 0$, $L' > L_2 > L^*$. But since $\mu_X(L) - (1+h)L$ is strictly decreasing in L for all $L > L^*$, $\frac{d}{dL} u[\phi(L,h,\delta^*),L] < 0$ for all $L > L_2$. It follows that $u(r',L') < u(\bar{r},L_2)$, i.e. conditions (3.1)-(3.3) are satisfied at $r = \bar{r}$ and $L = L_2$. Since any other point satisfying conditions (3.1) and (3.2) violates (3.3), this equilibrium will be unique.

Since all firms continue to receive loans, an immediate implication of Proposition 1 is that the total volume of credit and investment will fall if $\phi_L > 0$ in the initial equilibrium and will rise if $\phi_L < 0$. Thus, the aggregate effects of the loan rate ceiling will be as predicted by the naive model of Section I only if there is rationing to begin with. Whether total lending increases or decreases, however, all borrowers will clearly be worse off than in the absence of the ceiling.[7]

2. We have assumed above that the ceiling $\bar{r}$ exceeds $\min_L \phi(L,h,\delta^*)$. If $\bar{r} < \min_L \phi(L,h,\delta^*)$, there will exist no loan size at which the bank can realize expected profits per loan of δ^*. In the case of zero administrative costs or of unrestricted entry to the industry, the imposition of such a ceiling will of course force all banks to shut down. However, if administrative costs are nonzero and entry to the industry is restricted, so that banks earn positive total expected profits in the initial equilibrium, this need not be the case.

Let us suppose that $\bar{r}$ is too low to yield expected profits per loan of $\delta^* = \delta(M/\bar{N})$ but high enough for $\delta(r,L,h)$ to exceed the break-even level $\min \frac{C(m)}{m}$. Since $\delta < \delta(M/\bar{N})$ and $m_i = m(\delta)$ for all i, $\sum_1^{\bar{N}} m_i < M$. From equilibrium condition (E.2') it then follows that $u(r,L) = 0$ or $\delta(r,L,h) = \max_{r,L} \delta(r,L,h)$ subject to $r \leq \bar{r}$. It was shown earlier that the first possibility violates equilibrium condition (E.3'). If on the other hand $m = m(\delta)$ and $\delta(r,L,h) = \max_{r,L} \delta(r,L,h)$ subject to $r \leq \bar{r}$, condition (E.3') will clearly be satisfied. Thus, the new equilibrium loan rate must be $\bar{r}$ and the new equilibrium loan size $Q(\bar{r},h)$, the value of L that maximizes $\delta(\bar{r},L,h)$. In the new equilibrium, Type II credit rationing will occur. That is, since $m(\delta)\bar{N} < M$, some firms will obtain loans while other, identical firms receive no credit at all. Furthermore, since $\delta(r,Q(r,h),h)$ is a decreasing function of r and since $dm/d\delta > 0$, the number of firms which do receive loans will fall as the ceiling $\bar{r}$ is reduced. The above remarks are summarized in the following proposition:

Proposition 2. Suppose that h is exogenous, and that a ceiling of $\bar{r}$ is imposed on the loan rate, where $\bar{r} < \underset{L}{\text{Min}}\ \phi(L,h,\delta^*)$. If there are no administrative costs or if entry is unrestricted, no loans will be made by banks. If administrative costs are nonzero and entry is restricted, some firms will continue to receive credit as long as $\delta(\bar{r},Q(\bar{r},h),h) > \text{Min}\ \frac{C(m)}{m}$. For those firms the loan rate will be $\bar{r}$ and the loan size $Q(\bar{r},h)$. The total number of loans supplied by all banks will be less than M, and will be smaller the lower is $\bar{r}$.

It is not difficult to see that the total volume of credit and investment, $m\bar{N}L$, may either rise or fall when administrative costs are nonzero and entry is restricted. The total number of loans made by banks will always be smaller, but as shown in Figure 6 the size of each loan may increase. It should also be noted that those firms fortunate enough to receive loans may enjoy higher expected profits than in the absence of the loan rate ceiling. Of course, banks and firms which fail to receive credit will be worse off.

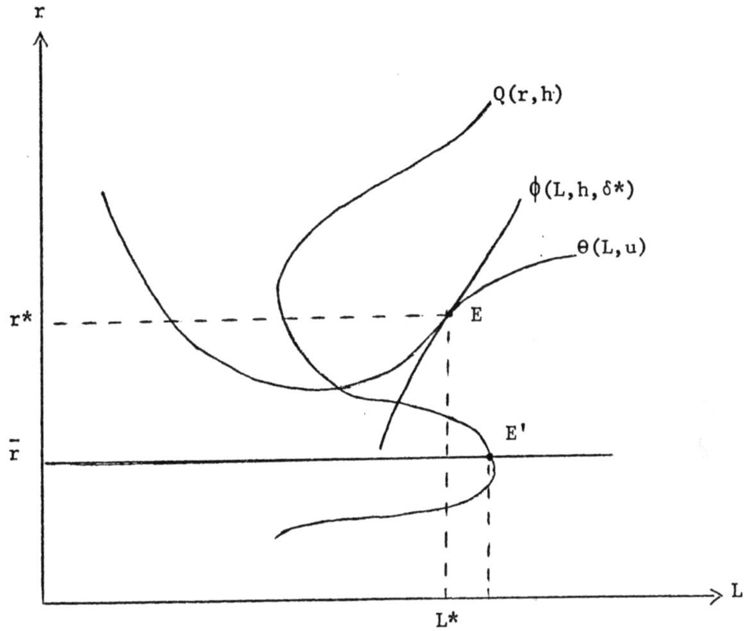

Case of $Q(\bar{r},h) > L^*$

Figure 6

C. h endogenous

We now turn to the more interesting case in which the opportunity rate h is endogenous. We shall assume that the volume of funds a bank can lend are limited to the deposits it can attract. The opportunity rate h may then be interpreted as the interest rate paid on deposits. Each bank behaves competitively in that it takes h as given, but the total volume of deposits the industry as a whole can attract increases with h. This implies that h may be expressed as an increasing function of the total volume of bank credit: $h = \Omega(\sum_{1}^{N} m_i L)$, with $\Omega' > 0$.

In contrast to the case in which h is exogenous, interest rate ceilings will affect the welfare of depositors as well as that of banks and firms. In particular, the possibility now arises that a ceiling on the loan rate will benefit borrowers at the expense of depositors. Ceilings may in fact be imposed by the government with precisely this objective in mind. In this section we shall establish the circumstances in which this result will be achieved, as well as determining the impact of the ceiling on the total volume of credit and investment.

Allowing h to be endogenous not only enriches the model but also complicates it considerably. It is no longer possible to restrict our attention to a single family of bank iso-profit curves in r-L space, since a change in h from the initial equilibrium level will cause each of those curves to shift. To deal with this problem, we shall define a new function $\tilde{\phi}(L,\delta)$ which is a generalization of the function $\phi(L,h,\delta)$. It indicates that value of r such that expected profits per loan equal δ when the deposit rate h is just high enough so that loans of size L can be made to all M firms. We proceed by establishing certain properties of the curve $\tilde{\phi}(L,\delta^*)$, where δ^* is as before the value of expected profits per loan in the initial equilibrium. Together with equilibrium conditions (E.1)-(E.6), these properties will enable us to determine the characteristics of the new equilibrium.

$\tilde{\phi}(L,\delta)$ is formally defined to be that value of r such that $\delta(r,L,\Omega(ML)) = \delta$. If $\mu_X(L) - (1+h)L > \delta$, there will exist a unique value of r satisfying this equation, since $\delta(\hat{r}(L),L,h) = \mu_X(L) - (1+h)L$ for all h and $\partial\delta/\partial r > 0$ for $r < \hat{r}(L)$. Given the function $\tilde{\phi}(L,\delta)$, we can trace out a family of curves in r-L space, with higher curves corresponding to higher values of δ. Since $\delta^* = \delta(r^*,L^*,h^*)$ and $h^* = \Omega(ML^*)$, the curve $\tilde{\phi}(L,\delta^*)$ will intersect the iso-profit locus $\phi(L,h^*,\delta^*)$ at the equilibrium loan size L^*. Also, $\Omega' > 0$ implies $\Omega(ML) \gtrless h^*$ as $L \gtrless L^*$. From $\partial\delta/\partial r > 0$ and $\partial\delta/\partial h \leq 0$ it follows that $\tilde{\phi}(L,\delta^*)$ will lie below $\phi(L,h^*,\delta^*)$ for all $L < L^*$ and above it for all $L > L^*$. To determine the market equilibrium under a loan rate ceiling, we must establish several additional properties of the curve $\tilde{\phi}(L,\delta^*)$. Proofs are given in Appendix A.

<u>Property 1.</u> Suppose $\delta^* = 0$. There then exists an $\bar{\bar{L}} > L^*$ such that (a) the function $\tilde{\phi}(L,\delta^*)$ is defined at each L in the interval $(0,\bar{\bar{L}})$; (b) $\delta(r,L,\Omega(ML)) < 0$ for all $L > \bar{\bar{L}}$; and (c) $\lim_{L\to\bar{\bar{L}}} \tilde{\phi}(L,\delta^*) = \hat{r}(\bar{\bar{L}})$.

<u>Property 2.</u> Suppose $\delta^* = 0$. Then $\tilde{\phi}_L(L,\delta^*) > 0$ and $\phi_L(L,\Omega(ML),\delta^*) > 0$.[8]

Properties 1 and 2 describe the curve $\tilde{\phi}(L,\delta^*)$ for the case of zero administrative costs. As shown in Figure 7, the curve is upward sloped throughout and approaches the locus $\hat{r}(L)$ as L approaches $\bar{\bar{L}}$. At each value of L, the curve will intersect a zero-profit locus corresponding to a given value of h. In Figure 7, for example, the curves $\tilde{\phi}(L,0)$ and $\phi(L,\Omega(ML'),0)$ intersect at L'; along the former curve the deposit rate h increases with L while along the latter it remains fixed at $\Omega(ML')$. Each zero-profit locus intersected by the curve $\tilde{\phi}(L,0)$ will have slope $\phi_L(L,\Omega(ML),0) > 0$.

The reason for the positive slope of the curve $\tilde{\phi}(L,0)$ is not difficult to see. Since $\delta(r,L,\Omega(ML)) = 0$, $\partial\delta/\partial L < 0$ at each point on the curve. Thus, an increase in L with h held constant must decrease expected profits per loan. But the change in L will also raise h by increasing the total volume of deposits ML; since $\partial\delta/\partial h < 0$, this also tends to reduce δ. Therefore, expected profits per loan can remain equal to zero only if the increase in L is accompanied by an increase in r.

<u>Property 3.</u> Suppose $\delta^* > 0$. There then exists an $\bar{L} < L^*$ and an $\bar{\bar{L}} > L^*$ such that (a) the function $\tilde{\phi}(L,\delta^*)$ is defined at each L in the interval $(\bar{L},\bar{\bar{L}})$; (b) $\delta(r,L,\Omega(ML)) < \delta^*$ for all $L > \bar{\bar{L}}$; (c) $\lim_{L\to\bar{L}} \tilde{\phi}(L,\delta^*) = \hat{r}(\bar{L})$ and $\lim_{L\to\bar{\bar{L}}} \tilde{\phi}(L,\delta^*) = \hat{r}(\bar{\bar{L}})$; (d) $\lim_{L\to\bar{L}} \tilde{\phi}_L(L,\delta^*) < 0$ and $\lim_{L\to\bar{\bar{L}}} \tilde{\phi}_L(L,\delta^*) = +\infty$; and (e) $\lim_{L\to\bar{L}} \phi_L(L,\Omega(ML),\delta^*) = -\infty$ and $\lim_{L\to\bar{\bar{L}}} \phi_L(L,\Omega(ML),\delta^*) = +\infty$.

<u>Property 4.</u> Suppose $\delta^* > 0$. There then exists an $\hat{L}$, $\bar{L} < \hat{L} < \bar{\bar{L}}$, such that $\phi_L(L,\Omega(ML),\delta^*) \gtrless 0$ as $L \gtrless \hat{L}$ and $\tilde{\phi}_L(L,\delta^*) > 0$ for $L \geq \hat{L}$.

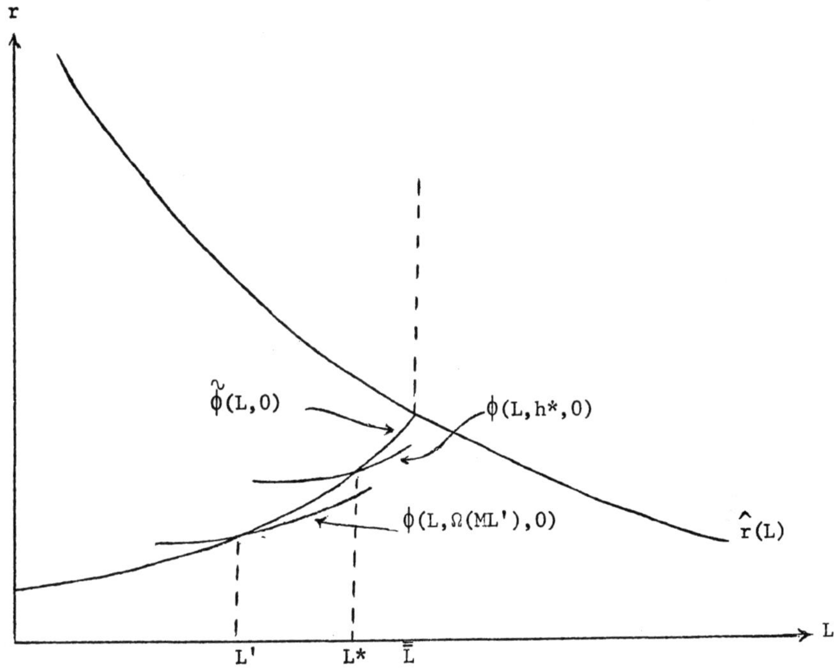

Case of $\delta^* = 0$

Figure 7

Properties 3 and 4 refer to the case of nonzero administrative costs, which is illustrated in Figure 8. The curve $\tilde{\phi}(L,\delta^*)$ will be negatively sloped for L close to $\bar{L}$ and positively sloped for L close to $\bar{\bar{L}}$. At $\hat{L}$, $\tilde{\phi}(L,\delta^*)$ will be positively sloped and will intersect an iso-profit locus $\phi(L,\Omega(M\hat{L}),\delta^*)$ with zero slope. For any larger L, $\tilde{\phi}(L,\delta^*)$ will be upward sloped and will intersect an iso-profit locus with positive slope. For smaller L, the curve $\tilde{\phi}(L,\delta^*)$ may have either positive or negative slope but it will always intersect a negatively sloped iso-profit locus.

The reason the curve $\tilde{\phi}(L,\delta^*)$ will have negative slope for some values of L is that $\partial\delta/\partial L$ may be positive when $\delta^* > 0$. An increase in L will in this event have two opposing effects on expected profits per loan. If the deposit rate h were held constant, the increase in loan size would raise δ. But h will increase as the total volume of credit ML rises, and this tends to reduce δ. When the first effect outweighs the second, as happens in the vicinity of $\bar{L}$, expected profits per loan can remain equal to δ^* only if r falls.

As shown in Figure 8, there may exist a "break" in the curve when $\delta^* > 0$, i.e. $\tilde{\phi}(L,\delta^*)$ may be defined over some interval to the left of $\bar{L}$. Also, there may exist more than one point at which the derivative $\tilde{\phi}_L$ vanishes. However, if the marginal deposit rate Ω' is nondecreasing, or if it is decreasing at a sufficiently small rate, these possibilities may be ruled out:

<u>Property 5.</u> Suppose that $\delta^* > 0$ and that $L\Omega''/\Omega' > -2$. Then $\delta(r,L,\Omega(ML)) < \delta^*$ for all $L < \bar{L}$. Also, the curve $\tilde{\phi}(L,\delta^*)$ will be U-

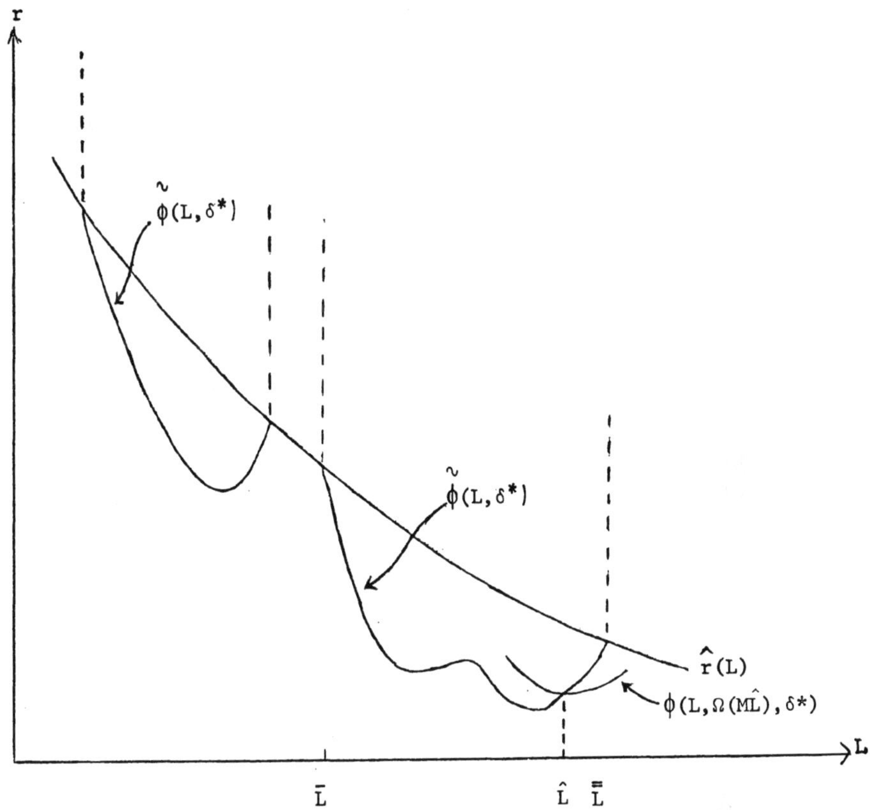

Case of $\delta^* > 0$

Figure 8

shaped, i.e. there will exist some $\tilde{L}$, $\bar{L} < \tilde{L} < \bar{\bar{L}}$, such that $\tilde{\phi}_L \gtreqless 0$ as $L \gtreqless \tilde{L}$.

We are now prepared to evaluate the impact of a loan rate ceiling. As in the case of h exogenous, the nature of the new equilibrium will depend on the height of the ceiling.

1. Consider first a loan rate ceiling $\bar{r}$ such that $\tilde{\phi}(L,\delta^*) < \bar{r} < r^*$. For $\delta^* > 0$, $\hat{L}$ is defined as in Property 4; the natural extension of the definition to the case of $\delta^* = 0$ is $\hat{L} \equiv 0$. The first step in determining the new market equilibrium is to show that conditions (E.1)-(E.6) can be satisfied only at a point on the curve $\tilde{\phi}(L,\delta^*)$. To do this, we must establish that all M firms will receive loans in the new equilibrium and that expected profits per loan will equal δ^*.

Equilibrium conditions (E.3') and (E.5b) have already been seen to imply $\delta(r,L,h) = \delta^*$ if administrative costs are negligible or entry to the banking industry is free. Also, if administrative costs are nonzero and entry is restricted, conditions (E.1) and (E.3') imply $\delta(r,L,h) \leq \delta^*$, with the equality holding when the total number of loans supplied equals M. Thus, to establish that the new equilibrium combination of r and L will lie on the curve $\tilde{\phi}(L,\delta^*)$, it remains only to show that all firms will receive loans. Suppose that this is not the case, i.e. that $\sum_1^N m_i < M$ in the new equilibrium. Equilibrium condition (E.2') then implies that firms earn zero expected profits or that banks operate on their offer curves. But in Appendix B it is shown that in both cases $\delta(r,L,h)$ must exceed δ^* if equilibrium conditions (E.3') and

(E.4) are to be satisfied. Since this possibility has already been ruled out, all firms will indeed receive loans in the new equilibrium.

From the above remarks and from equilibrium conditions (E.3'), (E.4), and (E.6), it is clear that a particular combination of r, L, and h will represent an equilibrium if and only if

(3.1) $r \leq \bar{r}$

(3.2) $\delta(r,L,h) = \delta^*$

(3.3) $\nexists$ an $r' \leq \bar{r}$ and L' such that $\delta(r',L',h) > \delta(r,L,h)$ and $u(r',L') \geq u(r,L)$

(3.4) $h = \Omega(ML)$

The equilibrium r and L must therefore lie on the curve $\mathfrak{F}(L,\delta^*)$, at a point on or below the horizontal line $r = \bar{r}$. In the case of h exogenous, we determined the exact location of the new equilibrium by finding that point on the iso-profit curve $\phi(L,h,\delta^*)$ which satisfied conditions (3.1) and (3.3). In the present case, a different value of h and thus a different iso-profit curve corresponds to each point on the curve $\mathfrak{F}(L,\delta^*)$. A point on the curve $\mathfrak{F}(L,\delta^*)$ will therefore represent an equilibrium if and only if it is also the point on the corresponding iso-profit curve which satisfies condition (3.3). Together with Properties 1-4 above, this allows us to determine the new equilibrium loan rate and loan size. It is a remarkable result that the direction of change in the equilibrium loan size will depend on the nature of the initial equilibrium in the same way as when h is exogenous. This relationship is expressed by the following proposition:

Proposition 3. Suppose that each bank takes h as given, but that h is an increasing function of total deposits. Suppose further that a ceiling of $\bar{r}$ is imposed on the loan rate, with $\tilde{\phi}(\hat{L},\delta^*) < \bar{r} < r^*$.

(a) If $\phi_L(L^*,h^*,\delta^*) > 0$, the new equilibrium will occur at loan rate $\bar{r}$ and loan size $L_1 < L^*$, where L_1 is the maximum value of L such that $\tilde{\phi}(L,\delta^*) \leq \bar{r}$.

(b) If $\phi_L(L^*,h^*,\delta^*) < 0$, the new equilibrium will occur at loan rate $\bar{r}$ and loan size L_2, where L_2 is any value of L such that $L^* < L < \hat{L}$ and $\tilde{\phi}(L,\delta^*) = \bar{r}$. If $L\Omega''/\Omega' > -2$, this equilibrium will be unique.

Proof: (a) At $r = \bar{r}$ and $L = L_1$, conditions (3.1), (3.2) and (3.4) are clearly satisfied. It remains to show that (3.3) is also satisfied. Now from $\tilde{\phi}(\hat{L},\delta^*) < \bar{r} < r^*$ and Properties 2 and 4 of the curve $\tilde{\phi}(L,\delta^*)$, it follows that $\hat{L} < L_1 < L^*$ and $\phi_L(L_1,\Omega(ML_1),\delta^*) > 0$. This implies that L_1 is the maximum value of L such that $\phi(L,\Omega(ML_1),\delta^*) \leq \bar{r}$. Let $L_1^* = \mathcal{L}(\Omega(ML_1))$, the equilibrium loan size that would prevail if h were fixed at $\Omega(ML_1)$ and if no loan rate ceiling were imposed. Then, since $L_1 < L^*$ implies $\Omega(ML_1) < h^*$ and since $d\mathcal{L}/dh < 0$, $L_1^* > L^* > L_1$. From Proposition 1a it follows that condition (3.3) will be satisfied at $r = \bar{r}$, $L = L_1$, and $h = \Omega(ML_1)$.

To see that equilibrium can occur only at $r = \bar{r}$ and $L = L_1$, consider any other combination of r and L--say r_3 and L_3--satisfying conditions (3.1), (3.2), and (3.4). Then $r_3 = \tilde{\phi}(L_3,\delta^*) \leq \bar{r}$ which from the definition of L_1 implies $L_3 < L_1$. Now, Properties 2 and 4 imply either (i) $\phi_L(L_3,\Omega(ML_3),\delta^*) > 0$ and $r_3 < \bar{r}$ or (ii) $\phi_L(L_3,\Omega(ML_3),\delta^*) < 0$ and $r_3 \leq \bar{r}$. In either case, there must exist an $\varepsilon > 0$ such that

$\phi(L,\Omega(ML_3),\delta^*) < \bar{r}$ for $L_3 < L < L_3 + \varepsilon$. Also, $L_3 < L_1 < L^*$ implies $\Omega(ML_3) < h^*$ and thus $L_3^* > L^* > L_3$. But from the proof of Proposition 1a we know that along the iso-profit locus $\phi(L,\Omega(ML_3),\delta^*)$, $du/dL > 0$ for all $L < L_3^*$. Thus, condition (3.3) is not satisfied at $r = r_3$ and $L = L_3$.

(b) From Property 4, $\tilde{\phi}(\hat{L},\delta^*) < \bar{r} < r^*$, and $\phi_L(L^*,h^*,\delta^*) < 0$, it follows that there will exist at least one value of L, say L_2, such that $L^* < L < \hat{L}$ and $\tilde{\phi}(L,\delta^*) = \bar{r}$. At $r = \bar{r}$ and $L = L_2$, conditions (3.1), (3.2), and (3.4) are clearly satisfied. We now show that (3.3) is also satisfied. Since $L_2 < \hat{L}$, $\phi_L(L_2,\Omega(ML_2),\delta^*) < 0$. Thus, L_2 is the minimum value of L such that $\phi(L,\Omega(ML_2),\delta^*) \leq \bar{r}$. Also, $L_2 > L^*$ implies $\Omega(ML_2) > h^*$ and thus $L_2^* < L^* < L_2$. From Proposition 1b it follows that condition (3.3) will be satisfied at $r = \bar{r}$, $L = L_2$, and $h = \Omega(ML_2)$.

To see that equilibrium can occur only at $r = \bar{r}$ and an $L = L_2$, consider any other combination of r and L--say r_4 and L_4--satisfying conditions (3.1), (3.2), and (3.4). Then $r_4 = \tilde{\phi}(L_4,\delta^*) \leq \bar{r}$. Suppose first that $L_4 > L^*$. In this event either (i) $r_4 < \bar{r}$ or (ii) $r_4 = \bar{r}$ and $\phi_L(L,\Omega(ML_4),\delta^*) > 0$. In either case, there must exist an $\varepsilon > 0$ such that $\phi(L,\Omega(ML_4),\delta^*) < \bar{r}$ for $L_4 - \varepsilon < L < L_4$. Also, $L_4 > L^*$ implies $\Omega(ML_4) > h^*$ and thus $L_4^* < L^* < L_4$. But from the proof of Proposition 1b we know that along the locus $\phi(L,\Omega(ML_4),\delta^*)$, $du/dL < 0$ for all $L > L_4^*$. Thus condition (3.3) cannot be satisfied at $r = r_4$ and $L = L_4$. Now suppose that $L_4 < L^*$. Then since Property 4 implies $\phi_L(L,\Omega(ML_4),\delta^*) < 0$, there must exist an $\varepsilon > 0$ such that $\phi(L,\Omega(ML_4),\delta^*)$

$< \bar{r}$ for $L_4 < L < L_4 + \varepsilon$. Also, $L_4 < L^*$ implies $\Omega(ML_4) < h^*$ and thus $L_4^* > L^* > L_4$. But along the locus $\phi(L,\Omega(ML_4),\delta^*)$, $du/dL > 0$ for all $L < L_4^*$. Condition (3.3) can therefore not be satisfied at $r = r_4$ and $L = L_4$.

We already know from Property 5 that if $L\Omega''/\Omega' > -2$, the locus $\tilde{\phi}(L,\delta^*)$ will be U-shaped. There can thus exist only one L_2 such that $L^* < L_2 < \hat{L}$ and $\tilde{\phi}(L_2,\delta^*) = \bar{r}$. This completes the proof.

Proposition 3 is illustrated in Figures 9 and 10. In the first case, the bank iso-profit curve $\phi(L,h^*,\delta^*)$ is positively sloped at the initial equilibrium point E. This implies that banks would be better off if they could make smaller loans at the prevailing loan rate $(\partial\delta/\partial L < 0)$, while firms would prefer to receive larger loans at that rate $(\partial u/\partial L > 0)$. That is, credit is rationed in the initial equilibrium. The new equilibrium will occur at E', at the intersection of the line $r = \bar{r}$ with the last positively sloped segment of the curve $\tilde{\phi}(L,\delta^*)$. Since the size of each loan is reduced, and since all firms continue to receive loans, the total volume of credit and investment must fall.

Figure 10 illustrates the second case, in which the iso-profit curve $\phi(L,h^*,\delta^*)$ is negatively sloped at the initial equilibrium E. In this case, banks would prefer to make larger loans at the equilibrium loan rate $(\partial\delta/\partial L > 0)$ while firms would prefer to borrow and invest less at that rate $(\partial u/\partial L < 0)$. The new equilibrium will occur at point E', E", or E‴, at a value of L greater than L^* but less than $\hat{L}$. Although the line $r = \bar{r}$ may intersect the curve $\tilde{\phi}(L,\delta^*)$ at a point to

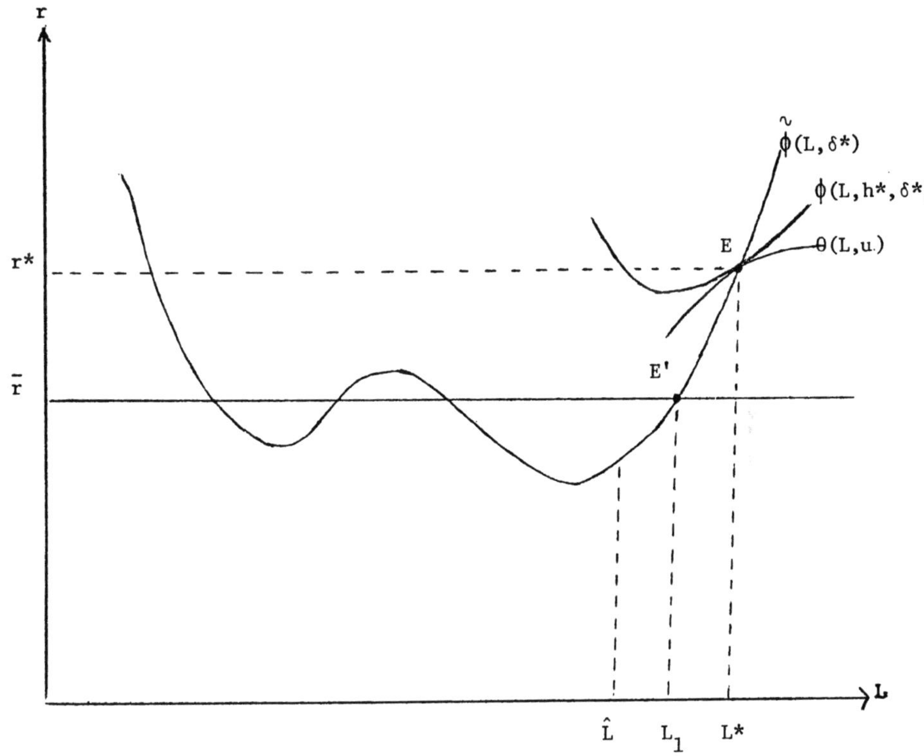

Case of $\phi_L(L^*,h^*,\delta^*) > 0$

Figure 9

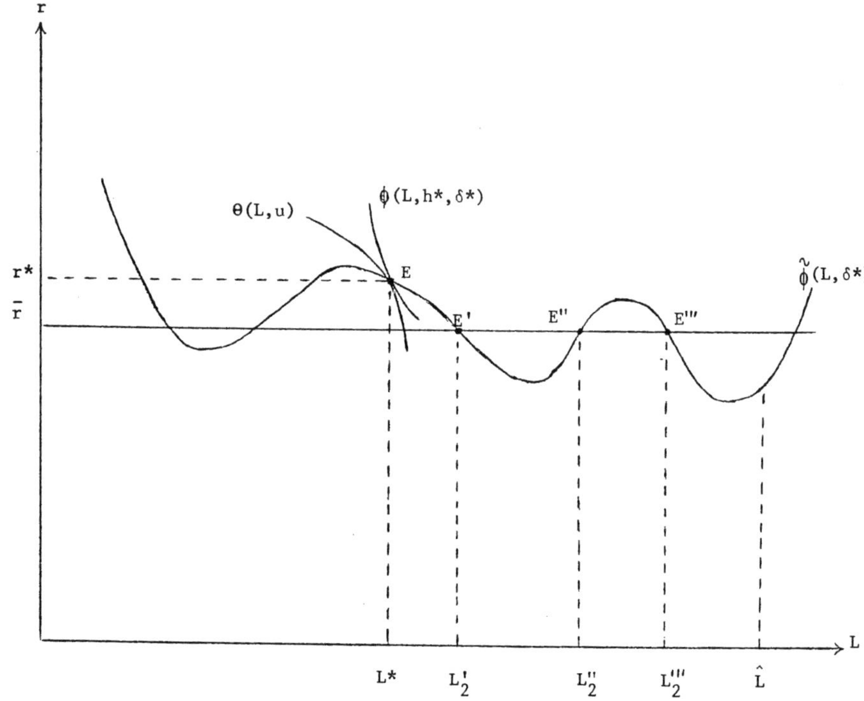

Case of $\phi_L(L^*,h^*,\delta^*) < 0$

Figure 10

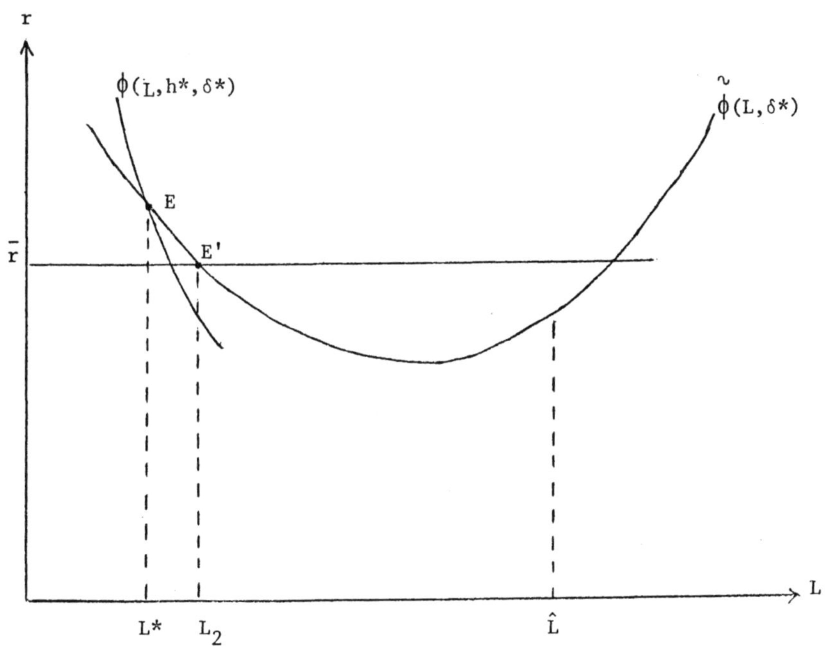

Case of LΩ"/Ω'>-2

Figure 11

the left of E, such a point cannot represent an equilibrium. Thus, the size of each loan and the total volume of credit and investment must increase as a result of the ceiling. If $L\Omega''/\Omega' > -2$, as in Figure 11, the new equilibrium will also be unique.

Since h is an increasing function of the total volume of credit, it is clear that all depositors will be made worse off by the ceiling if $\phi_L(L^*,h^*,\delta^*) > 0$ and better off if $\phi_L(L^*,h^*,\delta^*) < 0$. The effect of the ceiling on the welfare of borrowers is not quite so obvious. We noted in the previous section that when the deposit rate is exogenous, the imposition of a ceiling on the loan rate must make each borrower worse off if all firms continue to receive loans. This is because the expected total profits of borrower and lender, $\mu_X(L) - (1+h)L$, are maximized in the initial equilibrium but not in the new equilibrium, and because banks' expected profits per loan δ remain unchanged by the ceiling. In the present case, in which h is not fixed but varies with the total volume of deposits and loans, it is again true that the quantity $\mu_X(L) - (1+h)L$ fails to attain a maximum in the new equilibrium and that δ remains equal to δ^*. Thus, if the deposit rate h rises, all borrowers must be worse off than in the absence of the ceiling. But since h may also decrease, the possibility now exists that each firm will enjoy higher expected profits as a result of the ceiling. It is easily shown, in fact, that when $\phi_L(L^*,h^*,\delta^*) > 0$ all borrowers will at first be made better off as the ceiling $\bar{r}$ is reduced below the initial equilibrium loan rate r*:

Proposition 4. Suppose that h is an increasing function of total deposits and that a ceiling of $\bar{r}$ is imposed on the loan rate. If $\phi_L(L^*,h^*,\delta^*) > 0$, the expected profits of each firm in equilibrium will at first increase as $\bar{r}$ is reduced below r^*. On the other hand, if $\phi_L(L^*,h^*,\delta^*) < 0$, all firms will be worse off for any $\bar{r}$ such that $\tilde{\phi}(\hat{L},\delta^*) < \bar{r} < r^*$.

Proof: Expected profits of the firm are $u(r,L) = \hat{\delta}(L) - \delta(r,L,\Omega(ML))$, where $\hat{\delta}(L) = \mu_X(L) - [1 + \Omega(ML)]L$. As we move along the curve $\tilde{\phi}(L,\delta^*)$, $\delta(r,L,\Omega(ML))$ remains constant. Thus, $\frac{d}{dL}\,u(\tilde{\phi}(L,\delta^*),L) = d\hat{\delta}/dL = d\mu_X/dL - [1 + \Omega(ML)] - ML\Omega'$. At $L = L^*$, $d\mu_X/dL - [1 + \Omega(ML)] = 0$. Since $\Omega' > 0$ and $d^2\mu_X/dL^2 < 0$, this implies $\frac{d}{dL}\,u(\tilde{\phi}(L,\delta^*),L) < 0$ for all $L \geq L^*$. If $\phi_L(L^*,h^*,\delta^*) > 0$, we know from Proposition 3a that the new equilibrium point must move to the left along the curve $\tilde{\phi}(L,\delta^*)$ as the ceiling $\bar{r}$ is reduced below r^*. Therefore, since $du/dL < 0$ at L^*, the expected profits of each borrower will at first increase. If on the other hand $\phi_L(L^*,h^*,\delta^*) < 0$ and $\tilde{\phi}(\hat{L},\delta^*) < \hat{r} < r^*$, Proposition 3b implies that the new equilibrium point will lie on the curve $\tilde{\phi}(L,\delta^*)$ at an $L > L^*$. Thus, since $du/dL < 0$ for all $L \geq L^*$, the expected profits of each borrower must be lower in the new equilibrium.

2. Until this point we have assumed that the ceiling $\bar{r}$ is sufficiently high for conditions (3.1)-(3.4) to be satisfied at some value of L. Let us now suppose that $\bar{r}$ is so low that these conditions cannot be fulfilled. This will clearly be the case if $\bar{r} < \min_L \tilde{\phi}(L,\delta^*)$; Appendix C demonstrates that it will also occur if $\bar{r} < \tilde{\phi}(\hat{L},\delta^*)$ and

$\phi_L(L^*,h^*,\delta^*) > 0$.[9] In determining the new market equilibrium, it will be important to distinguish between (1) the case of zero administrative costs or free entry, in which each bank must earn zero total expected profits in equilibrium, and (2) the case of nonzero administrative costs and restricted entry, in which positive expected profits are possible. We shall refer to the former as the "zero-profit" case and to the latter as the "positive-profit" case.

It is not difficult to show that some firms will be unable to obtain loans in the new equilibrium, if one exists. By our assumption about $\bar{r}$, any point lying on the curve $\tilde{\phi}(L,\delta^*)$ must fail to satisfy conditions (3.1) and (3.3). Since (3.1) and (3.3) were taken directly from equilibrium conditions (E.3') and E.6), and since (E.4) requires $h = \Omega(\sum_1^N m_i L)$, it follows that $\delta(r,L,h) = \delta^*$ and $\sum_1^N m_i = M$ cannot both hold in the new equilibrium. Clearly, $\delta(r,L,h) < \delta^*$ and $\sum_1^N m_i = M$ cannot be satisfied simultaneously either. In the zero-profit case this would imply $\pi(r,L,m,h) < 0$ and in the positive profit case $m_i \neq m(\delta)$; in both cases equilibrium condition (E.3') would be violated. We have already seen, moreover, that $\delta(r,L,h)$ cannot exceed δ^* in equilibrium. Thus, by process of elimination, $\sum_1^N m_i < M$ in the new equilibrium, i.e. not all firms will receive loans.

Now, from equilibrium condition (E.2'), $\sum_1^N m_i < M$ implies either $u(r,L) = 0$ or $\delta(r,L,h) = \underset{r,L}{\text{Max}}\ \delta(r,L,h)$ subject to $r \leq \bar{r}$. In demonstrating that all firms must receive loans if $\bar{r}$ exceeds $\tilde{\phi}(\hat{L},\delta^*)$, we noted that $u(r,L) = 0$, $\sum_1^N m_i < M$, and conditions (E.3') and (E.4) imply $\delta(r,L,h) > \delta^*$. As shown in Appendix B, this is true regardless of the level of the ceiling. Thus, since equilibrium requires $\delta(r,L,h) \leq \delta^*$, the possibility that $u(r,L) = 0$ can be ruled out in the present case. The only remaining possibility is that $\delta(r,L,h) = \underset{r,L}{\text{Max}}\ \delta(r,L,h)$ subject to $r \leq \bar{r}$, i.e. that $r = \bar{r}$ and $L = Q(\bar{r},h)$ in the new equilibrium. At such an r and L, equilibrium condition (E.3') will clearly be satisfied. To determine whether the complete set of equilibrium conditions is satisfied, we must consider the zero-profit and positive-profit cases separately.

Let $S = \sum_{1}^{N} m_i$, the total number of loans granted by banks. Then in the zero-profit case, a particular combination of L, h, and S will satisfy equilibrium conditions (E.1)-(E.6) if and only if

$$L = Q(\bar{r},h)$$

$$h = \Omega(SL)$$

$$\delta(\bar{r},L,h) = \delta^*$$

$$S < M$$

Clearly an equilibrium with $L > 0$ will not exist in the absence of administrative costs, since $\delta(r,L,h) = 0$ and $L = Q(r,h)$ imply $Q(r,h) = 0$. It is shown in Appendix C, however, that when administrative costs are nonzero there must exist a unique and nontrivial solution to the above set of restrictions if $\delta(r,L,h) > \text{Min}\ \frac{C(m)}{m}$ at $r = \bar{r}$, $h = \Omega(0)$, and $L = Q(\bar{r},\Omega(0))$.

In the positive-profit case δ must be treated as endogenous; in addition, however, the total number of loans must be restricted to equal $m(\delta)\bar{N}$ for any $\delta > \text{Min}\ \frac{C(m)}{m}$. Thus, the equilibrium values of L, h, S, and δ are those for which

$$L = Q(\bar{r},h)$$

$$h = \Omega(SL)$$

$$\delta = \delta(\bar{r},L,h)$$

$$\delta \geq \text{Min}\ \frac{C(m)}{m}$$

$$S = m(\delta)\bar{N}$$ [10]

$$S < M$$

As shown in Appendix C, a unique solution will exist provided $\delta(\bar{r},Q(\bar{r},\Omega(0)),\Omega(0)) > \text{Min}\ \frac{C(m)}{m}$.

Thus, if administrative costs are nonzero and if $\bar{r}$ is sufficiently high that $\delta(\bar{r},Q(\bar{r},\Omega(0)),\Omega(0)) > \text{Min}\ \frac{C(m)}{m}$, the new equilibrium will involve Type II credit rationing. This will be true whether or not entry to the banking industry is restricted.[11] Also, as might be expected, the number of firms unable to obtain credit will be greater the lower is the ceiling on the loan rate. These results are summarized in the following proposition:

<u>Proposition 5.</u> Suppose that h is an increasing function of total deposits and that a ceiling of $\bar{r}$ is imposed on the loan rate. Suppose further that either (1) $\bar{r} < \text{Min}_{L}\ \tilde{\phi}(L,\delta^*)$ or (2) $\bar{r} < \tilde{\phi}(\hat{L},\delta^*)$ and $\phi_L(L^*,h^*,\delta^*) > 0$. If there are no administrative costs, all banks will shut down. If administrative costs are nonzero and if $\delta(\bar{r},Q(\bar{r},\Omega(0)),\Omega(0)) > \text{Min}\ \frac{C(m)}{m}$, some firms will receive loans in the

new equilibrium but others will not. For those firms which do receive credit, the loan rate will be $\bar{r}$ and the loan size $Q(\bar{r},h)$. The total number of loans supplied by all banks will be smaller the lower is $\bar{r}$.

From the characteristics of the bank's offer curve, it is not difficult to see that the equilibrium loan size may increase as a result of the ceiling on $\bar{r}$. In the positive-profit case that increase may be sufficient to offset the decline in the number of loans, so that the total volume of credit and investment rises. Appendix C demonstrates that in the zero-profit case this can occur only if $\phi_L(L^*,h^*,\delta^*) < 0$.

Firms that find themselves unable to borrow in the new equilibrium will of course be worse off than before the ceiling was imposed. However, those firms which continue to receive credit may benefit from the ceiling, provided either h or δ fall.[12]

D. Relationship to the naive model

It should not be surprising that the naive credit model can be obtained as a special limiting case of the model employed here. In particular, when investment projects are riskless and administrative costs are negligible, our model reduces to the simple one described in Section I. To show this, we first derive the characteristics of the preceiling equilibrium under these special assumptions. We then apply equilibrium conditions (E.1)-(E.6) of Section III.A. to determine the effects of imposing a ceiling on the loan rate.

If investment is riskless, the outcome of each project will be a function only of the size of the loan--i.e. $x = \psi(L)$, with $\psi(0) = 0$, $\psi' > 0$, and $\psi'' < 0$. The bank's profits from a loan of size L at rate r are thus $\delta(r,L,h) = \min\{\psi(L),(1+r)L\} - (1+h)L$; the borrowing firm's profits, on the other hand, are $u(r,L) = \max\{\psi(L) - (1+r)L,0\}$. The distribution of the income from the project between borrower and lender is illustrated in Figure 12.

Now, in the absence of any ceiling on the loan rate, equilibrium will be determined by conditions (E.1)-(E.5) of Section II. Since administrative costs are assumed to be negligible, condition (E.3) requires that banks earn zero profits per loan; furthermore, the size of each loan must equal $\underline{L}(h)$, the value of L that maximizes $\delta(r,L,h) + u(r,L) = \psi(L) - (1+h)L$, given h. As shown in Figure 13, the bank's zero iso-profit curve $\phi(L,h,0)$ is a horizontal line at $r = h$. Equilibrium will occur at E, the point of tangency of this curve with a customer iso-profit locus $\theta(L,u)$. Since both curves have zero slope at

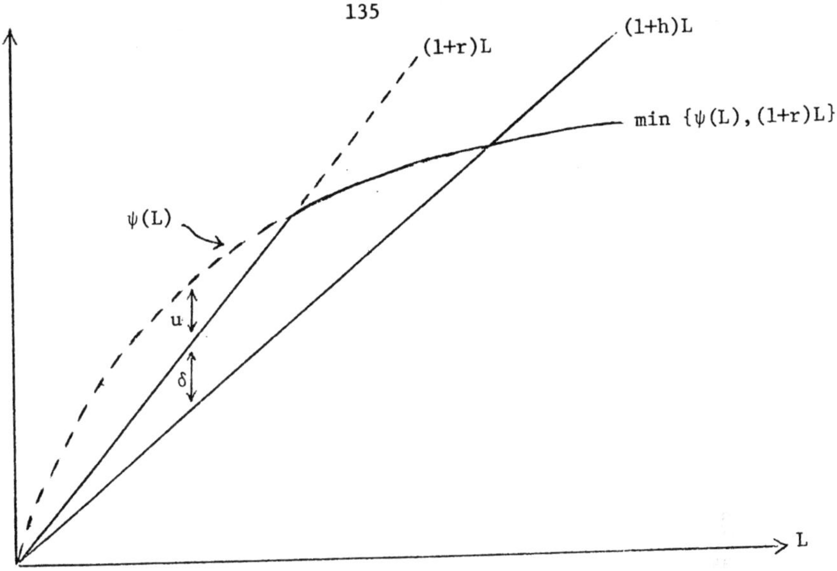

r,h given

Figure 12

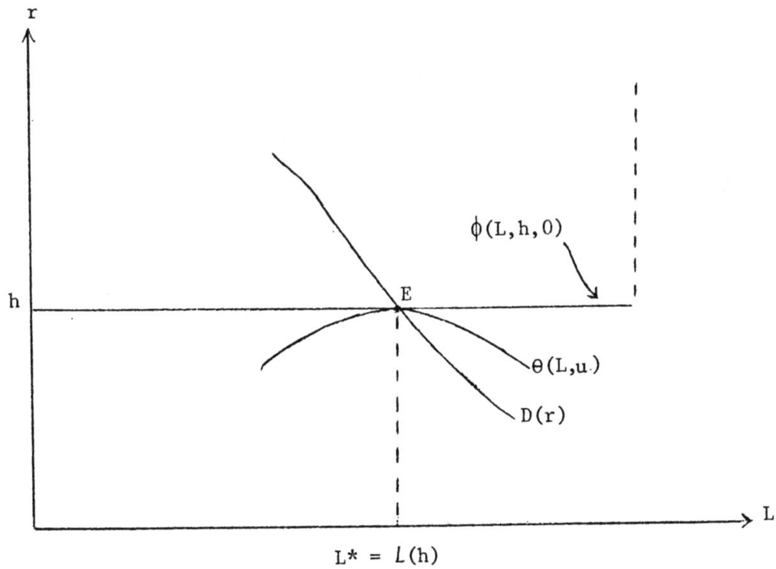

Figure 13

this point, $\partial\delta/\partial L = \partial u/\partial L = 0$. Thus, in the preceiling equilibrium, the firm will receive precisely that amount of credit $D(r)$ which maximizes its profits at the prevailing loan rate.[13]

Let L_T be the total volume of funds loaned by the banking industry. Since $r = h$, $L_T = MD(r)$, and $h = \Omega(L_T)$, the market equilibrium may be represented by the intersection of an aggregate supply curve $\Omega(L_T)$ and an aggregate demand curve $MD(r)$. Since $\partial^2 u/\partial L^2 < 0$ and $\partial^2 u/\partial L\partial r < 0$ imply $dD/dr < 0$, the aggregate demand curve will be downward sloping, as assumed in the naive model of Section I. The supply schedule will be perfectly elastic if h is taken as exogenous, and upward sloping if h is endogenous.

Let us now assume that a ceiling of $\bar{r}$ is imposed on the loan rate, where $\bar{r} < r^*$. Condition (E.3') of Section III.A. requires that banks continue to earn zero profits in the new equilibrium. If h is exogenous, it follows immediately that all banks will be compelled to shut down. Suppose alternatively that h is endogenous, i.e. that $h = \Omega(L_T)$ with $\Omega' > 0$. If $h > \bar{r}$, banks will earn negative profits, violating (E.3'). If $h < \bar{r}$, $\delta(r,L,h) = 0$ requires $r = h$ and thus $r < \bar{r}$. But in this case (E.3') can be satisfied only at $L = \mathcal{L}(h) = D(h)$. Furthermore, since $u(r,L) > 0$ and $\delta(r,L,h) = 0 < \underset{L}{\text{Max}}\ \delta(\bar{r},L,h)$, condition (E.2') implies $\sum_{1}^{N} m_i = M$. Thus, the total volume of credit must be $L_T = MD(h) > MD(r^*)$, where the inequality follows from $h < \bar{r} < r^*$ and $dD/dr < 0$. Since $\Omega' > 0$, this is clearly inconsistent with the requirement that $h = \Omega(L_T)$. Thus, in the new equilibrium it must be true that $h = r = \bar{r}$. As in the naive model, this determines the total volume of credit as the value of L_T at which $\Omega(L_T) = \bar{r}$.

Since the bank's zero iso-profit curve is horizontal and since $h = \bar{r}$, equilibrium condition (E.3') is satisfied at all points on the curve. Also, since $\delta(r,L,h) = 0 = \underset{L}{\text{Max}}\ \delta(\bar{r},L,h)$ in the new equilibrium, condition (E.2') cannot be used to rule out the possibility that $\sum_1^N m_i < M$. Thus, both the size of each loan and the total number of loans are indeterminate. It will be recalled that this was also true of the model presented in Section I.

The special case we have been examining provides some insight into the role of uncertainty in the more general version of the model. Introducing uncertainty in the outcome of the investment project has two effects. First, it shifts the aggregate supply schedule upwards from $\Omega(L_T)$ to $\phi(L_T/M,0)$, as shown in Figure 14. If the increase in the riskiness of the investment project leaves the expected outcome unchanged for all values of L--i.e. if it takes the form of a "mean-preserving spread"--the equilibrium loan size that prevails in the absence of a loan rate ceiling, L*, will be unaffected. However, the imposition of a ceiling on the loan rate will have a smaller impact on total credit and investment when investment projects are risky. More precisely, a given difference between the initial equilibrium loan rate r* and the ceiling $\bar{r}$ will produce a smaller decline in total credit.[14] The explanation is clear. In a zero-profit equilibrium with risky investment projects, banks always make larger loans than are optimal at the prevailing loan rate ($\partial\delta/\partial L < 0$). If the loan rate is forced downward by means of a ceiling, the bank's profits can remain equal to zero

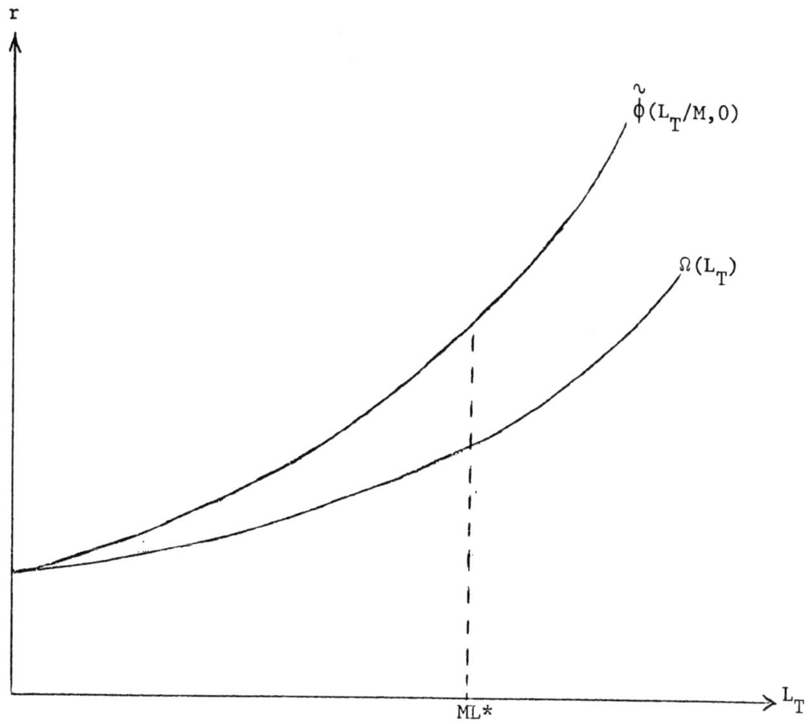

Figure 14

only if (i) the size of each loan is reduced or (ii) the deposit rate h falls. Each effect obviously implies a reduction in total credit, and since both effects are at work the required reduction will be smaller than if only the second were operating, as is the case when investment projects are riskless. If h is exogenous, the existence of the first effect also explains why a ceiling on the loan rate need not force banks to shut down.

The second result of introducing uncertainty is to make determinate the distribution of bank credit among firms under a loan rate ceiling. If investment projects are risky, the bank's zero iso-profit curve must have positive slope. Consequently, equilibrium condition (E.3') will be satisfied at only one point on the curve rather than at all points. Together with condition (E.2'), this allows us to determine the number of firms which receive credit, the size of each loan, and the effect on borrowers' expected profits.[15]

IV. The short-run impact of monetary policy

The analysis of Section III lends itself naturally to the following question: what will be the impact of changes in underlying monetary conditions on the volume and distribution of bank credit, when the loan rate is for some reason sticky? To investigate this question, we shall suppose that the function Ω shifts upward but that the loan rate is fixed at the initial long-run equilibrium level. The equilibrium conditions are then exactly the same as for the case of a loan rate ceiling, except that the constraint on r is now an equality. For the sake of brevity, we shall consider here only the case in which the schedule $\Omega(\sum_{1}^{N} m_i L)$ is perfectly elastic, i.e. the case of h exogenous.

Let h_1 be the initial value of h and h_2 the new value; let r_1^* and L_1^* be the long-run equilibrium loan rate and loan size corresponding to h_1; and let r_2^* and L_2^* be the long-run equilibrium values of r and L corresponding to h_2. From $L_i^* = \mathcal{L}(h_i)$ and $d\mathcal{L}/dh < 0$, it follows that $L_2^* < L_1^*$. In the long run, then, the increase in h will cause the size of each loan to fall and thus also the total volume of credit and investment. It was shown in Chapter I, however, that the effect of a change in h on the long-run equilibrium loan rate is unambiguous only if $\phi_L(L_1^*, h_1, \delta^*) \leq 0$. Whenever this condition does hold, an increase in h will raise the long-run equilibrium loan rate; but if $\phi_L(L_1^*, h_1, \delta^*) > 0$, the possibility exists that r* will fall.

To begin with, let us suppose that the increase in h is sufficiently small that $\underset{L}{\text{Min}}\ \phi(L, h_2, \delta^*) < r_1^*$. Then by essentially the same argument given in Section III.B. for the case of $\bar{r} > \min_L \phi(L,h,\delta^*)$, it can be shown that all firms will continue to receive loans in the new short-run equilibrium (if one exists) and that expected profits per loan must remain equal to δ^*. Together with equilibrium condition (E.3') this implies that a particular value of L will represent a short-run equilibrium if and only if

(4.1) $\delta(r_1^*,L,h_2) = \delta^*$

(4.2) $\nexists$ an L' such that $\delta(r_1^*,L',h_2) > \delta(r_1^*,L,h_2)$

and $u(r_1^*,L') \geq u(r_1^*,L)$

The first condition implies that the new short-run equilibrium point must lie at an intersection of the bank iso-profit locus $\phi(L,h_2,\delta^*)$ with the horizontal line $r = r_1^*$. But, since $\partial\delta/\partial r > 0$ and $\partial\delta/\partial h < 0$, the curve $\phi(L,h_2,\delta^*)$ must lie strictly above the curve $\phi(L,h_1,\delta^*)$, as shown in Figure 15. An immediate implication is that if an equilibrium does exist--i.e. if condition (4.2) is satisfied at one of the two points of intersection--the size of each loan will fall if $\phi_L(L_1^*,h_1,\delta^*) > 0$ and rise if $\phi_L(L_1^*,h_1,\delta^*) < 0$. In the first case, banks are initially providing larger loans than they would like at the prevailing loan rate ($\partial\delta/\partial L < 0$); thus, for expected profits per loan δ to remain unchanged, the increase in h must be offset by a reduction in L. Conversely, if banks are initially making smaller loans than they would like ($\partial\delta/\partial L > 0$), expected profits per loan can remain constant only if L increases.

Whether a short-run equilibrium exists at all, and the exact location of the equilibrium point, will depend on condition (4.2). These questions are addressed in the following proposition, which we state without proof:

Proposition 6. Suppose that h increases from h_1 to h_2, but that the loan rate remains fixed at r_1^* in the short run. Suppose further that $\min_L \phi(L,h_2,\delta^*) < r_1^*$. Finally, let $\bar{L}$ and $\bar{\bar{L}}$ be the minimum and maximum values of L such that $\phi(L,h_2,\delta^*) = r_1^*$.

(a) If $\phi_L(L_1^*,h_1,\delta^*) > 0$ and $r_2^* \geq r_1^*$, a short-run equilibrium will exist; the new equilibrium loan size will be $\bar{L}$ when $L_2^* < \bar{L}$ and $\bar{\bar{L}}$ when $L_2^* > \bar{\bar{L}}$. If $r_2^* < r_1^*$, a short-run equilibrium may not exist; if it does it will occur at either $\bar{L}$ or $\bar{\bar{L}}$.[16]

(b) If $\phi_L(L_1^*,h_1,\delta^*) < 0$, a short-run equilibrium will exist; the new equilibrium loan size will be $\bar{L} > L_1^* > L_2^*$.

Proposition 6 is illustrated in Figures 15a and 15b. In each case the initial long-run equilibrium occurs at E_1, the new short-run equilibrium at E_1', and the new long-run equilibrium at E_2. Since all firms continue to receive credit, the increase in h will have the same effect on total credit and investment as it has on loan size. It will be recalled that in the naive model of Section I restrictive monetary policy leads to a decline in total credit if the loan rate is sticky; also, the reduction is greater than that which ultimately occurs after the loan rate has adjusted to the new long-run equilibrium level. These results allowed us to draw certain conclusions about the short-run effectiveness

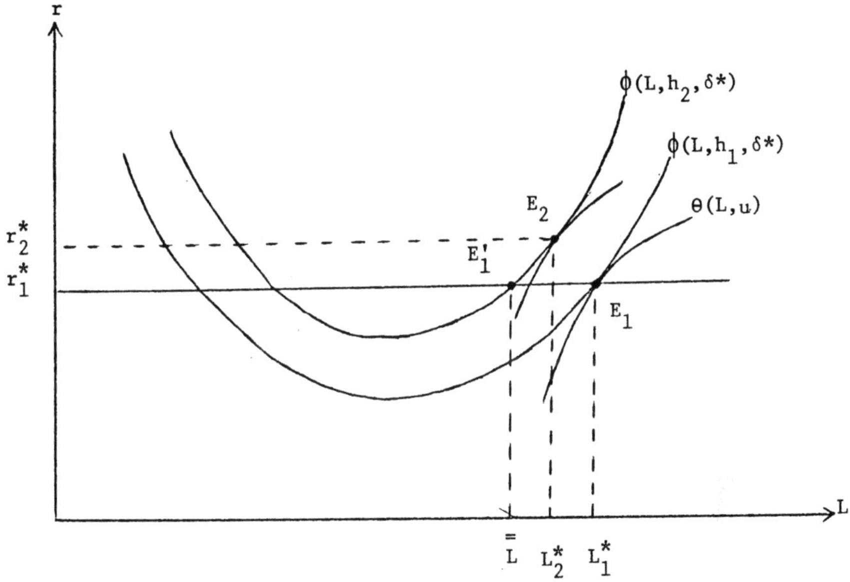

Case of $\phi_L(L_1^*,h_1,\delta^*)>0$

Figure 15a

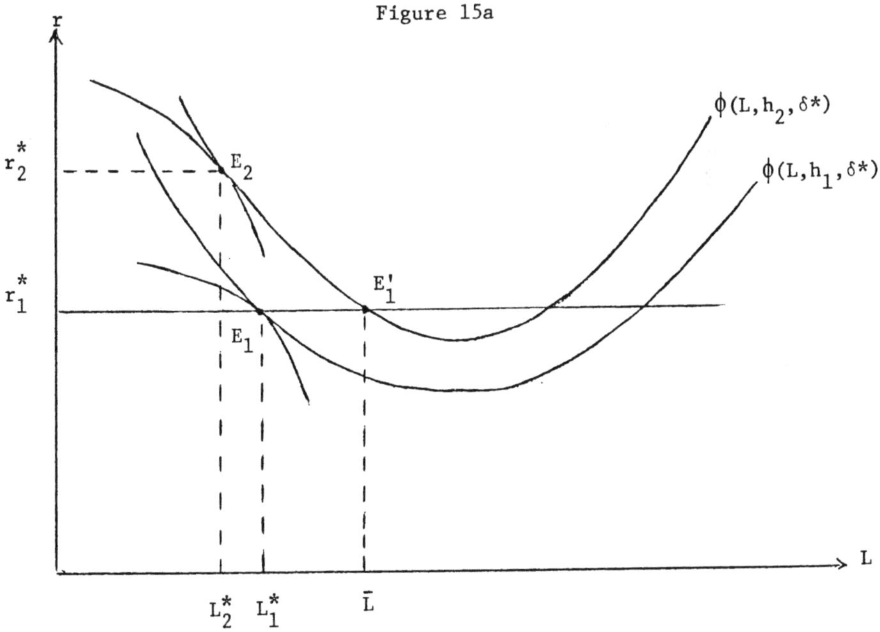

Case of $\phi_L(L_1^*,h_1,\delta^*)<0$

Figure 15b

of monetary policy. In the present case, however, total credit and investment will decline only if $\phi_L(L_1^*, h_1, \delta^*) > 0$, i.e. only if there is rationing in the initial equilibrium. If $\phi_L(L_1^*, h_1, \delta^*) < 0$, as in Figure 15b, the short-run impact of restrictive monetary policy will be exactly opposite to that indicated by the naive model. Furthermore, even though credit must fall when $\phi_L(L_1^*, h_1, \delta^*) > 0$, the reduction may well be <u>less</u> than that which occurs over the long run.

Let us now suppose that the increase in h is large enough that expected profits of δ^* cannot be realized at any value of L as long as r remains fixed at r_1^*. Clearly all banks will be forced to shut down if they were earning zero total expected profits in the initial equilibrium. However, as in the case of $\bar{r} < \min_L \phi(L,h,\delta^*)$ in Section III.B., this need not occur if banks were earning positive total expected profits before the increase in h--i.e. if administrative costs are nonzero and entry to the banking industry is restricted. Provided h_2 is low enough for banks to earn nonnegative total expected profits at loan rate r_1^*, there will exist a short-run equilibrium in which banks operate on their offer curves, making loans of size $Q(r_1^*, h_2)$. As long as r remains fixed at r_1^*, some firms will receive loans while others do not. The number of firms which do receive credit will be $m(\delta)\bar{N}$, where δ is the value of the bank's expected profits per loan when $r = r_1^*$, $h = h_2$, and $L = Q(r_1^*, h_2)$.

Since $\delta(r,Q(r,h),h)$ is decreasing in h and since $dm/d\delta > 0$, the number of loans granted by banks will be lower the higher is h_2. Since $\partial Q/\partial h < 0$, the total volume of credit $m\bar{N}Q$ will also vary inversely with

h_2. However, only in the case of $\phi_L(L_1^*, h_1, \delta^*) \geq 0$ can we be sure that total credit will be lower than in the initial long-run equilibrium. If $\phi_L(L_1^*, h_1, \delta^*) \geq 0$, $Q(r_1^*, h_2) < Q(r_1^*, h_1) \leq L_1^*$; since both the size of each loan and the number of loans are reduced, total credit will fall. But when $\phi_L(L_1^*, h_1, \delta^*) < 0$, it is entirely possible that $L_1^* < Q(r_1^*, h_2) < Q(r_1^*, h_1)$. If the increase in the size of each loan is sufficiently large, it will offset the decline in the number of loans, causing total lending to rise.

V. Conclusions

In Chapter I we saw that firms would generally fail to receive the amount of credit they demanded at the equilibrium loan rate, and banks make smaller or larger loans than they desired at that rate, if (1) there existed a risk of default on each loan and diminishing marginal returns to investment, or (2) costs of administration depended on the number of loans that a bank makes rather than the volume of its lending. The first factor was seen to lead to an equilibrium in which firms received smaller loans than they desired at the prevailing loan rate and banks made larger loans than were optimal at that rate, and the second factor to an equilibrium in which the opposite condition held.

The model introduced in Chapter I has been employed in this chapter to evaluate the impact of a ceiling on the loan rate. By treating default risk and administrative costs in an explicit manner we have been able to determine what the effects of such a ceiling will be on the distribution of bank credit among borrowers and on the welfare of each of the different groups involved (banks, borrowers, and depositors). These are questions which cannot be answered by the conventional or "naive" model, which simply posits an aggregate demand for credit inversely related to the loan rate and an aggregate supply of deposits that is an increasing function of the deposit rate. Our analysis also suggests that the aggregate effects of a ceiling may be quite different from those indicated by the conventional model.

We have seen that both the aggregate and distributive effects depend on the relative significance of default risk and administrative costs. Our findings may be summarized as follow:

(1) When there exists a risk of default but no cost of administration, the imposition of a ceiling will cause a decrease in the size of each loan and in total lending. If the supply of deposits to the banking industry is less than perfectly elastic, the equilibrium deposit rate will also fall. In the new equilibrium all firms will continue to receive credit, unless the ceiling is so low that banks are forced to shut down altogether. If the deposit rate is exogenous, each borrower will be worse off despite the reduction in the loan rate. However, if the deposit rate is endogenous, the expected profits of each firm will at first increase as the ceiling is reduced below the initial equilibrium loan rate. Depositors will always be harmed by the ceiling.

(2) Introducing costs of administration which depend on the number of loans made by the bank alters the above conclusions in two important respects. First, it need no longer be true that all firms receive credit in the postceiling equilibrium. In general, there will exist a critical level such that all firms are able to obtain loans when the ceiling lies above that level and some firms are denied credit when the ceiling lies below it. Second, the possibility arises that the ceiling will lead to an <u>increase</u> in total lending and the deposit rate. Provided the ceiling lies above the critical level just mentioned, this will occur whenever administrative costs are sufficiently high that

firms initially receive larger loans (i.e. undertake larger investment projects) than they would desire. In this case the effect of the ceiling on the welfare of borrowers and depositors will also be different than before: Borrowers will experience a decline in expected profits, even if the ceiling lies only slightly below the initial equilibrium loan rate; depositors, on the other hand, will find themselves better off in the postceiling equilibrium.

As we have indicated, the above results may be applied to a closely related question--the impact of monetary policy on the volume and distribution of bank lending when loan rates are inflexible. For example, if a restrictive monetary policy raises the average opportunity cost of making loans and if the loan rate is fixed in the short run, total lending will generally contract when administrative costs are small and expand when those costs are high. Also, if the increase in the average opportunity cost of lending is sufficiently great, some firms will be denied credit altogether. This analysis may be of particular relevance to countries such as Finland and Sweden in which loan rates are inflexible because commercial banks are required to maintain them in a fixed relationship to the central bank discount rate.[17]

In Chapter I we distinguished between two types of credit rationing--that in which the individual borrower receives a smaller loan than he would desire at the quoted loan rate, and that in which some firms are able to obtain loans while other identical firms are not. We also observed that credit could not be rationed in the second sense in an unrestricted competitive equilibrium. In the next chapter we shall see that this type of rationing can occur in the absence of any constraints on the loan rate, provided there is moral hazard in the lending process. When moral hazard exists, unsatisfied firms may not always be able to obtain credit by offering to pay a higher rate of interest than banks are currently charging. In this respect, moral hazard may perform much the same role as a ceiling on the loan rate.

Appendix A

Properties 1-5 of the curve $\tilde{\phi}(L,\delta^*)$ are proved below.

Property 1. Suppose $\delta^* = 0$. There then exists an $\bar{\bar{L}} > L^*$ such that (a) the function $\tilde{\phi}(L,\delta^*)$ is defined at each L in the interval $(0,\bar{\bar{L}})$; (b) $\delta(r,L,\Omega(ML)) < 0$ for all $L > \bar{\bar{L}}$; and (c) $\lim_{L\to\bar{\bar{L}}} \tilde{\phi}(L,\delta^*) = \hat{r}(\bar{\bar{L}})$.

Proof: Let $\hat{\delta}(L) = \delta(\hat{r}(L),L,\Omega(ML)) = \mu_x(L) - [1 + \Omega(ML)]L$. Since $r^* < \hat{r}(L^*)$ and $\delta(r^*,L^*,\Omega(ML^*)) = 0$, $\hat{\delta}(L^*) > 0$. Also, since $d\mu_x/dL = 1 + \Omega(ML)$ at $L = L^*$ and since $d^2\mu_x dL^2 < 0$ and $\Omega' > 0$, $\lim_{L\to\infty} \hat{\delta}(L) = -\infty$. There must therefore exist an $\bar{\bar{L}} > L^*$ such that $\delta(\bar{\bar{L}}) = 0$. Now

$$\text{(A.1)} \qquad \frac{d\hat{\delta}}{dL} = \frac{d\mu_x}{dL} - [1 + \Omega(ML)] - ML\Omega'$$

Our assumptions about ψ ensure that $d\mu_x/dL < \mu_x(L)/L$ for all $L > 0$. Thus, $d\hat{\delta}/dL < 0$ if $L > 0$ and $\hat{\delta}(L) \leq 0$. Since $\hat{\delta}(\bar{\bar{L}}) = 0$, this implies $\hat{\delta}(L) > 0$ for $0 < L < \bar{\bar{L}}$ and $\hat{\delta}(L) < 0$ for $L > \bar{\bar{L}}$. Statements (a), (b), and (c) follow immediately.

Property 2. Suppose $\delta^* = 0$. Then $\tilde{\phi}_L(L,\delta^*) > 0$ and $\phi_L(L,\Omega(ML),\delta^*) > 0$.

Proof: From $\delta(\tilde{\phi}(L,\delta^*),L,\Omega(ML)) = \delta^*$, it follows that

$$\tilde{\phi}_L(L,\delta^*) = -\frac{1}{\delta_r}(\delta_L - ML\Omega')$$

where the partial derivatives $\delta_r(r,L,h)$ and $\delta_L(r,L,h)$ are evaluated at $r = \tilde{\phi}(L,\delta^*)$ and $h = \Omega(ML)$. Also, $\phi_L(L,\Omega(ML),\delta^*) = -\delta_L/\delta_r$. Thus, since

$L > 0$ and $\delta(r,L,h) = 0$ imply $\delta_L(r,L,h) < 0$, both $\phi_L(L,\Omega(ML),0)$ and $\tilde{\phi}_L(L,0)$ must be positive.

<u>Property 3.</u> Suppose $\delta^* > 0$. There then exist an $\bar{L} < L^*$ and an $\bar{\bar{L}} > L^*$ such that (a) the function $\tilde{\phi}(L,\delta^*)$ is defined at each L in the interval $(\bar{L},\bar{\bar{L}})$; (b) $\delta(r,L,\Omega(ML)) < \delta^*$ for all $L > \bar{\bar{L}}$; (c) $\lim_{L\to\bar{L}} \tilde{\phi}(L,\delta^*) = \hat{r}(\bar{L})$ and $\lim_{L\to\bar{\bar{L}}} \tilde{\phi}(L,\delta^*) = \hat{r}(\bar{\bar{L}})$; (d) $\lim_{L\to\bar{L}} \tilde{\phi}_L(L,\delta^*) < 0$ and $\lim_{L\to\bar{\bar{L}}} \tilde{\phi}_L(L,\delta^*) = +\infty$; and (e) $\lim_{L\to\bar{L}} \phi_L(L,\Omega(ML),\delta^*) = -\infty$ and $\lim_{L\to\bar{\bar{L}}} \phi_L(L,\Omega(ML),\delta^*) = +\infty$.

Proof: As in the proof of Property 1, let $\hat{\delta}(L) = \delta(\hat{r}(L),L,\Omega(ML))$. Since $r^* < \hat{r}(L^*)$ and $\delta(r^*,L^*,\Omega(ML^*)) = \delta^*$, $\hat{\delta}(L^*) > \delta^*$. Now at L^*, $d\mu_x/dL - [1 + \Omega(ML)] = 0$. Thus, since $d^2\mu_x/dL^2 < 0$ and $\Omega' > 0$, $d\hat{\delta}/dL = d\mu_x/dL - [1 + \Omega(ML)] - ML\Omega' < 0$ for all $L \geq L^*$. As we saw earlier, $\lim_{L\to\infty} \hat{\delta}(L) = -\infty$; also, $\mu_x(0) = 0$ implies $\hat{\delta}(0) = 0$. There must therefore exist an $\bar{L} < L^*$ and an $\bar{\bar{L}} > L^*$ such that $\hat{\delta}(\bar{L}) = \hat{\delta}(\bar{\bar{L}}) = \delta^*$, $\hat{\delta}(L) > \delta^*$ for $\bar{L} < L < \bar{\bar{L}}$, and $\hat{\delta}(L) < \delta^*$ for $L > \bar{\bar{L}}$. Parts (a), (b), and (c) of the property follow immediately.

It will be recalled from the proof of Property 2 that $\tilde{\phi}_L(L,\delta^*) = -\frac{1}{\delta_r}(\delta_L - ML\Omega')$ and $\phi_L(L,\Omega(ML),\delta^*) = -\frac{\delta_L}{\delta_r}$, where δ_r and δ_L are evaluated at $r = \tilde{\phi}(L,\delta^*)$ and $h = \Omega(ML)$. Now

$$\lim_{L\to\bar{\bar{L}}} \delta_L(\tilde{\phi}(L,\delta^*),L,\Omega(ML))$$

$$= \delta_L(\lim_{L\to\bar{\bar{L}}} \tilde{\phi}(L,\delta^*),\bar{\bar{L}},\Omega(M\bar{\bar{L}}))$$

$$= \delta_L(\hat{r}(\bar{\bar{L}}),\bar{\bar{L}},\Omega(M\bar{\bar{L}}))$$

$$= \left.\frac{d\mu_x}{dL}\right|_{L=\bar{\bar{L}}} - [1 + \Omega(M\bar{\bar{L}})] < 0$$

where the inequality follows from $\bar{\bar{L}} > L^*$. Thus, since $\lim_{r \to \hat{r}(L)} \delta_r(r,L,h) = 0$,

$$\lim_{L \to \bar{\bar{L}}} \tilde{\phi}_L(L,\delta^*) = +\infty$$

and

$$\lim_{L \to \bar{\bar{L}}} \phi_L(L,\Omega(ML),\delta^*) = +\infty$$

Similarly,

$$\lim_{L \to \bar{L}} \delta_L(\tilde{\phi}(L,\delta^*),L,\Omega(ML))$$

$$= \left.\frac{d\mu_x}{dL}\right|_{L=\bar{L}} - [1 + \Omega(M\bar{L})] > 0$$

which implies

$$\lim_{L \to \bar{L}} \phi_L(L,\Omega(ML),\delta^*) = -\infty$$

Finally, $\tilde{\phi}(L,\delta^*) < \hat{r}(L)$, $\lim_{L \to \bar{L}} \tilde{\phi}(L,\delta^*) = \hat{r}(\bar{L})$, and $d\hat{r}/dL < 0$ imply

$$\lim_{L \to \bar{L}} \tilde{\phi}_L(L,\delta^*) < 0$$

<u>Property 4.</u> Suppose $\delta^* > 0$. There then exists an $\hat{L}$, $\bar{L} < \hat{L} < \bar{\bar{L}}$, such that $\phi_L(L,\Omega(ML),\delta^*) \gtreqless 0$ as $L \gtreqless \hat{L}$ and $\tilde{\phi}_L(L,\delta^*) > 0$ for $L \geq \hat{L}$.

Proof: From part (e) of Property 3, $\phi_L(L,\Omega(ML),\delta^*)$ is negative for L sufficiently close to $\bar{L}$ and positive for L sufficiently close to $\bar{\bar{L}}$. There must therefore exist some intermediate value of L, say $\hat{L}$, at which $\phi_L(L,\Omega(ML),\delta^*) = 0$. Now, when evaluated at $r = \tilde{\phi}(L,\delta^*)$ and $h = \Omega(ML)$, the partial derivative $\delta_L(r,L,h)$ may be treated as a function of L alone, with

$$\frac{d}{dL}\delta_L = \delta_{rL}\tilde{\phi}_L + \delta_{LL} - M\Omega'$$

$$(A.2) \qquad = -\frac{\delta_{rL}}{\delta_r}(\delta_L - ML\Omega') + \delta_{LL} - M\Omega'$$

$$= \delta_{LL} - \frac{\delta_{rL}}{\delta_r}\delta_L + M\Omega'[\frac{\delta_{rL}L}{\delta_r} - 1]$$

But

$$\frac{\delta_{rL}}{\delta_r} = \frac{1 - G(\hat{y}) - Lg(\hat{y})\,\partial\hat{y}/\partial L}{L[1-G(\hat{y})]} < \frac{1}{L}$$

where the inequality follows from $\partial\hat{y}/\partial L > 0$. Thus,

$$\frac{d}{dL}\delta_L < \delta_{LL} - \frac{\delta_{rL}}{\delta_r}\delta_L$$

Since $\delta_{LL} < 0$, it follows that $\frac{d}{dL}\delta_L < 0$ whenever $\delta_L = 0$: once δ_L becomes negative as we move along the locus $\tilde{\phi}(L,\delta^*)$ from $\bar{L}$ to $\bar{\bar{L}}$, it must remain so. Since $\phi_L = -\delta_L/\delta_r$, this implies $\phi_L(L,\Omega(ML),\delta^*) < 0$ for $\bar{L} < L < \hat{L}$ and $\phi_L(L,\Omega(ML),\delta^*) > 0$ for $\hat{L} < L < \bar{\bar{L}}$. Also, since $\tilde{\phi}_L = -\frac{1}{\delta_r}(\delta_L - ML\Omega')$, $\tilde{\phi}_L(L,\delta^*) > 0$ for $L \geq \hat{L}$.

It remains to show that $\phi_L(L,\Omega(ML),\delta^*) < 0$ at any $L < \bar{L}$ for which the function $\tilde{\phi}(L,\delta^*)$ is defined. Consider any $L < \bar{L}$ for which $\tilde{\phi}(L,\delta^*)$ is defined. Clearly there must exist an L' and L" such that (i) $L' < L < L'' < \bar{L}$; (ii) $\tilde{\phi}(L,\delta^*)$ is defined at each L in the interval (L',L"); and (iii) $\lim_{L\to L'} \tilde{\phi}(L,\delta^*) = \hat{r}(L')$ and $\lim_{L\to L''} \tilde{\phi}(L,\delta^*) = \hat{r}(L'')$. Thus

$$\lim_{L\to L'} \delta_L(\tilde{\phi}(L,\delta^*),L,\Omega(ML)) = \left.\frac{d\mu_x}{dL}\right|_{L=L'} - [1 + \Omega(ML')]$$

$$\lim_{L\to L''} \delta_L(\tilde{\phi}(L,\delta^*),L,\Omega(ML)) = \left.\frac{d\mu_x}{dL}\right|_{L=L''} - [1 + \Omega(ML'')]$$

Since $L' < L'' < \bar{L} < L^*$, both these expressions are positive; $\delta_L(\tilde{\phi}(L,\delta^*),L,\Omega(ML))$ will therefore be positive for L sufficiently close to L' or L". Since $\delta_L(\tilde{\phi}(L,\delta^*),L,\Omega(ML)) = 0$ always implies $\frac{d}{dL}\delta_L < 0$, it follows that $\delta_L(\tilde{\phi}(L,\delta^*),L,\Omega(ML)) > 0$ and thus $\phi_L(L,\Omega(ML),\delta^*) < 0$ for all L such that $L' < L < L''$. This completes the proof of Property 4.

<u>Property 5.</u> Suppose that $\delta^* > 0$ and that $L\Omega''/\Omega' > -2$. Then $\delta(r,L,\Omega(ML)) < \delta^*$ for all $L < \bar{L}$. Also, the curve $\tilde{\phi}(L,\delta^*)$ will be U-shaped, i.e. there will exist some $\tilde{L}$, $\bar{L} < \tilde{L} < \bar{\bar{L}}$, such that $\tilde{\phi}_L \gtreqless 0$ as $L \gtreqless \tilde{L}$.

Proof: Differentiating the expression for $d\hat{\delta}/dL$ in (A.1) with respect to L yields

$$\frac{d^2\hat{\delta}}{dL^2} = \frac{d^2\mu_x}{dL^2} - M(L\Omega'' + 2\Omega')$$

Since $L\Omega''/\Omega' > -2$ and $d^2\mu_x/dL^2 < 0$, $d^2\hat{\delta}/dL^2 < 0$. This implies $\delta(r,L,\Omega(ML)) \leq \hat{\delta}(L) < \delta^*$ for all $L < \bar{L}$.

To prove the second part of the property, recall that $\tilde{\phi}_L(L,\delta^*) = -\frac{1}{\delta_r}(\delta_L - ML\Omega')$. Differentiating this expression with respect to L we obtain

$$\tilde{\phi}_{LL}(L,\delta^*) = -\frac{1}{\delta_r}\left[\frac{d}{dL}\delta_L - M(L\Omega'' + \Omega')\right] - (\delta_L - ML\Omega')\frac{d}{dL}\left(\frac{1}{\delta_r}\right)$$

Now from (A.2), $\tilde{\phi}_L(L,\delta^*) = 0$ implies

$$\frac{d}{dL}\delta_L = \delta_{LL} - M\Omega'$$

and thus

$$\tilde{\phi}_{LL}(L,\delta^*) = -\frac{1}{\delta_r}\left[\delta_{LL} - ML(\Omega'' + 2\Omega')\right] > 0$$

From part (d) of Property 3 it then follows that there must exist some $\tilde{L}$, $\bar{L} < \tilde{L} < \bar{\bar{L}}$, such that $\tilde{\phi}_L \gtreqless 0$ as $L \gtreqless \tilde{L}$.

Appendix B

In this appendix we show that $\sum_{1}^{N} m_i = M$ in the new equilibrium if the loan rate ceiling $\bar{r}$ satisfies $\tilde{\phi}(\hat{L},\delta^*) < \bar{r} < r^*$.

Suppose that $\sum_{1}^{N} m_i < M$. Then from equilibrium condition (E.2') it follows that either (1) $u(r,L) = 0$ or (2) $\delta(r,L,h) = \underset{r,L}{\text{Max}}\ \delta(r,L,h)$ subject to $r \leq \bar{r}$. Consider the first possibility. In this case, equilibrium condition (E.3') requires $L = \mathcal{L}(h)$, since $u(r,L) = 0$ implies $\partial\delta/\partial L = d\mu_x/dL - (1+h)$. Also, equilibrium condition (E.4) requires $h = \Omega(SL)$, where $S \equiv \sum_{1}^{N} m_i$. Let $h(S)$ and $L(S)$ be the solution to

$$h = \Omega(SL), \quad L = \mathcal{L}(h)$$

Then, since $dh/dS > 0$, $\frac{d}{dS}\{\mu_x(L(S)) - [1 + h(S)]L(S)\} < 0$. But at $S = M$, $\mu_x(L(S)) - [1 + h(S)]L(S) = \mu_x(L^*) - (1+h^*)L^* > \delta(r^*,L^*,h^*) = \delta^*$. Thus, $S \equiv \sum_{1}^{N} m_i < M$ implies $\mu_x(L(S)) - [1 + h(S)]L(S) > \delta^*$; since $\delta(r,L,h) = \mu_x(L) - (1+h)L$ when $u(r,L) = 0$, this violates the condition $\delta(r,L,h) \leq \delta^*$.

Consider next the possibility that $\delta(r,L,h) = \underset{r,L}{\text{Max}}\ \delta(r,L,h)$ subject to $r \leq \bar{r}$. In this case, $L = Q(\bar{r},h)$ and $\delta_L(r,L,h) = 0$. But $L > 0$ and $L = Q(r,h)$ imply $\delta(r,L,h) > 0$, which violates the condition $\delta(r,L,h) \leq \delta^*$ for the case in which $\delta^* = 0$. To complete the proof, we shall show that the condition $\delta(r,L,h) \leq \delta^*$ will also be violated if $\delta^* > 0$.

As before, equilibrium condition (E.4) requires $h = \Omega(SL)$. Let $\tilde{Q}(r,S)$ be that value of L such that

$$\text{(B.1)} \qquad \delta_L(r,L,\Omega(SL)) = 0$$

where the expression on the left is the partial derivative $\delta_L(r,L,h)$ evaluated at $h = \Omega(SL)$. The value of L satisfying (B.1) will be unique, since $\delta_{LL} + \delta_{Lh}S\Omega' = \delta_{LL} - S\Omega' < 0$. At loan size $L = \tilde{Q}(r,S)$ and deposit rate $h = \Omega(SL)$, expected profits per loan are

$$\text{(B.2)} \qquad \tilde{\delta}(r,S) \equiv \delta(r,\tilde{Q}(r,S),\Omega(S\tilde{Q}(r,S)))$$

Differentiating (B.2) with respect to S and taking into account (B.1), we obtain

$$\frac{\partial\tilde{\delta}}{\partial S} = \delta_L \frac{\partial\tilde{Q}}{\partial S} - \tilde{Q}\Omega'[\tilde{Q} + S\frac{\partial\tilde{Q}}{\partial S}]$$

$$= -\tilde{Q}\Omega'[\tilde{Q} + S\frac{\partial\tilde{Q}}{\partial S}]$$

From (B.1),

$$\delta_{LL}\frac{\partial\tilde{Q}}{\partial S} - \Omega'[\tilde{Q} + S\frac{\partial\tilde{Q}}{\partial S}] = 0$$

and

$$\frac{\partial\tilde{Q}}{\partial S} = \frac{\Omega' Q}{\delta_{LL} - \Omega' S} < 0$$

This implies $\tilde{Q} + S\frac{\partial\tilde{Q}}{\partial S} > 0$ and thus $\partial\tilde{\delta}/\partial S < 0$. Differentiating (B.2) with respect to r yields

$$\frac{\partial\tilde{\delta}}{\partial r} = \delta_r + \delta_L\frac{\partial\tilde{Q}}{\partial r} - \tilde{Q}\Omega' S\frac{\partial\tilde{Q}}{\partial r}$$

$$= \delta_r - \tilde{Q}\Omega' S\frac{\partial\tilde{Q}}{\partial r}$$

But (B.1) implies

$$\frac{\partial \tilde{Q}}{\partial r} = - \frac{\delta_{rL}}{\delta_{LL} - \Omega' S}$$

and thus

$$\frac{\partial \tilde{\delta}}{\partial r} = \delta_r [1 + \frac{\tilde{Q}\Omega' S}{\delta_{LL} - \Omega' S} \frac{\delta_{rL}}{\delta_r}]$$

It was shown in the proof of Property 4 in Appendix A that $\frac{\delta_{rL}}{\delta_r} < \frac{1}{L}$. Since $\frac{\tilde{Q}\Omega' S}{\delta_{LL} - \Omega' S} < 0$, it follows that

$$\frac{\partial \tilde{\delta}}{\partial r} > \delta_r [1 + \frac{\Omega' S}{\delta_{LL} - \Omega' S}] = \frac{\delta_r \delta_{LL}}{\delta_{LL} - \Omega' S} > 0$$

From the definition of $\hat{L}$ in Property 4, $r = \tilde{\phi}(\hat{L}, \delta^*)$ and $S = M$ imply $\tilde{\delta}(r,S) = \delta^*$. Since $\partial \tilde{\delta}/\partial r > 0$ and $\partial \tilde{\delta}/\partial S < 0$, it follows that $\tilde{\delta}(r,S) > \delta^*$ for any $r > \tilde{\phi}(L, \delta^*)$ and $S < M$. Thus, if $r = \bar{r}$, $L = \tilde{Q}(r,S)$, $h = \Omega(SL)$, and $S < M$, expected profits per loan $\delta(r,L,h)$ will exceed δ^*. This completes the proof.

Appendix C

This appendix is concerned with the case in which the ceiling $\bar{r}$ is too low for conditions (3.1)-(3.4) of Section III.C.1. to be realized. We first show that conditions (3.1)-(3.4) cannot be satisfied if $\bar{r} < \tilde{\phi}(\hat{L},\delta^*)$ and $\phi_L(L^*,h^*,\delta^*) > 0$. Next, we establish the circumstances in which the alternative equilibrium conditions given in Section III.C.2. can be met, and prove that the new equilibrium will be unique. This is done first for the zero-profit case and then for the positive-profit case. Finally, it is shown that in the zero-profit case the deposit rate and the total volume of credit must fall if $\bar{r} < \tilde{\phi}(\hat{L},\delta^*)$ and $\phi_L(L^*,h^*,\delta^*) > 0$.

1. Suppose that $\bar{r} < \tilde{\phi}(\hat{L},\delta^*)$ and that $\phi_L(L^*,h^*,\delta^*) > 0$. Consider any combination of r and L--say r_3 and L_3--which satisfies conditions (3.1), (3.2), and (3.4). Then $r_3 = \tilde{\phi}(L_3,\delta^*) \leq \bar{r}$. From $\bar{r} < \tilde{\phi}(\hat{L},\delta^*)$ and Property 4 it follows that $L_3 < \hat{L}$ and $\phi_L(L_3,\Omega(ML_3),\delta^*) < 0$. There will thus exist an $\varepsilon > 0$ such that $\phi(L,\Omega(ML_3),\delta^*) < \bar{r}$ for $L_3 < L < L_3 + \varepsilon$. Also, $\phi_L(L^*,h^*,\delta^*) > 0$ implies $L^* > \hat{L} > L_3$. As in the proof of Proposition 3, let $L_3^* = \mathcal{L}(\Omega(ML_3))$, the value of L that maximizes $\mu_{\underset{\sim}{x}}(L) - (1+h)L$ given $h = \Omega(ML_3)$. Then since $L_3 < L^*$ implies $\Omega(ML_3) < h^*$ and since $d\mathcal{L}/dh < 0$, $L_3^* > L^* > L_3$. But along the locus $\phi(L,\Omega(ML_3),\delta^*)$, $du/dL > 0$ for all $L < L_3^*$. Therefore, since $\phi(L,\Omega(ML_3),\delta^*) < \bar{r}$ for $L_3 < L < L_3 + \varepsilon$, condition (3.3) cannot be satisfied at $r = r_3$ and $L = L_3$.

2. The equilibrium conditions for the zero-profit case are

$$\text{(C.1)} \qquad L = Q(\bar{r},h)$$

(C.2) $h = \Omega(SL)$

(C.3) $\delta(\bar{r},L,h) = \delta^*$

(C.4) $S < M$

In Appendix B we defined $\tilde{Q}(r,S)$ to be the value of L satisfying $L = Q(r,h)$ and $h = \Omega(SL)$. This value was shown to be unique, given r and S. We also defined $\tilde{\delta}(r,S)$ to equal $\delta(r,\tilde{Q}(r,S),\Omega(S\tilde{Q}(r,S)))$, and showed that $\partial\tilde{\delta}/\partial r > 0$, $\partial\tilde{\delta}/\partial S < 0$.

If $\delta^* = 0$, conditions (C.1) and (C.3) require $L = 0$. Suppose alternatively that $\delta^* = \text{Min}\,\frac{C(m)}{m} > 0$, i.e. that administrative costs are nonzero. From the definition of $\tilde{\delta}(r,S)$ it is clear that equations (C.1)-(C.3) are satisfied at any S for which $\tilde{\delta}(\bar{r},S) = \delta^*$. Also, if such an S exists it will be unique, since $\partial\tilde{\delta}/\partial S < 0$. Let $\hat{r} = \tilde{\delta}(\hat{L},\delta^*)$. From $\partial\tilde{\delta}/\partial S < 0$ it follows that $\underset{S}{\text{Max}}\,\tilde{\delta}(\bar{r},S) = \tilde{\delta}(\bar{r},0) = \delta(\bar{r},Q(\bar{r},\Omega(0)),\Omega(0))$. Furthermore, $\bar{r} < \hat{r}$, $\tilde{\delta}(\hat{r},M) = \delta^*$, $\partial\tilde{\delta}/\partial r > 0$, and $\partial\tilde{\delta}/\partial S < 0$ imply $\tilde{\delta}(\bar{r},S) < \delta^*$ for all $S \geq M$. Thus, there will exist a nontrivial solution to the complete set of equilibrium conditions (C.1)-(C.4) if and only if $\delta(\bar{r},Q(\bar{r},\Omega(0)),\Omega(0)) > \delta^* = \text{Min}\,\frac{C(m)}{m}$.

In terms of Figure 16, the new equilibrium occurs at E, the point at which the horizontal line $\delta = \delta^*$ intersects the curve $\tilde{\delta}(\bar{r},S)$. The existence of a point of intersection is ensured by $\tilde{\delta}(\bar{r},0) > \delta^*$ and $\tilde{\delta}(\bar{r},M) < \delta^*$; its uniqueness follows from the negative slope of the curve $\tilde{\delta}(\bar{r},S)$. A decrease in the ceiling will cause $\tilde{\delta}(\bar{r},S)$ to shift downward; thus, the equilibrium value of S will fall.

3. The equilibrium conditions for the positive-profit case are

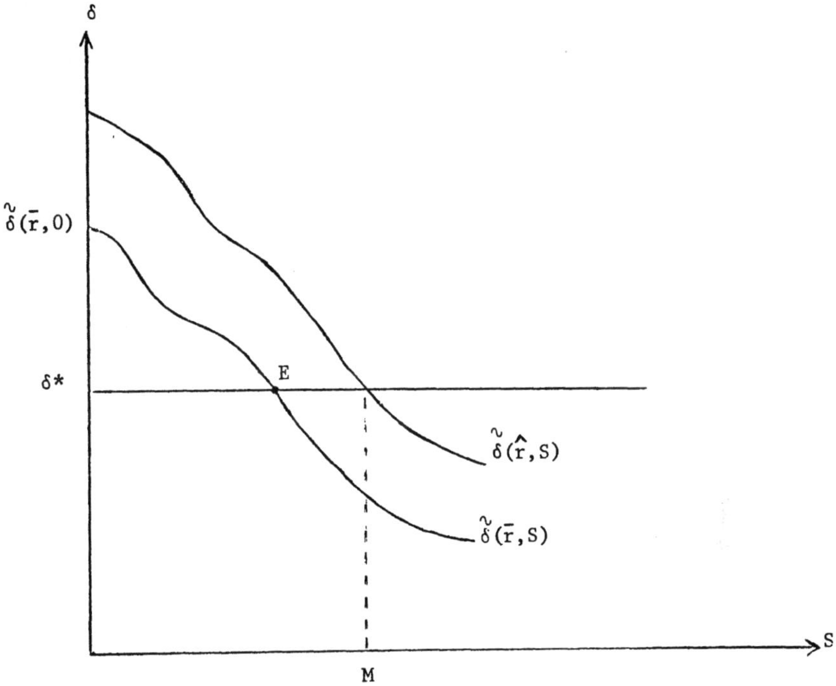

Zero-profit case

Figure 16

$$(C.5) \qquad L = Q(\bar{r},h)$$

$$(C.6) \qquad h = \Omega(SL)$$

$$(C.7) \qquad \delta = \delta(\bar{r},L,h)$$

$$(C.8) \qquad \delta \geq \text{Min } \frac{C(m)}{m}$$

$$(C.9) \qquad S = m(\delta)\bar{N} \text{ if } \delta > \text{Min } \frac{C(m)}{m}$$

$$0 \leq S \leq m(\delta)\bar{N} \text{ if } \delta = \text{Min } \frac{C(m)}{m}$$

$$(C.10) \qquad S < M$$

Given S, the value of L which satisfies the first two equations is $\tilde{Q}(\bar{r},S)$. At that value of L, expected profits per loan are $\tilde{\delta}(\bar{r},S) = \delta(\bar{r},\tilde{Q}(\bar{r},S),\Omega(S\tilde{Q}(\bar{r},S)))$. Thus conditions (C.5)-(C.9) are satisfied at any δ and S such that (i) $\delta = \tilde{\delta}(\bar{r},S) > \text{Min } \frac{C(m)}{m}$ and $S = m(\delta)\bar{N}$ or (ii) $\delta = \tilde{\delta}(\bar{r},S) = \text{Min } \frac{C(m)}{m}$ and $0 \leq S \leq m(\delta)\bar{N}$. Since $\partial\tilde{\delta}/\partial S < 0$ and $dm/d\delta > 0$ for all $\delta > \text{Min } \frac{C(m)}{m}$, such a δ and $S > 0$ will exist if and only if $\tilde{\delta}(\bar{r},0) = \delta(\bar{r},Q(\bar{r},\Omega(0)),\Omega(0)) > \text{Min } \frac{C(m)}{m}$. From $\partial\tilde{\delta}/\partial S < 0$ and $dm/d\delta > 0$ it also follows that this combination of δ and S will be unique. Finally, since $\tilde{\delta}(\hat{r},M) = \delta^*$, $m(\delta^*)\bar{N} = M$, $\bar{r} < \hat{r}$, and $\partial\tilde{\delta}/\partial r > 0$, condition (C.10) will be satisfied.

In Figure 17a, the new equilibrium occurs at E, the point of intersection of the curves $S = m(\delta)\bar{N}$ and $\delta = \tilde{\delta}(\bar{r},S)$. Since $\delta > \text{Min } \frac{C(m)}{m}$ in this example, banks continue to earn positive expected profits π. This is not the case in Figure 17b, in which $\delta = \text{Min } \frac{C(m)}{m}$ in the new equilibrium. In this instance, no bank will earn positive profits and some banks will shut down altogether. Each bank which does stay in business will offer that number of loans m which minimizes the average cost $\frac{C(m)}{m}$. Note that in either case a decrease in the ceiling will shift the curve $\tilde{\delta}(\bar{r},S)$ downward, reducing the total number of loans S granted by banks.

4. In the zero-profit case, equilibrium requires $\delta(\bar{r},Q(\bar{r},h),h) = \delta^*$. Now $\delta(r,Q(r,h),h)$ may be treated as a function of r and h alone. Since $L = Q(r,h)$ implies $\delta_L = 0$, the partial derivatives of this function are

$$\text{(C.11)} \qquad \frac{\partial}{\partial r}\delta(r,Q(r,h),h) = \delta_r + \delta_L \frac{\partial Q}{\partial r} = \delta_r > 0$$

$$\text{(C.12)} \qquad \frac{\partial}{\partial h}\delta(r,Q(r,h),h) = \delta_L \frac{\partial Q}{\partial h} + \delta_h = \delta_h < 0$$

Let $\hat{h} = \Omega(M\hat{L})$ and $\hat{r} = \tilde{\phi}(\hat{L},\delta^*)$. Clearly $\delta(\hat{r},Q(\hat{r},\hat{h}),\hat{h}) = \delta^*$, which from (C.11) and $\bar{r} < \hat{r}$ implies $\delta(\bar{r},Q(\bar{r},\hat{h}),\hat{h}) < \delta^*$. From (C.12) it then follows that the equilibrium condition $\delta(\bar{r},Q(\bar{r},h),h) = \delta^*$ can hold only if $h < \hat{h}$ (see Figure 18).

Suppose $\phi_L(L^*,h^*,\delta^*) > 0$. Then $L^* > \hat{L}$, which implies $h^* = \Omega(ML^*) > \Omega(M\hat{L}) = \hat{h}$. Since the new equilibrium value of h must be lower than $\hat{h}$, it must also be lower than h^*. The new equilibrium values of S and L must therefore satisfy $SL < ML^*$, i.e. total credit will fall as a result of the ceiling.

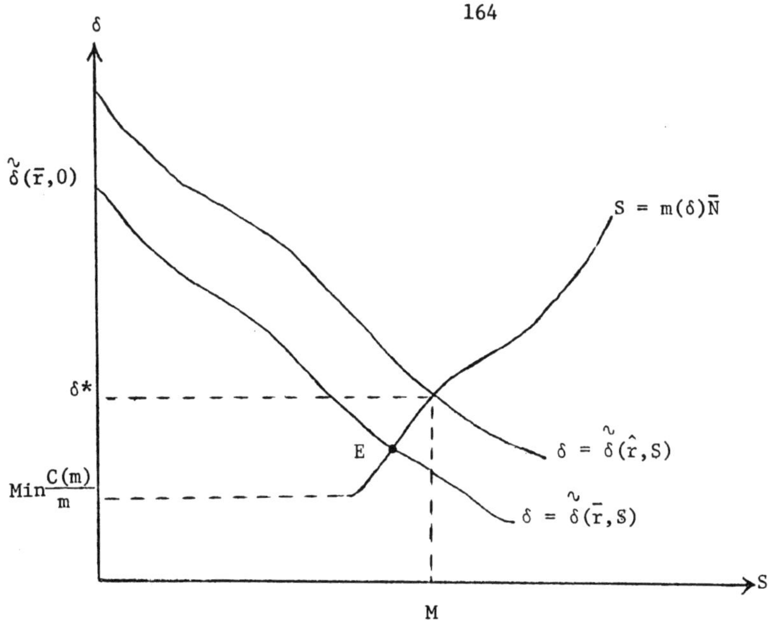

Positive-profit case

Figure 17a

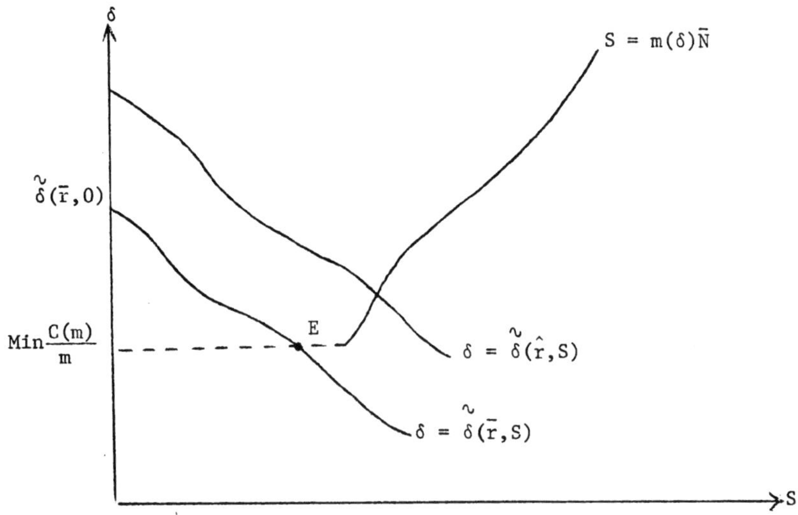

Positive-profit case

Figure 17b

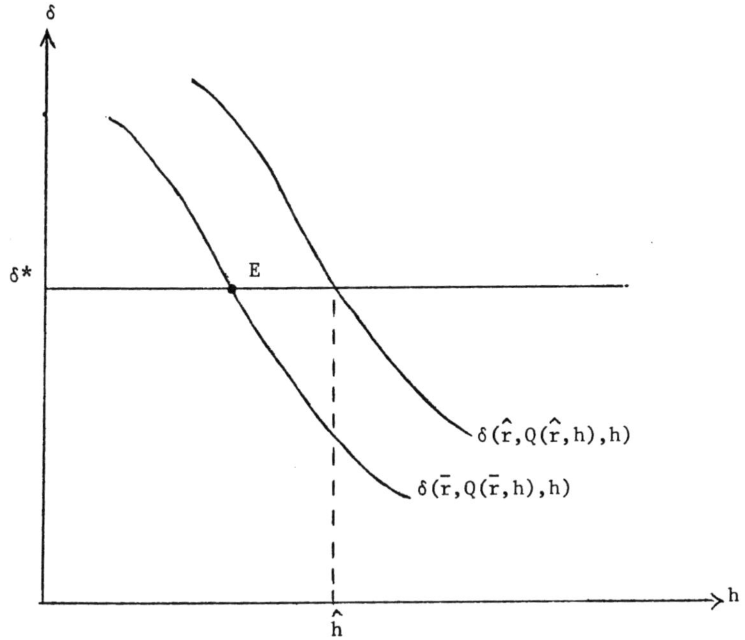

Figure 18

Footnotes

1 Throughout this chapter it is assumed that firms have identical investment projects. The model may be extended, along the lines indicated in Chapter I, to take account of differences among firms; however, the preliminary work which I have done suggests that this does not affect the basic results presented here.

2 In Chapter I it was shown that this assumption is unnecessary if the bank making the first loan always has priority over the firm's assets. In particular, in the equilibrium described below no bank will have an incentive to make a loan to a customer who has already borrowed from another bank. This can also be shown to be the case in each of the equilibria described in Section III.

3 As in Chapter I, we shall refer to δ as the bank's expected profits per loan. It should be remembered, however, that δ is calculated gross of administrative costs.

4 In restating the conditions on p. 47 we have taken into account that $\psi(0,y) = 0$ implies $\mu_x(0) = 0$.

5 This assertion may appear sufficiently obvious to not require further comment. However, it may be justified as follows. Let r_j be the loan rate charged th j^{th} firm and L_j the size of the loan it receives. Then in a competitive equilibrium, one of two possibilities must hold. Either

(i) $u(r_j,L_j) = u(r_k,L_k)\ \forall\ j$ and k

or

(ii) $\pi_i = \underset{r,L,m}{\text{Max}}\ \pi(r,L,m,h)$ s.t. $r \leq \bar{r}\ \forall\ i$

That is, one firm can be worse off than another in equilibrium only if each bank has absolutely no incentive to alter the terms of its loans.

Suppose (i) holds, and let $\bar{u} = u(r_j,L_j)$. Then for any firm j receiving a loan, it must be true in equilibrium that $\delta(r_j,L_j,h) = \underset{r,L}{\text{Max}}\ \delta(r,L,h)$ s.t. $u(r,L) \geq \bar{u}$ and $r \leq \bar{r}$; otherwise, the bank would be able to increase its expected profits from each loan without losing any customers. But the solution to this maximization problem is easily seen to be unique. Thus, r and L must be the same for all firms which receive credit.

Suppose alternatively that (ii) holds. For each loan j made by a bank, this implies $r_j = \bar{r}$ and $L_j = Q(\bar{r},h)$. Once again, banks will charge the same loan rate and grant loans of the same size to all customers.

6 Let $\hat{L}(r)$ be the inverse of the function $\hat{r}(L)$. Then $u(r^*,L^*) > 0$ implies $\hat{L}(r^*) > L^*$. But $u(r,L) = 0$, $d\hat{L}/dr < 0$, and $r \leq \bar{r} < r^*$ imply $L \geq \hat{L}(r) > \hat{L}(r^*)$. Thus, $L > L^* = \mathcal{L}(h)$.

7 The borrower's expected profits are $u(r,L) = [\mu_X(L) - (1+h)L] - \delta(r,L,h)$. Since the first term falls and the second remains con-

stant, $u(r,L)$ must be lower in the new equilibrium.

8 $\phi_L(L,\Omega(ML),\delta^*)$ is to be interpreted as the partial derivative $\phi_L(L,h,\delta^*)$ evaluated at $h = \Omega(ML)$.

9 The remaining possibility is that $\underset{L}{\text{Min}}\ \tilde{\phi}(L,\delta^*) < \bar{r} < \tilde{\phi}(\hat{L},\delta^*)$ and $\phi_L(L^*,h^*,\delta^*) < 0$. It is not difficult to show that in this case there will exist at least one combination of r and L satisfying conditions (3.1)-(3.4). As in Proposition 3b, the equilibrium loan rate will be $\bar{r}$ and the equilibrium loan size L_2, where $\tilde{\phi}(L_2,\delta^*) = \bar{r}$ and $L^* < L_2 < \hat{L}$. In addition, however, there will exist an equilibrium identical to that described below.

10 If $\delta = \text{Min}\ \frac{C(m)}{m}$, so that total expected profits of each bank equal zero, the appropriate restriction is $0 \leq S \leq m(\delta)\bar{N}$. When the second inequality holds, fewer than $\bar{N}$ banks will remain in business.

11 It will be recalled from the previous section that when h is exogenous and $\bar{r} < \underset{L}{\text{Min}}\ \phi(L,h,\delta^*)$, Type II credit rationing occurs only in the positive-profit case, i.e. only if entry is restricted. In the zero-profit case all banks are compelled to shut down, since the reduction in the loan rate cannot be offset by a fall in the deposit rate.

12 If h increases, the total expected profits of borrower and lender, $\mu_x(L) - (1+h)L$, will fall. In the zero-profit case, δ remains constant; thus, if h rises, the borrower must be worse off than in

the absence of the ceiling. However, in the positive-profit case, δ will be lower in the new equilibrium; the borrower may therefore enjoy higher expected profits even if h increases as a result of the ceiling.

13 In contrast to the case of risky investment projects, it will always be possible to define a demand curve D(r) indicating the borrowing firm's optimal loan size at each r. This follows from $\partial^2 u/\partial L^2 = \psi'' < 0$.

14 The partial derivative of $\tilde{\phi}(L_T/M,0)$ with respect to L_T is

$$-\frac{1}{M\delta_r}(\delta_L - ML\Omega') > -\frac{\delta_L}{M\delta_r} + \Omega'$$

where the inequality follows from $\delta_r < L$. Thus, the curve $\tilde{\phi}(L_T/M,0)$ is steeper than $\Omega(L_T)$ at all values of L_T.

15 We have been assuming that there are no administrative costs of making loans. When such costs do exist, it will be possible to determine the impact of a loan rate ceiling on the distribution of bank credit even if investment projects are riskless. The reason is that the equilibrium iso-profit curve $\phi(L,h,\delta^*)$ will not have zero slope. When administrative costs are present, the equilibrium value of δ must be positive; and if investment projects are riskless, the bank's iso-profit curves will be negatively sloped for all $\delta > 0$. The impact of a loan rate ceiling in this case will be as indicated in Propositions 1b and 3b above.

16 If it is possible to define a demand curve D(r) such that $\partial u/\partial L \gtreqless 0$ as $L \lesseqgtr D(r)$, a short-run equilibrium must exist even when $r_2^* < r_1^*$. Furthermore, the new equilibrium loan size will always be $\bar{\bar{L}}$.

17 For a discussion of such practices, see [1].

References

[1] Jaffee, Dwight M. and Myhrman, Johan, "Monetary Policy in Small, Open, Economies: The Nordic Countries," August 1975

[2] McKinnon, Ronald I., Money and Capital in Economic Development (Washington, D.C., Brookings, 1973)

[3] Shaw, Edward S., Financial Deepening in Economic Development (New York, Oxford University Press, 1973)

[4] Tobin, James and Brainard, William C., "Financial Intermediaries and the Effectiveness of Monetary Controls," American Economic Review, May 1963

[5] Tucker, Donald P., "Credit Rationing, Interest Rate Lags, and Monetary Policy Speed," Quarterly Journal of Economics, February 1968

CHAPTER III. MORAL HAZARD AND EQUILIBRIUM CREDIT RATIONING

Introduction

In Chapter I it was seen that when there is risk of default, competitive equilibrium in the market for bank loans is fully compatible with credit rationing, in the sense that each firm may receive a smaller loan than it desires at the interest rate charged by the bank. We also noted, however, that in the absence of interest rate ceilings a competitive equilibrium could not arise in which some firms were able to obtain loans while other, identical firms were not. The purpose of the present chapter is to show that equilibrium rationing may occur in this second sense when there is "moral hazard" in the lending process. This will be seen to have important implications not only for the efficiency of resource allocation, but also for the effectiveness of monetary policy in controlling aggregate demand.

In general, firms will have a variety of investment projects to choose from. Associated with each project will be a probability distribution of the future income or net cash flow generated by the investment. The firm's expected profits from an investment--i.e. the expected surplus of income over debt repayment--will obviously depend on which project is chosen, as well as on the terms of the loan received. Similarly, as long as there exists a possibility of default on the loan, the bank's expected profits will be a function not only of the loan rate it charges and the volume of credit it extends, but also of the particular characteristics of the project in which the funds are invested.

In the case of any fixed-payment debt such as corporate bonds or commercial bank loans, the payment which the lender receives is a concave but not linear function of the total income generated by the borrower's investment project. The lender receives all the income from the project when the outcome is less than or equal to the principal and interest on the loan, but does not share in any excess over that fixed amount. When the outcome of the project is uncertain, this feature of fixed-payment debt can give rise to an important conflict of interest between lender and borrower. If two investment projects yield the same expected total income but differ in "riskiness"--in the sense used by Rothschild and Stiglitz ([6]), that one project has greater weight in the tails of the probability distribution of its outcome--the expected income of the lender must always be lower, and the expected income of the borrower higher, for the riskier of the two projects. That is, the share of the borrower in the total expected income from the project will be an increasing function of its riskiness.

In general, however, the projects available to the borrower will differ not only in riskiness but also in the total income which each is expected to generate. Stated alternatively, changes in the riskiness of a project need not be "mean-preserving." If a borrower is risk-neutral and can alter the characteristics of his project in such a way as to increase both the riskiness of the project and the total expected return, he will want to do so. Beyond some point, however, it may not be possible to achieve further increases in risk without reducing the total expected return from the project. In this event the borrower will face a tradeoff between the total expected income from the project and the share of that expected return to which he is entitled. One result is that the mix of project characteristics which maximizes the borrower's expected profits from a loan will not be that which maximizes the total expected return from the project. Equally important, for our purposes, is that the borrower's optimal tradeoff between risk and total expected return will generally vary with the terms of the loan. It is because of this that the bank may face a problem of "moral hazard" if it is unable to specify all the characteristics of the borrower's investment project in the loan contract or if it cannot ensure that the borrower will live up to such agreements. Just as an insurance company will consider the effect of a policy on the insured's probability of having an accident, so will the bank want to take into account any indirect effect the terms of a loan might have on the probability distribution of the outcome of the borrower's investment project.

In the absence of moral hazard, the bank's expected revenues from a loan are an increasing function of the interest rate it charges. As a result, a competitive equilibrium cannot exist in which some firms are able to obtain loans while other, identical firms are not. Firms without credit would be willing to pay a slightly higher rate of interest than banks were currently charging in order to obtain a loan, and banks would be happy to make loans at that higher interest rate since their expected profits would be increased.

When the borrower's choice of project characteristics depends on the terms of the loan, however, the net effect of an increase in the loan rate may well be to reduce the bank's expected profits from a loan. We shall see below that a borrower will respond to a rise in the loan rate by choosing a project with higher risk and lower total expected return. Such a change in project characteristics will tend to reduce the bank's expected revenues from a loan and may even offset the favorable direct effect of the increase in the loan rate. Thus, if it is not possible to commit a borrower to a fully specified set of project characteristics, a bank may be unwilling to accomodate--at a higher rate of interest than it is currently charging--those firms which have not been able to obtain credit elsewhere. It is important to note that this unwillingness on the part of the bank does not result from any inherent difference between firms which have been fortunate enough to receive credit and firms which have not. Rather, it arises from the bank's recognition that at any rate of interest higher than it is currently charging, firms will choose projects so risky as to offset the increase in the amount due on the loan.

Much of this chapter is concerned with establishing the precise conditions under which this kind of equilibrium credit rationing will occur. Of no less interest, however, are the implications which this type of credit rationing has for the efficiency of resource allocation and the effectiveness of monetary policy. We shall see first that resources may not be allocated optimally if some firms are denied credit in equilibrium. In particular, given the mix of project characteristics selected in equilibrium and the total volume of lending, it may be possible to increase the net expected return to investment by distributing credit more evenly. As was shown in Chapter I, distortions of this nature do not result when banks ration credit in the alternative sense of providing each of their customers with a smaller loan than he desires.

The other implication which we emphasize in this chapter concerns the effectiveness of monetary policy in controlling aggregate demand. If investment is financed primarily through bank loans, and if all firms must receive credit in equilibrium, monetary policy can affect total investment only by changing the size of loan granted to each firm. Policy measures which tend to reduce the relative attractiveness of bank deposits to wealth holders will generally lead to an increase in the equilibrium deposit rate, and as a result, some decline in the equilibrium loan size (see Chapter I). But if the marginal returns to individual investment projects are sharply diminishing, the increase in the deposit rate will produce only a small reduction in the size of each loan. Aggregate investment will be "interest-inelastic," and this will be true even if customers were initially receiving smaller loans than they desired.

However, if the initial equilibrium is one in which banks ration credit by refusing to lend to some borrowers, monetary policy will not affect the rate of interest paid on bank deposits, the rate of interest charged on loans, or the size of each loan--it will affect instead the number of firms which are able to obtain loans, increasing the extent of credit rationing in the case of a monetary contraction and reducing it in the case of a monetary expansion. Thus, as argued by proponents of the availability doctrine, monetary policy may have a significant impact on investment even if the scale of each project is highly insensitive to changes in interest rates. This also is an implication which the alternative concept of credit rationing does not have.

In Section I we present the model in its most general form and set forth the conditions for a competitive equilibrium when there is moral hazard in the lending process. By way of introduction, we show how these conditions determine an equilibrium in the limiting case in which the size of each project is fixed, and then consider the implications of credit rationing for the effectiveness of monetary policy in this special case.

Section II established general restrictions on the probability distribution of the project outcome which ensure that the indirect effect of an increase in the loan rate will be to reduce the bank's expected profits from a loan. In Section III we consider an important case in which these restrictions are satisfied. In this case investment is "putty-clay." The firm must decide when it makes its investment how much labor, raw materials, or other factors of production it will employ at the end of the period with its newly installed capital stock, but is uncertain as to what the wage or the price of its output will be at that time. We examine in detail the particular case in which the technology of production is Cobb-Douglas and the probability distribution of prices is uniform. In the process we show how competitive equilibrium is derived when projects are of variable size; discuss the various factors which determine whether the equilibrium is one in which banks ration credit, in the sense of refusing to lend to certain borrowers; and show that monetary policy will have a greater impact on investment when the initial equilibrium is of this nature. Although the putty-clay model provides the frame of reference for this discussion, our results will be seen to have somewhat wider applicability. In the following section, we explain the implications of equilibrium rationing for the efficiency of resource allocation.

An interesting problem, which arises only in the presence of moral hazard, is that a bank may have an incentive to make a second loan to a firm which has already borrowed from another bank, even if the bank which made the first loan has priority over the firm's assets in the event of default. We first take note of this possibility in Section I, when we present the conditions for a competitive equilibrium, but consider it at much greater length in Section V. The last section of the paper summarizes our major conclusions.

To avoid any possible confusion, we will adopt the same terminology employed in Chapter II to distinguish between the two varieties of equilibrium credit rationing. Thus, Type I credit rationing will be said to exist when the individual customer receives a smaller loan than he would desire at the interest rate charged by the bank. Type II rationing, on the other hand, will refer to a situation in which some firms receive loans while other, identical firms do not. As should be evident by now, a major theme of this chapter is that the two types of credit rationing differ significantly both in their causes and in their implications.

I. The basic model

A. Assumptions

As in Chapters I and II, we shall assume that firms undertake one-period investment projects which can be financed only by borrowing from banks. The outcome of each project is nonnegative and may be interpreted as the end-of-period value of the firm. We suppose that all firms have identical investment projects.

The outcome x of a representative project is assumed to be uncertain. In particular, it has a cumulative distribution function F which depends both on the amount of credit L obtained by the firm (i.e. the size of the investment) and on a one-dimensional project characteristic γ. Unless otherwise stated, we shall assume that F is differentiable in both x and γ. We define x_m and x_M, the lower and upper bounds on x, so that

$$F(x_M,L,\gamma) = 1, \quad F(x,L,\gamma) < 1 \text{ for all } x < x_M$$

$$x_m F(x_m,L,\gamma) = 0, \quad F(x,L,\gamma) > 0 \text{ for all } x > x_m$$

We do not rule out the possibility that the limits x_m and x_M will vary with L and γ. For convenience, we suppose that the end-of-period value of the firm will be zero if the firm does not undertake any investment--i.e. $F(0,0,\gamma) = 1$.

The bank's revenues from a loan are $R = \min\{x,(1+r)L\}$, where r is the loan rate. Thus, if the borrower does not obtain additional credit elsewhere, the bank's expected revenues from a loan will be

$$\mu_R(r,L,\gamma) = \int_{x_m}^{z} xF_x(x,L,\gamma)dx + z\int_{z}^{x_M} F_x(x,L,\gamma)dx \tag{1}$$

$$= z - \int_{x_m}^{z} F(x,L,\gamma)dx$$

where z = (1+r)L, the principal and interest on the loan. The borrower's profits from a loan are simply x-R. Its expected profits are thus

$$u(r,L,\gamma) = \int_{z}^{x_M} (x-z)F_x(x,L,\gamma)dx \tag{2}$$

$$= x_M - z - \int_{z}^{x_M} F(x,L,\gamma)dx$$

The total expected outcome of the project, μ_x, is equal to the sum of the bank's expected revenues μ_R and the borrower's expected profits u, or

$$\mu_x(L,\gamma) = \int_{x_m}^{x_M} xF_x(x,L,\gamma)dx = x_M - \int_{x_m}^{x_M} F(x,L,\gamma)dx \tag{3}$$

Since the end-of-period value of the firm is assumed to equal zero in the absence of a loan, $\mu_x(0,\gamma) = 0$.

As in Chapters I and II, we assume that both banks and firms attempt to maximize expected profits, i.e. that all agents are risk-neutral. Excluding costs of administration, the bank's expected profits from an individual loan are

$$\delta(r,L,\gamma,h) = \mu_R(r,L,\gamma) - (1+h)L$$ [1]

where $(1+h)L$ is the opportunity cost to the bank of making the loan. The opportunity rate h may be interpreted as the rate of return which the bank could earn on some alternative riskless investment or as the rate of interest which it must pay to obtain deposits. The bank's total expected profits from m identical loans are

$$\pi(m,\delta) = m\delta - C(m)$$

where C(m) is the total cost of administration incurred by the bank. In Chapters I and II we allowed for the possibility that the marginal costs of administration C'(m) would be at first decreasing and then increasing in m. To simplify matters, we shall assume in this paper that there is a fixed cost c of administering each loan, i.e. that C(m) = cm.

The properties of an equilibrium in the market for bank loans will depend crucially on the manner in which the project characteristic γ is determined. We shall assume that at any loan rate r and loan size L, the borrower is free to choose that value of γ which maximizes his expected profits $u(r,L,\gamma)$. In other words, the bank is unable to control directly the characteristics of a borrower's investment project by specifying them in the loan contract. This may be the case either because the bank finds it difficult to determine whether the borrower has lived up to the contract (i.e. selected the project characteristics to which he has agreed), or because it does not have adequate means of penalizing the borrower for violation of the agreement. Although the bank cannot exercise direct control over the characteristics of the investment project, we shall suppose that it does know which value of γ

the borrower will choose at each combination of r and L.

In practice, loan agreements generally do include a number of covenants with the borrower ([3], [5]). In the case of "term" loans (i.e. medium or long-term loans to business firms), the borrower is often obligated to maintain working capital above a specified level and to limit spending on illiquid fixed assets. Also, agreements frequently forbid the firm to pledge its assets as security for other loans, and limit the total amount of additional borrowing the firm can undertake. From the periodic financial statements that borrowers are almost always required to furnish, the bank may have little difficulty in verifying whether provisions of this nature are being violated. However, provisions so general may leave the firm considerable latitude to take actions which are favorable to its interests and harmful to those of the bank. Furthermore, even if it were possible for the bank to specify the characteristics of the investment project in such detail as to leave the borrower no legal right to take such actions, the mere perusal of financial reports would be unlikely to establish whether the borrower was fulfilling the agreement; thus, the cost to the bank of verifying compliance, e.g. of employing loan supervisors with the necessary technological expertise, could be very large indeed. Finally, the formal penalty for violation of the loan agreement, which in most instances is that the entire loan become due at once, may not give the borrower sufficient incentive to comply fully.[2]

B. Equilibrium conditions

Let us assume for the moment that each firm can take out only one bank loan at a time. Also, let m_i be the number of loans supplied by the ith bank, N the number of banks (which need not be fixed), and M the number of firms with investment projects. Then, given that borrowers can choose whatever value of γ they wish, the conditions for a competitive equilibrium may be stated as

(E.1) $\sum_{1}^{N} m_i \leq M$

(E.2) $\sum_{1}^{N} m_i < M$ only if (i) $\max_{\gamma} u(r,L,\gamma) = 0$ or (ii) r, L, and γ maximize $\delta(r,L,\gamma,h)$ subject to the constraint that γ maximize $u(r,L,\gamma)$

(E.3a) $\nexists$ an r', L', and γ' such that (i) γ' maximizes $u(r',L',\gamma)$; (ii) $\delta(r',L',\gamma',h) > \delta(r,L,\gamma,h)$; and (iii) $u(r',L',\gamma') \geq u(r,L,\gamma)$

(E.3b) $\nexists$ an m' such that $\pi(m',\delta) > \pi(m_i,\delta)$

(E.4) $h = \Omega(\sum_{1}^{N} m_i L)$

Condition (E.1) expresses the constraint that the total number of loans supplied by banks cannot exceed the number of firms with investment projects. Condition (E.2) states that some firms will fail to obtain loans in equilibrium only if (i) borrowers cannot earn positive expected profits at the prevailing loan terms r and L; or (ii) at those terms, banks are earning the maximum expected profits which can be achieved from a loan given that the borrower is free to choose γ. Condition (E.3a) ensures that no bank will have an incentive to alter the terms of its loans, i.e. that alternative combinations of r and L which the bank could offer would either fail to increase its expected profits per loan or would cause it to lose customers to competing banks. Similarly, condition (E.3b) guarantees that a bank will have no incentive to alter the number of its loans, m. Finally, (E.4) indicates that the opportunity rate h is a function of the total volume of lending by all banks, $L_T \equiv \sum_1^N m_i L$. As in Chapters I and II, we assume $\Omega' \geq 0$.

The equilibrium condition which gives rise to the possibility of Type II rationing is (E.2). Of course, if $\underset{\gamma}{\text{Max}}\, u(r,L,\gamma) = 0$, each firm will be just indifferent between receiving a loan and not receiving one; the fact that some firms may not receive loans in this case is therefore not particularly interesting. The more significant case is that in which firms which would like to borrow at the prevailing loan terms are unable to do so. As indicated in part (ii) of condition (E.2), this can occur only if the prevailing loan terms are already the most advantageous possible to banks. Only under these circumstances will banks be unwilling to accommodate, at a different interest rate or loan size, firms which have been unable to obtain credit.

For given values of L and γ, increases in the loan rate will raise the bank's expected revenues and expected profits from a loan until the loan rate becomes so high that default is certain, at which point the expected profits of the borrower become equal to zero. Thus, δ can attain a maximum at an r and L for which $\underset{\gamma}{\text{Max}}\ u(r,L,\gamma) > 0$ only if a further increase in the loan rate would cause the borrower to choose a value of γ less favorable to the bank. In other words, if the borrower's optimal choice of γ can be represented by the function $\gamma^*(r,L)$, we require that $\frac{\partial \mu_R}{\partial \gamma} \frac{\partial \gamma^*}{\partial r}$ be negative. Furthermore, this adverse indirect effect of an increase in the loan rate must be sufficiently strong to offset the favorable direct effect, $\frac{\partial \mu_R}{\partial r}$. That is, the condition

$$\frac{\partial \mu_R}{\partial r} + \frac{\partial \mu_R}{\partial \gamma} \frac{\partial \gamma^*}{\partial r} = 0$$

must hold.

If projects are of fixed size $\bar{L}$, we need be concerned only with the effect of changes in the loan rate on the bank's expected profits. However, in the more general case in which the size of the project is variable, we must also consider whether banks could earn higher expected profits by making smaller or larger loans; only if this is not possible will some firms be denied credit in equilibrium. Thus, for Type II rationing to occur, the net effect on δ of a marginal increase in loan size, taking into account any induced change in γ, must be zero:

$$\frac{\partial \delta}{\partial L} + \frac{\partial \delta}{\partial \gamma} \frac{\partial \gamma^*}{\partial L} = \frac{\partial \mu_R}{\partial L} - (1+h) + \frac{\partial \mu_R}{\partial \gamma} \frac{\partial \gamma^*}{\partial L} = 0$$

The crucial role played by the assumption that the borrower is free to choose γ can perhaps best be perceived by considering how equilibrium would be determined under alternative circumstances. Let us suppose that the project characteristic γ can be specified in the loan contract and that borrowers always choose that value of γ to which they have agreed (e.g. because there exist adequate means of enforcing the contract). In this case, γ is simply another attribute of the loan in addition to its size L. A bank will therefore offer that combination of r, L, and γ which yields the highest expected profits per loan δ without causing it to lose customers to competing banks. Only equilibrium conditions (E.2) and (E.3a) are affected, and they are replaced by

(E.2') $\sum_{1}^{N} m_i < M$ only if $u(r,L,\gamma) = 0$

(E.3a') $\nexists$ an r', L', and γ' such that $\delta(r',L',\gamma',h) > \delta(r,L,\gamma,h)$ and $u(r',L',\gamma') \geq u(r,L,\gamma)$

It will be noted from (E.2') that an equilibrium cannot exist in which firms that would like to obtain credit--i.e. that are not just indifferent to receiving a loan at the prevailing loan terms--are unable to do so. If $u(r,L,\gamma) > 0$, any firm which has been unable to obtain credit will be willing to take a loan at the same L and γ and a somewhat higher loan rate; and since a bank can be sure that the borrower will implement the project characteristic γ to which he has agreed (rather than that which would maximize his expected profits), it will always be happy to make a loan at those more favorable terms. It should also be observed from condition (E.3a') that the equilibrium values of L and γ will be Pareto-optimal, in the sense of maximizing the combined expected profits of lender and borrower, $\delta(r,L,\gamma,h)$ + $u(r,L,\gamma) = \mu_x(L,\gamma) - (1+h)L$. We shall see that this is not generally true when the borrower can choose whatever value of γ he wishes.

Before stating equilibrium conditions (E.1)-(E.4), we made the assumption that each firm can take out only one loan. Now, in Chapter I, we derived the equilibrium for a competitive loan market under the assumption that each firm took out only one loan. We then showed that in this equilibrium no bank would have an incentive to make a second loan, provided that the bank making the first loan always had priority over the firm's assets in the event of default. In the equilibrium described by conditions (E.1)-(E.4), however, there may exist an incentive for banks to make these second loans. The possibility arises because the borrower is free to choose a different value of γ for his project when he takes out a second loan, i.e. because the bank making the first loan cannot commit the borrower to a given project characteristic γ. Only in this case is it possible for a second loan to reduce the expected profits of the bank which made the first loan, and only in these circumstances can a bank earn positive expected profits from a second loan while leaving the borrower no worse off than before.

In Section V we will consider this problem in some detail. At that time we will prove that an incentive to make second loans can exist in an equilibrium described by conditions (E.1)-(E.4), and establish sufficient conditions to rule out this possibility. In the meantime, it will be assumed either that a bank can forbid its customers to seek additional financing from other banks for the same project, or that it can require prior consent for any second loan. It should be noted that the problem does not arise in the special case to which we turn now, in which the size of each project is fixed.

C. The case of fixed project size

Later in this chapter, when we take up particular examples in which the project outcome x has a cumulative distribution function of the form $F(x,L,\gamma)$, we will show in detail how conditions (E.1)-(E.4) can be used to derive the competitive market equilibrium. However, rather than postpone all discussion of the determination of equilibrium, let us consider briefly the limiting case in which the size of each investment project is fixed. Through consideration of this case, we can immediately appreciate the implications of Type II rationing for the effectiveness of monetary policy.

Let $\bar{L}$ be the technologically fixed project size. The expected profits of the bank are then $\delta(r,\bar{L},\gamma,h) = \mu_R(r,\bar{L},\gamma) - (1+h)\bar{L}$. Let us suppose that the bank's expected revenues μ_R attain a maximum, subject to the constraint that the borrower is free to choose γ, at some loan rate r^* which is not so high that default on the loan is certain; as we know, this presumes that increases in the loan rate beyond r^* have an adverse indirect effect on the bank's expected revenues, through induced changes in γ. Finally, let $\hat{\delta}(\bar{L},h)$ be the constrained maximum of δ with respect to r, i.e. the expected profits earned by the bank at loan rate r^* when the borrower chooses γ so as to maximize his own expected profits $u(r^*,\bar{L},\gamma)$.

From equilibrium condition (E.3b) it is clear that δ^*, the expected profits yielded by each loan in equilibrium, must be equal to c, the cost to the bank of administering a loan: when $\delta > c$, banks will attempt to expand their loans, and when $\delta < c$, they will attempt to contract them. Now, since the bank's maximum expected profits $\hat{\delta}(\bar{L},h)$ are strictly decreasing in h, there will exist a unique opportunity rate h' such that $\hat{\delta}(\bar{L},h) \gtreqless \delta^*$ as $h \lesseqgtr h'$. But from condition (E.4) we know that the opportunity rate h can be expressed as a nondecreasing function of the total number of loans S granted by all banks: $h = \Omega(S\bar{L})$, where $S \equiv \sum_{1}^{N} m_i$. It follows immediately that the equilibrium will be characterized by Type II rationing if and only if $\Omega(M\bar{L}) > h'$.[3] When this condition holds, banks cannot grant loans to all M firms and at the same time earn sufficient expected profits per loan to cover the cost of administration, c. The total number of firms S* receiving credit will be that value of S for which $\Omega(S\bar{L}) = h'$, as shown in Figure 1a. Since the loan rate charged will be that value r* which maximizes δ, both conditions (E.2) and (E.3a) will be satisfied.

When the opposite condition $\Omega(M\bar{L}) < h'$ holds, the equilibrium must be one in which all firms receive credit. This case is illustrated in Figure 1b. From (E.2) we know that banks will grant fewer than M loans in equilibrium only if they are charging that loan rate r* which maximizes δ. But if fewer than M loans are made, the opportunity rate h will be so low that maximum expected profits per loan $\hat{\delta}(\bar{L},h)$ exceed $\delta^* = c$. Since banks will wish to increase lending whenever $\delta > c$, this obviously cannot represent an equilibrium. Thus, in equilibrium all firms will receive credit, h will equal $\Omega(M\bar{L})$, and the equilibrium loan rate will be such that banks earn expected profits per loan $\delta^* = c$. Also, condition (E.3a) requires that the loan rate not exceed r*: if r did exceed r*, a bank could increase its expected profits per loan, without

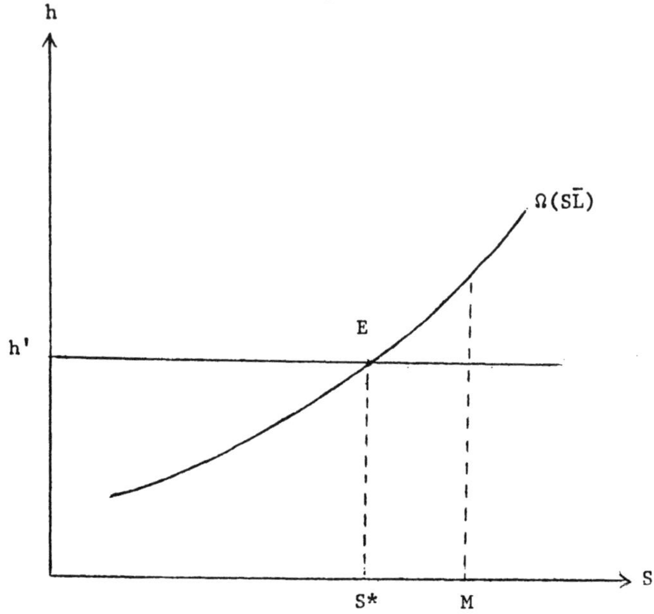

Figure 1a: Fewer than M firms receive credit

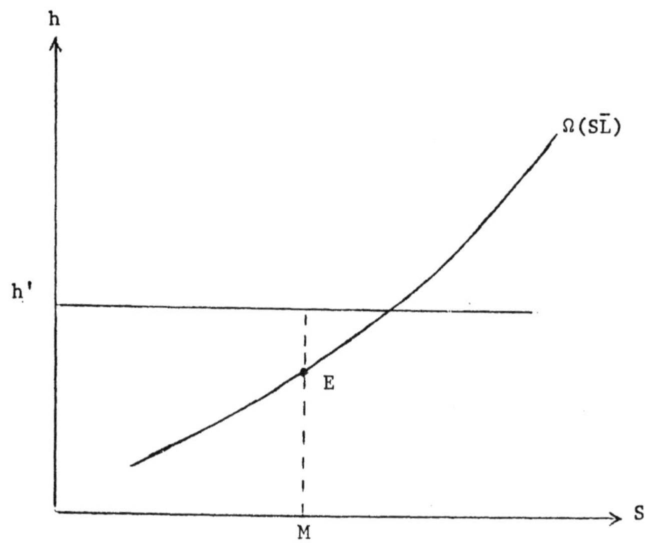

Figure 1b: All firms receive credit

losing customers to competitors, by simply reducing the loan rate to r^*.

Monetary policy can be viewed as affecting the market for bank loans through shifts in the function Ω which relates the opportunity rate h to the total volume of bank lending L_T. In this framework, a tightening of monetary policy corresponds to an upward shift in Ω and an easing of monetary policy to a downward shift in Ω. Since the size of each project is technologically fixed, it is clear that monetary policy can affect total lending and investment only by changing the total number of loans S granted by banks. Let us suppose first that the initial equilibrium is one in which all firms are able to obtain loans, i.e. that $\Omega(M\bar{L}) < h'$. In this case any downward shift in Ω or any upward shift in Ω which leaves $\Omega(M\bar{L})$ less than h' will have no effect on the number of loans granted and thus no effect on total lending and investment. The impact of monetary policy will be felt only on the equilibrium opportunity rate and on the equilibrium loan rate, which adjusts to maintain expected profits per loan at the equilibrium level $\delta^* = c$.

However, if the initial equilibrium is characterized by Type II rationing, i.e. if some firms are being denied credit, matters will be quite different. As shown in Figure 2, a tightening of monetary policy will in this case reduce the total number of loans S* made by banks, and thus also the total volume of lending and investment, $L_T = S^*L$. Since h must remain equal to h' for banks to remain in business (i.e. for the cost of administration c not to exceed δ), any upward shift in the function Ω must be accompanied by a decrease in total lending. Conversely, an easing of monetary policy, as reflected in a downward shift in Ω, must lead to an increase in the number of firms receiving credit and in total lending and investment. Thus, when Type II rationing is present, monetary policy can be effective in controlling investment even when each firm's demand for credit is completely interest-rate inelastic. As we noted in Chapter I, the existence of Type I rationing, in which all firms receive credit but are granted smaller loans than they desire, does not have this implication.

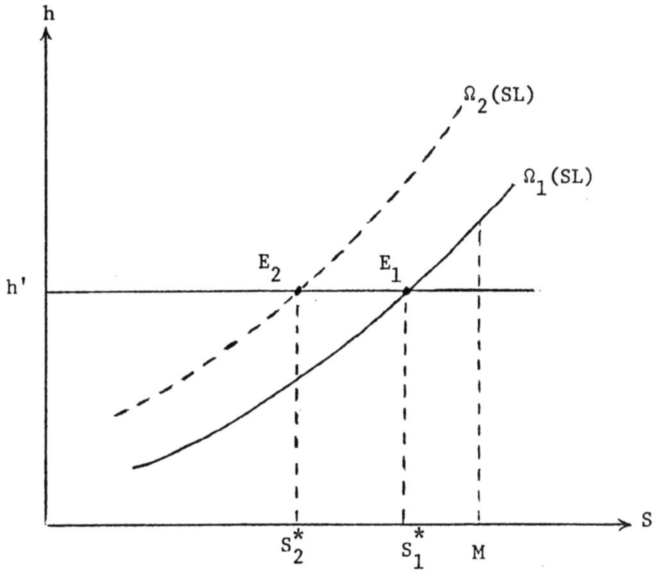

Figure 2

II. Conditions for the existence of moral hazard

In Section I we saw that an equilibrium with Type II rationing could occur only if the indirect effect of an increase in the loan rate were to reduce the bank's expected revenues from a loan. For this to happen, increases in the loan rate must lead the borrower to alter the characteristics of his investment project, and thus also the probability distribution of the project's outcome, in a way which is harmful to the interests of the bank. We have referred to this state of affairs as a problem of "moral hazard" because it is analogous to those situations in insurance markets in which the terms of a policy affect the insured's probability of having an accident, e.g. by causing him to behave more carelessly.

In the first part of this section we will establish restrictions on the cumulative distribution function $F(x,L,\gamma)$ which ensure that increases in the loan rate do cause the borrower to alter γ in a manner harmful to the bank. The more important of these restrictions may be summarized as follows: (1) an increase in the parameter γ always increases the riskiness of the distribution of x, in the sense of shifting weight from the center of the distribution to the tails; and (2) as the parameter γ is increased, the total expected outcome of the project at first increases but eventually begins to decline.

The significance of the first condition is that it creates a potential conflict of interest between borrower and lender. When the outcome of an investment project is high, the borrower realizes as profit the entire excess over the fixed amount due on the loan. Because of limited liability, however, he does not experience correspondingly large losses when the outcome of the project is very low. As a result, a change in project characteristics which raises the probability of both very low and very high outcomes will tend to increase the expected profits of the borrower and reduce those of the bank. The role of the second condition is to ensure that this effect is sufficiently strong to cause the borrower to choose a risky project, but not so great as to cause him to choose the riskiest project available.

In the latter part of this section, we apply our results to the general class of cases in which the outcome of the investment project can be expressed as a function $\psi(L,\gamma,y)$, where y is a random variable or "state of the world" whose probability distribution is independent of both L and γ. This class of cases includes as one member the model of putty-clay investment which will be presented in Section III.

A. By way of introduction, let us consider the case in which the riskiness of the distribution of x increases with γ while the total expected outcome of the project remains unchanged--i.e. the case in which any increase in γ represents a mean-preserving increase in risk, in the sense used by Rothschild and Stiglitz [6] and by Diamond and Stiglitz [1]. In this case, the cumulative distribution function $F(x,L,\gamma)$ must satisfy the two integral conditions

$$\int F_\gamma(x,L,\gamma)dx = 0, \quad \int_{x \leq x'} F_\gamma(x,L,\gamma)dx \geq 0 \text{ for all } x'$$

Rothschild and Stiglitz have shown that under these conditions, EU(x) will be nonincreasing in γ for all concave functions U. Since the bank's expected revenues from a loan are $R = \min\{x,(1+r)L\}$, and since this is a concave function of x, it follows that the bank's expected revenues $\mu_R(r,L,\gamma)$ will be nonincreasing in γ. Thus, since the total expected outcome of the project is independent of γ, the borrower's expected profits, $u(r,L,\gamma) = \mu_x(L) - \mu_R(r,L,\gamma)$, will be maximized by choosing the highest possible γ, i.e. by making the project as risky as possible. This result also follows directly from the integral conditions and the expression for the borrower's expected profits given in (2).

Obviously increases in the loan rate will have no indirect effect on the bank's expected profits in this case, because the borrower will choose the same value of γ at all interest rates. However, this result depends on the invariance of the total expected outcome μ_x with respect to γ. If increases in the parameter γ affect not only the riskiness of the project but also the total expected outcome μ_x, and if the impact on μ_x is adverse as γ becomes very large, the borrower may not wish to select the riskiest project available. In this event, the value of γ which the borrower does select can be expected to vary with the interest rate charged on the loan.

The specific assumptions which we shall make about the cumulative distribution function $F(x,L,\gamma)$ to ensure that increases in the loan rate have a negative indirect effect on the bank's expected revenues include the following:

<u>Assumption A.1.</u> (local single-crossing property) For each $L > 0$ and γ there exists an $\bar{x}$ such that $F_\gamma(x,L,\gamma) > 0$ for $x_m < x < \bar{x}$ and $F_\gamma(x,L,\gamma) < 0$ for $\bar{x} < x < x_M$.

<u>Assumption A.2.</u> For all L and γ, $x_m \leq L$.

<u>Assumption A.3.</u> $\bar{x} = x_m$ at $\gamma = \gamma_{min}$ and $\bar{x} = x_M$ at $\gamma = \gamma_{max}$.

Assumption A.1 corresponds to the concept of an increase in risk as a shift in probability density from the center of the distribution to the tails. For γ_2 <u>marginally</u> higher than γ_1, it implies that the cumulative distribution function $F(x,L,\gamma_2)$ can cross the cumulative distribution function $F(x,L,\gamma_1)$ only once and from above, as shown in Figure 3; it should be noted, however, that this single-crossing property need hold only for values of γ_2 close to γ_1. Assumption A.1 also implies that a marginal increase in γ will represent a mean-preserving

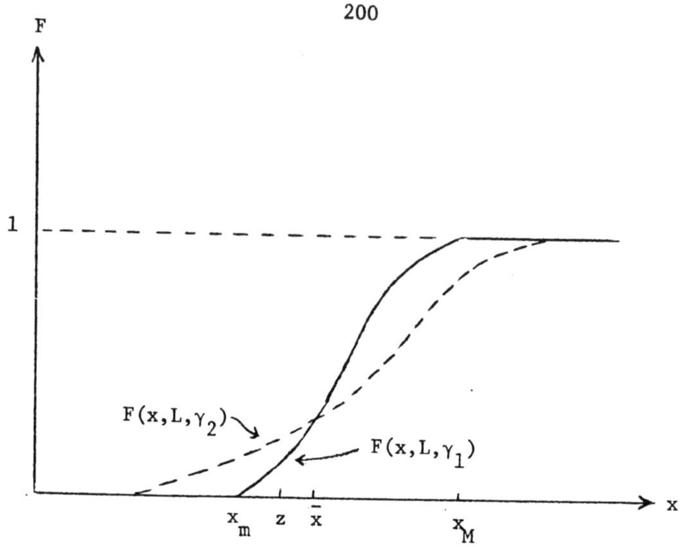

γ_2 marginally higher than γ_1

Figure 3

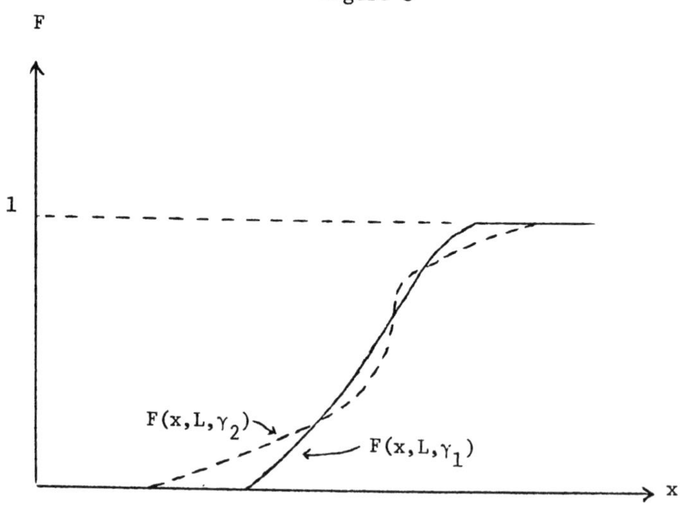

$\gamma_2 > \gamma_1$, $\bar{x}(\gamma_1) > x_m(\gamma_1)$

Figure 4

increase in risk, in the Rothschild-Stiglitz sense, whenever it leaves the total expected outcome μ_x unchanged.

Assumption A.2 guarantees that the principal and interest on a loan, z, will exceed the minimum possible outcome x_m, i.e. that there will exist a possibility of default on each loan. It is this possibility which allows a conflict of interest to arise between borrower and lender.

Finally, Assumption A.3 ensures that the borrower's expected profits will attain an interior optimum with respect to the project characteristic γ, i.e. that the borrower will select neither the least risky nor the riskiest project available. As γ is increased above its minimum possible level γ_{min}, the entire cumulative distribution function $F(x,L,\gamma)$ shifts downward, raising the expected profits of the borrower and the bank and the total expected outcome of the project. Conversely, as γ approaches its maximum possible level γ_{max}, the entire distribution of x shifts upward, reducing u, μ_R, and μ_x.

From Assumptions A.1, A.2, and A.3 it can be established that (a) whatever project the borrower chooses, a marginal increase in risk will reduce both the expected profits of the bank and the total expected outcome of the project; and (b) at a marginally higher loan rate the borrower will be able to increase his expected profits by selecting a riskier project. We first give an informal explanation for these results and then derive them more rigorously below.

Since corner solutions are excluded by Assumption A.3, the borrower's optimal project characteristic must clearly satisfy the first-order condition $u_\gamma(r,L,\gamma) = 0$. Together with Assumption A.1, this implies that a marginal increase in γ above the optimal level must shift the probability distribution F upward for at least some project outcomes x in excess of the principal and interest on the loan, z; if this were not the case--i.e. if the increase in γ shifted F downward for all possible outcomes $x > z$--the borrower could always increase his expected profits by choosing a slightly riskier project. But if a marginal increase in γ must shift F upward for at least some values of $x > z$, we know from the local single-crossing property that it must also raise F for any project outcome $x < z$ which has a nonzero probability of occurrence at the initial value of γ, i.e. for any value of x satisfying $x_m < x < z$[4] (see Figure 3). Such a shift in the probability distribution of x will clearly reduce the bank's expected revenues μ_R. Furthermore, since $u_\gamma = 0$ at the optimum and since $\mu_x = \mu_R + u$, it must also reduce the total expected outcome of the project μ_x.

It remains to explain why an increase in the loan rate should make it worthwhile to the borrower to increase the riskiness of his project. At the optimum, we have seen, a marginal increase in γ will shift F upward for outcomes x just above z and shift F downward for outcomes x significantly greater than z. The first effect tends to reduce the borrower's expected profits while the second effect tends to increase them by an equal amount. By raising the total amount z due on the loan, an increase in the loan rate narrows the range of outcomes over which the first effect applies. This raises the net gain to the borrower from a marginal increase in risk ($u_{r\gamma} > 0$).

The above results are stated more formally in the following proposition:

Proposition 1. Suppose that Assumptions A.1, A.2, and A.3 hold and that r and L satisfy $(1+r)L < x_M$ for some value of γ. Then at any value of γ which maximizes $u(r,L,\gamma)$, $\frac{\partial \mu_R}{\partial \gamma} = \frac{\partial \mu_x}{\partial \gamma} < 0$ and $\frac{\partial^2 u}{\partial r \partial \gamma} > 0$.

Proof: We first prove that the borrower's optimal value of γ must satisfy $\bar{x}(\gamma) > z$. Differentiating the expression for $u(r,L,\gamma)$ in (2) with respect to γ, we obtain

$$(4) \qquad u_\gamma(r,L,\gamma) = - \int_z^{x_M} F_\gamma(x,L,\gamma)dx$$

where $z \equiv (1+r)L$. Suppose that $u(r,L,\gamma)$ is maximized at a value of γ for which $\bar{x}(\gamma) \leq z$. From Assumption A.1 it follows that $F_\gamma(x,L,\gamma) < 0$ for $z < x < x_M$. But equation (4) then implies $u_\gamma(r,L,\gamma) > 0$. Since Assumption A.3 implies that u must attain a maximum at a value of γ such that $\gamma_{min} < \gamma < \gamma_{max}$, and since the first-order condition $u_\gamma = 0$ must hold at an interior optimum, this is a contradiction.

Now, differentiating the expression for μ_R in (3) with respect to γ yields

$$\frac{\partial \mu_R}{\partial \gamma} = - \int_{x_m}^{z} F_\gamma(x,L,\gamma)dx$$

Since $\bar{x}(\gamma) > z$ and since Assumption A.2 implies $x_m < z$, the integral must be positive at the borrower's optimal value of γ; that is, $\frac{\partial \mu_R}{\partial \gamma} < 0$. Furthermore, since $\mu_x = \mu_R + u$ and since $u_\gamma = 0$ at any γ which is optimal for the borrower, the inequality $\frac{\partial \mu_x}{\partial \gamma} < 0$ must also hold.

Finally, by differentiating the expression for u_γ in (4) with respect to r we obtain

$$\frac{\partial^2 u}{\partial r \partial \gamma} = LF_\gamma(z,L,\gamma)$$

But since $\bar{x}(\gamma) > z$ must hold at an optimal value of γ, $F_\gamma(z,L,\gamma) > 0$ and thus $\partial^2 u/\partial r \partial \gamma > 0$.

If the borrower's optimal choice of γ is unique at a particular r and L and if $\partial^2 u/\partial \gamma^2$ is strictly negative at those values, Proposition 1 implies

$$\frac{\partial \gamma^*}{\partial r} = - \frac{\partial^2 u/\partial r \partial \gamma}{\partial^2 u/\partial \gamma^2} > 0$$

Thus in this case $\frac{\partial \mu_R}{\partial \gamma} \frac{\partial \gamma^*}{\partial r}$ will be negative: a marginal increase in the loan rate will have an adverse indirect effect on the bank's expected revenues from the loan. However, our assumptions do not even ensure that the borrower's optimal project characteristic γ will be unique given the loan terms r and L. As a result we cannot conclude from Proposition 1 that an increase in the loan rate will always cause the borrower to choose a higher value of γ and that the increase in γ will always tend to reduce the bank's expected profits. We shall see that the addition of either Assumption A.4 or Assumption A.5 below suffices to establish this stronger result, even though they do not allow us to rule out the possibility of multiple optima.

Assumption A.4. $\bar{x}$ is a continuous function of γ, and is nondecreasing in γ for all γ such that $\bar{x} < x_M$.

Assumption A.5. (global single-crossing property) If $\gamma_2 > \gamma_1$, $F(x',L,\gamma_2) = F(x',L,\gamma_1)$ implies $F(x,L,\gamma_2) > F(x,L,\gamma_1)$ for $x_m(\gamma_1) < x < x'$ and $F(x,L,\gamma_2) < F(x,L,\gamma_1)$ for $x' < x < x_M(\gamma_1)$.

When Assumption A.4 holds in addition to A.1 it still need not be true that all pairs of distributions $F(x,L,\gamma_1)$ and $F(x,L,\gamma_2)$ obey the single-crossing property. However, for any $\gamma_1 < \gamma_2$ such that $\bar{x}(\gamma_1) > x_m(\gamma_1)$, $F(x,L,\gamma_2)$ must cross $F(x,L,\gamma_1)$ first from above, as shown in Figure 4. The alternative assumption we can make is A.5, which requires that all pairs of distributions obey the single-crossing property. Given either A.4 or A.5 it can be shown that any increase in γ above a level which is optimal for the borrower must shift the probability distribution F upward for all possible outcomes x less than the principal and interest z:

Lemma. Suppose that Assumption A.4 or Assumption A.5 holds in addition to Assumptions A.1, A.2, and A.3, and that r and L satisfy $(1+r)L < x_M$ for some value of γ. Then if $u(r,L,\gamma)$ attains a maximum at

γ^*, $\gamma > \gamma^*$ implies $F(x,L,\gamma) > F(x,L,\gamma^*)$ for all x satisfying $x_m(\gamma^*) < x \leq z$.

Proof: Suppose first that Assumption A.4 holds. From the proof of Proposition 1a, we know that $z < \bar{x}(\gamma^*)$. But from Assumptions A.1 and A.4 it can be shown that $x_M(\gamma') = \bar{x}(\gamma')$ implies $x_M(\gamma) = \bar{x}(\gamma)$ for all $\gamma > \gamma'$. Since $\bar{x}$ is assumed to be nondecreasing in γ for all γ such that $\bar{x}(\gamma) < x_M(\gamma)$, and since $z < \bar{x}(\gamma^*)$, this means that $x < \bar{x}(\gamma)$ or $x \geq x_M(\gamma)$ must hold for all $\gamma > \gamma^*$ and all x satisfying $x_m(\gamma^*) < x \leq z$. Since Assumption A.1 requires $F_\gamma(x,L,\gamma) > 0$ for $x_m(\gamma) < x < \bar{x}(\gamma)$, the lemma follows.

Suppose alternatively that Assumption A.5 holds. Then since $u(r,L,\gamma)$ attains a maximum at γ^*, $F(z,L,\gamma)$ must exceed $F(z,L,\gamma^*)$ for all $\gamma > \gamma^*$. To see this, suppose there exists a $\gamma' > \gamma^*$ such that $F(z,L,\gamma') \leq F(z,L,\gamma^*)$. Then Assumption A.5 implies $F(x,L,\gamma') < F(x,L,\gamma^*)$ for $z < x < x_M(\gamma^*)$ and thus

$$u(r,L,\gamma') - u(r,L,\gamma^*) = -\int_{x \geq z} [F(x,L,\gamma') - F(x,L,\gamma^*)]dx > 0$$

Since γ^* was assumed to maximize $u(r,L,\gamma)$, this is a contradiction. Thus, $F(z,L,\gamma) > F(z,L,\gamma^*)$ for all $\gamma > \gamma^*$, as we asserted to begin with. From Assumption A.5 it then follows that $F(x,L,\gamma) > F(x,L,\gamma^*)$ for all $\gamma > \gamma^*$ and x satisfying $x_m(\gamma^*) < x \leq z$.

The above lemma enables us to establish the major result of this section:

<u>Proposition 2.</u> Suppose that Assumption A.4 or A.5 holds, in addition to Assumptions A.1, A.2, and A.3. Suppose further that r and L satisfy $(1+r)L < x_M$ for some value of γ. Then

(a) for any value of γ which maximizes the borrower's expected profits $u(r,L,\gamma)$, the total expected outcome $\mu_x(L,\gamma)$ and the bank's expected revenues $\mu_R(r,L,\gamma)$ will both be lower at all higher values of γ and higher at some smaller value of γ;

(b) at any loan rate $r' > r$ which satisfies $(1+r')L < x_M$ for some γ, the borrower will always choose a higher value of γ than at loan rate r.

Proof: (a) Let γ^* be a value of γ at which $u(r,L,\gamma)$ is maximized. The Lemma then implies that $F(x,L,\gamma) > F(x,L,\gamma^*)$ for all $\gamma > \gamma^*$ and all x such that $x_m(\gamma^*) < x \leq z$. Thus, from the expression for μ_R in (1), it is clear that

$$\mu_R(r,L,\gamma) - \mu_R(r,L,\gamma^*) = -\int_{x \leq z} [F(x,L,\gamma) - F(x,L,\gamma^*)]dx < 0$$

for all $\gamma > \gamma^*$. Since $u(r,L,\gamma) \leq u(r,L,\gamma^*)$ for all γ and $\mu_x(L,\gamma) = \mu_R(r,L,\gamma) + u(r,L,\gamma)$, this implies that $\mu_x(L,\gamma) < \mu_x(L,\gamma^*)$ must also hold for all $\gamma > \gamma^*$. The existence of a $\gamma < \gamma^*$ for which $\mu_R(r,L,\gamma) > \mu_R(r,L,\gamma^*)$ and $\mu_x(L,\gamma) > \mu_x(L,\gamma^*)$ follows from Proposition 1a.

(b) Consider any r_1 and r_2 such that $r_2 > r_1$ and $z_2 < x_M$ for some γ, where $z_i \equiv (1+r_i)L$. Also, let γ_1^* be any γ at which $u(r_1,L,\gamma)$ is maximized. Now suppose that $u(r_2,L,\gamma)$ attains a maximum at some $\gamma_2 < \gamma_1^*$. From Assumption A.2, $x_m(\gamma_2) < z_1$; the Lemma thus implies $F(x,L,\gamma_1^*) >$

$F(x,L,\gamma_2)$ for $z_1 \leq x \leq z_2$. But in this case

$$u(r_1,L,\gamma_2) - u(r_1,L,\gamma_1^*) = u(r_2,L,\gamma_2) - u(r_2,L,\gamma_1^*)$$

$$- \int_{z_1}^{z_2} [F(x,L,\gamma_2) - F(x,L,\gamma_1^*)]dx$$

$$\geq - \int_{z_1}^{z_2} [F(x,L,\gamma_2) - F(x,L,\gamma_1^*)]dx > 0$$

where the next-to-last inequality follows from the assumption that γ_2 maximizes $u(r_2,L,\gamma)$. Since $u(r_1,L,\gamma)$ was assumed to attain a maximum at γ_1^*, this is a contradiction. Thus, $u(r_2,L,\gamma)$ cannot attain a maximum at a $\gamma < \gamma_1^*$. Finally, from the proof of Proposition 1 we know that $\bar{x}(\gamma_1^*) > z_1$ and thus

$$0 = u_\gamma(r_1,L,\gamma_1^*) = - \int_{z_1}^{x_M} F_\gamma(x,L,\gamma_1^*)dx$$

$$< - \int_{z_2}^{x_M} F_\gamma(x,L,\gamma_1^*)dx = u_\gamma(r_2,L,\gamma_1^*)$$

This means that γ_1^* cannot maximize $u(r_2,L,\gamma)$.

According to Proposition 2, an increase in the loan rate will always cause the borrower to choose a project which, at the initial loan rate, would yield lower expected revenues to the bank--i.e. the change in the loan rate will have an adverse indirect impact on the bank's expected revenues. This must be true even if the borrower's optimal choice of γ is not unique at either the new or the old loan rate.

B. We have established restrictions on the probability distribution $F(x,L,\gamma)$ which ensure that increases in the loan rate will cause the borrower to alter γ in a manner harmful to the interests of the bank. To appreciate the significance of these restrictions, however, we must move to a lower level of generality. As a first step in this direction, we turn our attention now to that class of cases in which the project outcome can be expressed as a function of L, γ, and a "state of the world" y whose probability distribution is independent of both L and γ. This class of cases is similar to that considered in Chapters I and II, and includes as one member the model of putty-clay investment which will be presented in Section III.[5]

We shall assume that the outcome of each investment project takes the particular form $x = \max\{0,\psi(L,\gamma,y)\}$, where y is a random variable with cumulative distribution function G(y) and $\psi_y > 0$. In adopting this formulation, we allow for the possibility that ψ may take on values less than zero, but assume that the firm can always avoid negative outcomes by abandoning the project after the realization of the random variable y. The bank's expected revenues in this case will be

$$(4)\quad \mu_R(r,L,\gamma) = z\int_{\hat{y}}^{y_{max}} g(y)dy + \int_{\tilde{y}}^{\hat{y}} \psi(L,\gamma,y)g(y)dy$$

where $\hat{y}$ is the value of the random variable y at which the outcome ψ is just sufficient to pay the principal and interest on the loan and $\tilde{y}$ is the minimum possible value of y at which ψ is nonnegative. The firm's expected profits are simply

$$(5)\quad u(r,L,\gamma) = \int_{\hat{y}}^{y_{max}} [\psi(L,\gamma,y) - (1+r)L]g(y)dy$$

We are interested in the conditions under which increases in the parameter γ will correspond to increases in the riskiness of x. In particular, we wish to know the circumstances under which the restrictions on the cumulative distribution function $F(x,L,\gamma)$ contained in Assumptions A.1–A.5 will be satisfied. As it happens, we do not need to impose any restrictions on G, the probability distribution of the random variable y, to ensure that these restrictions on F are fulfilled. For Assumptions A.1–A.5 to hold, it is sufficient that the function ψ obey

<u>Assumption B.</u>

$$\psi_y > 0,\quad \psi_{\gamma y} > 0,\quad \psi(L,\gamma,y_{min}) \leq L,\quad \psi_{\gamma\gamma} < 0$$

$$\psi_\gamma(L,\gamma_{max},y) < 0 < \psi_\gamma(L,\gamma_{min},y)$$

As is shown in Appendix A, the restrictions $\psi_y > 0$, $\psi_{\gamma\gamma} < 0$, and $\psi_{\gamma y} > 0$ ensure that Assumptions A.1, A.4, and A.5 are satisfied; the requirement $\psi(L,\gamma,y_{min}) \leq L$ is equivalent to Assumption A.2; and the condition that ψ_γ be positive for small values of γ and negative for large values of γ guarantees that A.3 holds. Although the reasons why an increase in γ corresponds to an increase in the riskiness of x in this case are less than obvious, an explanation of that correspondence will be postponed until the next section, when we take up the example of putty-clay investment.

Since Assumptions A.1-A.5 hold when ψ satisfies Assumption B, we know from Proposition 2 that an increase in the loan rate must have an adverse indirect effect on the bank's expected revenues from a loan--or, in other words, that $\frac{\partial \mu_R}{\partial \gamma} \frac{\partial \gamma^*}{\partial r} < 0$. As we noted in Section I, however, for an equilibrium with Type II rationing to occur it is necessary not only that this indirect effect be negative, but also that it be sufficiently negative to offset the favorable direct effect of an increase in the loan rate on the bank's expected revenues. That is, $\frac{\partial \mu_R}{\partial \gamma} \frac{\partial \gamma^*}{\partial r}$ must at some point exceed $\frac{\partial \mu_R}{\partial r}$ in absolute value. Assumptions A.1-A.5 do not ensure that this will occur.

To see whether the net effect $\frac{\partial \mu_R}{\partial r} + \frac{\partial \mu_R}{\partial \gamma} \frac{\partial \gamma^*}{\partial r}$ may be negative, let us consider what happens as the bank raises the loan rate toward that level $\hat{r}(L)$ at which default becomes certain. In the present case, $\hat{r}(L)$ is the loan rate at which the maximum possible outcome of the project is just sufficient to cover the debt repayment to the bank, or the value of r at which $(1+r)L = \underset{\gamma}{\text{Max}}\ \psi(L,\gamma,y_{max})$. It is not difficult to see that as r approaches this level, the state of the world $\hat{y}$ at which $\psi(L,\gamma,y) = z$ must approach y_{max}. Thus, $\lim_{r \to \hat{r}} \frac{\partial \mu_R}{\partial r} = \lim_{r \to \hat{r}} L[1-G(\hat{y})] = 0$. In other words, since the probability of default approaches one as the loan rate approaches $\hat{r}(L)$, the extent to which the bank can increase its expected revenues by raising the amount due on the loan becomes negligible.

As default becomes certain, however, any increase in γ will continue to have an appreciable effect on μ_R, because it will affect the expected value of the collateral on the loan, i.e. the amount the bank can expect to receive from the project in the event of default.[6] Thus, as r gets very close to $\hat{r}(L)$, an increase in the loan rate will have an adverse net effect on the bank's expected revenues if and only if it leads to a nonnegligible increase in the value of γ chosen by the borrower. In Appendix A it is shown that sufficient conditions for this to be the case--i.e. for $\lim_{r \to \hat{r}} \frac{\partial \gamma^*}{\partial r}$ to be nonzero--are that $0 < g(y_{max}) < \infty$ and that $g'(y_{max})$ be finite.

Thus, under relatively minor restrictions on the cumulative distribution function G, the bank's expected revenues from a loan of given size will reach a maximum at a loan rate which yields positive expected profits to the borrower. We saw in Section I that when project size is fixed, this is all that is required to ensure that Type II rationing occurs as either the number of firms with investment projects, the cost of administering each loan, or the opportunity rate becomes large. We also noted, however, that if the size of each project is a variable subject to negotiation, some firms can fail to receive credit in equilibrium only if it is also impossible for banks to increase their expected profits per loan by changing the size of the loan--i.e. if the condition $\frac{\partial \mu_R}{\partial L} - (1+h) + \frac{\partial \mu_R}{\partial \gamma} \frac{\partial \gamma^*}{\partial L} = 0$ is satisfied in addition to the condition $\frac{\partial \mu_R}{\partial r} + \frac{\partial \mu_r}{\partial \gamma} \frac{\partial \gamma^*}{\partial r} = 0$. To ensure that this occurs at some combination of r and L, additional restrictions on ψ and G are required. The nature of these restrictions will become clear in the next section.

III. A model with putty-clay investment

A. General description

In this section we examine an important case in which the project outcome takes the form $\psi(L,\gamma,y)$ and the function ψ satisfies Assumption B. Since Assumption B is satisfied, we know from the previous section that the cumulative distribution function $F(x,L,\gamma)$ must satisfy Assumptions A.1-A.5. This means that the borrower will always be able to increase the riskiness of x by choosing a higher value of γ; equally important, his incentive to do this will be greater the higher is the rate of interest charged on the loan.

In order to add to their capital stock over the course of the period, firms must take out bank loans. The amount of end-of-period capital stock K which an individual firm obtains from its investment is assumed to increase with the size of the investment (i.e. the size of the loan), but at a constant or decreasing rate: $K = \chi(L)$ with $\chi' > 0$ and $\chi'' \leq 0$. At the end of the period the firm hires labor and employs that labor with its newly installed machinery to produce output Q.

Investment is assumed to be "putty-clay": the firm can choose machinery of any labor intensity, but once that machinery is installed capital and labor must be used in fixed proportions. Thus, at the time it makes its investment decision, the firm must determine the amount of labor to be employed in production at the end of the period.[7] It is not essential for our purposes that the second input be labor;

it could just as well be a raw material or some other factor of production such as land.

For convenience, we shall suppose that the firm has no installed capital at the beginning of the period. In this case, the total output which the firm can produce at the end of the period will simply be a function of its end-of-period capital stock K and the required labor input N. But since $K = \chi(L)$, output can also be expressed as a function of L and N: $Q = Q(L,N)$. We assume that this function includes the end-of-period scrap value, if any, of the firm's machinery. In this case, the end-of-period value of the firm, i.e. the outcome of the investment project, is

$$x = \max\{pQ(L,N) - wN, 0\}$$

where p is the end-of-period price of the good and w the end-of-period wage rate.

The outcome of the investment project will be uncertain at the beginning of the period if the price p, the wage rate w, or the end-of-period output Q is stochastic. It will be assumed here that p alone is stochastic, and that the bank and firm share the same subjective probability distribution on p, G(p). However, our results would be unaffected if w were stochastic or if end-of-period output were $Q(L,N)(1+\varepsilon)$, with ε a random variable of zero mean.

In terms of our previous discussion, the planned labor input N corresponds to the parameter γ, the price p is equivalent to the random variable y, and the quantity $pQ-wN$ corresponds to ψ. For Assumption B to hold, it is therefore sufficient that $p_{min} = 0$ and that the production function $Q(L,N)$ satisfy

$$Q_N > 0, \quad Q_{NN} < 0$$

$$Q_N(L,0) = \infty, \quad Q_N(L,\infty) = 0$$

We shall further assume that the output which the firm can achieve from a given labor input N increases with its capital stock K but at a decreasing rate. Since $K = \chi(L)$ with $\chi' > 0$ and $\chi'' \leq 0$, this implies $Q_L > 0$ and $Q_{LL} < 0$. In Figures 6a, 6b, and 6c we have plotted the project outcome x as a function of N, L, and p respectively, taking into account the above restrictions on $Q(L,N)$. In keeping with earlier usage, $\hat{p}$ is defined to be the price at which the net cash flow $pQ\text{-}wN$ is just sufficient to repay the principal and interest on the loan, and $\tilde{p}$ to be the price at which the net cash flow equals zero.

It is important to note that if there are diminishing marginal returns to the installment of capital within a fixed time period (i.e. if $\chi'' < 0$), the end-of-period output of the firm will display decreasing returns to scale with respect to loan size L and planned labor input N even if Q is homogeneous of degree one in K and N. The existence of diminishing marginal returns to investment could reflect constraints on the managerial and administrative resources of the firm; in the literature on the theory of investment, this has been referred to as the "Penrose effect" ([2], [7]).

Why does a rise in the firm's planned labor input increase the riskiness of its investment project? Or, in other terms, why does N

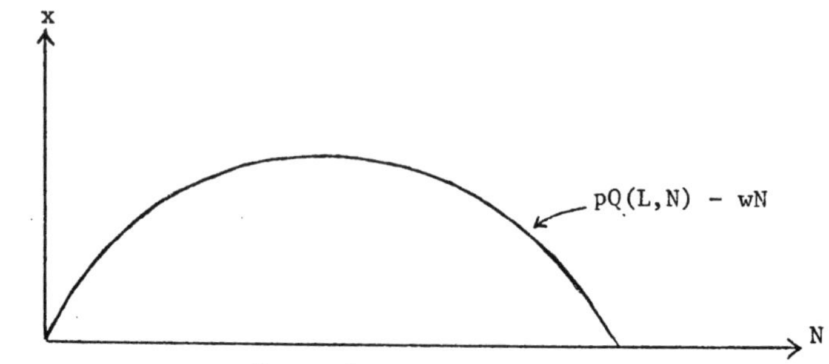

L, p given

Figure 6a

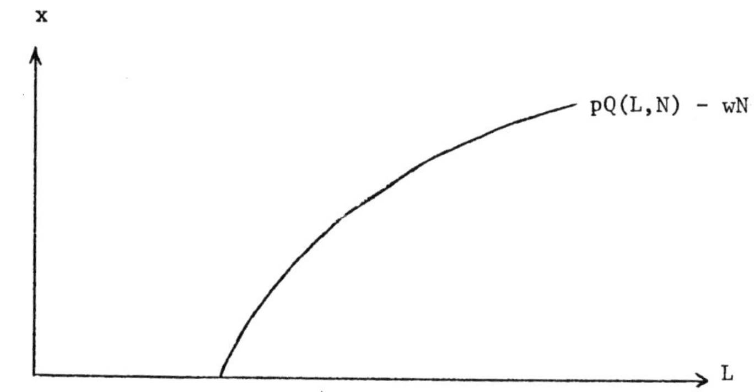

N, p given

Figure 6b

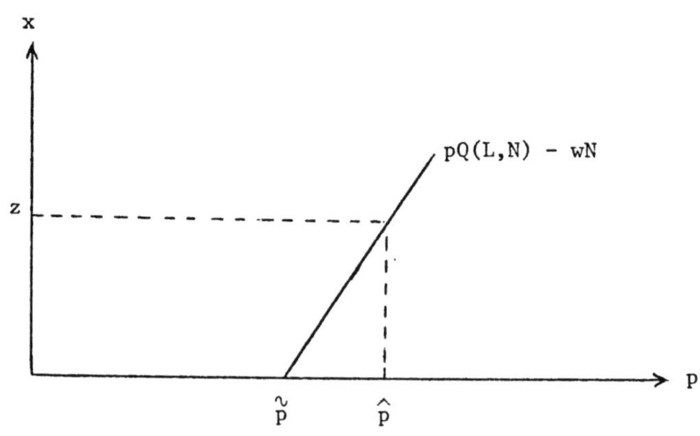

L, N given

Figure 6c

correspond to the parameter γ discussed earlier? A marginal increase in planned labor input has two effects: it raises the revenues pQ which the firm realizes at each price, and it increases the firm's total wage payments wN. At that price p* for which $pQ_N = w$, the two effects exactly offset each other and the marginal increase in labor input has no effect on the outcome of the project, pQ-wN. Thus, the probability that the outcome of the project will be less than or equal to p*Q-wN remains equal to G(p*). However, project outcomes less than p*Q-wN correspond to realizations of p less than p*, and at prices less than p*, a marginal increase in N will raise the firm's wage payments by more than its revenues. Since a higher price will be required to realize any given amount less than p*Q-wN, the probability that the actual outcome of the project will fall short of that amount must increase. By the converse argument, a marginal increase in planned labor input must also raise the probability that the outcome of the project exceeds any amount greater than p*Q-wN. Thus, the probability density of the outcome is shifted from the center of the distribution to the tails; in this sense, the firm can always increase the riskiness of the project by investing in machinery of greater labor intensity.

Since Assumptions A.1-A.5 are satisfied, Proposition 2 implies that at any loan rate and loan size the firm will purchase machinery of greater labor intensity than would maximize either the total expected outcome of the project or the expected revenues of the bank. Furthermore, a rise in the loan rate will cause the firm to increase its planned input of labor, reducing the expected outcome of the project and the expected revenues of the bank still further. Given the restrictions on the probability density g mentioned at the end of Section II, we know that this adverse indirect effect of an increase in r on the bank's expected revenues must at some point outweigh the favorable direct effect of such an increase. When project size is fixed, this fact suffices to establish the possibility of an equilibrium characterized by Type II rationing. In the more general case in which project size is variable, however, we cannot determine the properties of a competitive equilibrium without also considering the direct and indirect effects of changes in loan size. To do this, we require additional information about the technology of the firm.

The easiest possibility to analyze is that in which the end-of-period output of the firm is homogeneous of degree one in loan size and planned labor input. This will be the case if the firm's production function displays constant returns to scale with respect to capital and labor inputs and if in addition the installment of capital within a fixed time period is not subject to diminishing marginal returns. When the firm's technology is of this form, the expected revenues of the bank μ_R and the expected profits of the borrower u will both be homogeneous of degree one in loan size and labor input, given any loan rate. In Appendix A this property is employed with equilibrium conditions (E.1)-(E.4) to determine the characteristics of the competitive equilibrium and the conditions for its existence.[8] The principal results are summarized below:

<u>Proposition 3.</u> Suppose that Q displays constant returns to scale with respect to L and N. Let $1+\rho^*$ be the maximum value of the bank's

expected revenues at loan size L = 1, when the borrower is free to choose N. If there are no administrative costs and if $\Omega(0) < \rho^* < \Omega(\infty)$, a market equilibrium will exist. The equilibrium loan rate will be a value of r which maximizes the bank's expected revenues at all values of L; the equilibrium opportunity rate will be $h = \rho^*$; and the total volume of lending will be such that $\Omega(L_T) = \rho^*$. Both the equilibrium loan size and the number of firms which receive credit will be indeterminate; however, the labor intensity of investment N/L chosen by a borrower at the equilibrium loan rate will not depend on the size of the loan he receives.

Two features of this equilibrium are worth emphasizing. First, an equilibrium will exist only if the cost of administering each loan is zero. Because end-of-period output is homogeneous of degree one in L and N, a bank's expected revenues from a loan will always be proportional to the size of the loan. As a result, banks will have an incentive to expand loan size if average opportunity cost 1+h is less than average expected revenues $\frac{\mu_R}{L}$. If 1+h equals $\frac{\mu_R}{L}$, however, banks will earn expected profits $\delta = 0$ on each loan and will thus be unable to cover their costs of administration. The second point to be emphasized is that the distribution of credit among firms is indeterminate. The equilibrium may be one in which some firms are denied credit, but it may just as well be one in which all firms receive loans of equal size. The first possibility exists because each bank will be earning the maximum possible expected profits per loan at the equilibrium loan rate, and the second possibility because expected profits per loan are independent of loan size at that rate ($\delta = 0$ at all values of L).[9]

The more interesting and more relevant case, I believe, is that in which marginal returns to the scale of an investment project are diminishing. This is the case in which equiproportionate increases in the size of an investment and planned input of labor at the end of the period yield a less than proportionate increase in end-of-period output. To understand how a market equilibrium is determined in these circumstances, it will be necessary to make more specific assumptions about the form of the production function Q(L,N) and about the probability distribution of prices G(p). This we do below.

B. The case of Cobb-Douglas technology and uniform distribution of prices

In this section we consider a particular case of the putty-clay model in which it is possible to obtain an analytic solution to equilibrium conditions (E.1)-(E.4). In this case, the output which the firm can produce at the end of the period from an investment of size L and a labor input of N is

$$Q(L,N) = aL^{\beta}N^{\alpha}$$

where $0 < \beta < 1$, $0 < \alpha < 1$, and $a > 0$. Also, the end-of-period price p is distributed uniformly over the interval (0,s)--i.e. $g(p) = 1/s$ for $0 < p < s$. When Q is characterized by decreasing returns to scale (i.e. when $\alpha + \beta < 1$), we shall see that the competitive equilibrium may either be one in which all firms receive credit or one in which some firms receive loans while other, identical firms do not. We shall indicate the circumstances in which the second type of equilibrium is likely to occur, and also consider its implications for the effectiveness of monetary policy. Although the frame of reference for this discussion will be the particular example just mentioned, our results will be seen to have a wider applicability.

1. For any loan size L and loan rate r, there will exist a unique labor input N maximizing the borrower's expected profits, u. Let us define the labor intensity of the firm's investment as $n = N/L$. By partially differentiating u with respect to n, it can then be shown that the borrower will always choose that labor intensity of investment,

$n^*(r,L)$, which is the solution to the equation

$$(6)\quad asL^{-(1-\alpha-\beta)}n^{\alpha-1} + (1+r)n^{-1} - \frac{2-\alpha}{\alpha}w = 0$$

From (6) it is clear that the firm's optimal value of n will be an increasing function of the loan rate (as we know it must, from Proposition 2). Furthermore, an increase in the size of the loan will cause the firm to purchase machinery of lower labor intensity when the production function Q is characterized by decreasing returns to scale ($\alpha + \beta < 1$), machinery of greater labor intensity when Q displays increasing returns to scale ($\alpha + \beta > 1$), and machinery of unchanged labor intensity when Q is homogeneous of degree one in L and N ($\alpha + \beta = 1$).

At each loan size, there can be shown to exist a unique loan rate $r^*(L)$ which maximizes the bank's expected revenues $\mu_R(r,L,n)$ subject to the constraint that $n = n^*(r,L)$. At $r = r^*(L)$, the favorable direct effect on the bank's expected revenues of any increase in the loan rate will be offset by the unfavorable indirect effect which occurs via the change in the borrower's choice of n. Making use of (6) to solve the equation $0 = \frac{d}{dr}\mu_R(r,L,n^*(r,L))$, we find this value of r to be

$$(7)\quad 1+r^*(L) = \left(\frac{as}{w^{\alpha}}\right)^{\frac{1}{1-\alpha}} J^{\frac{\alpha}{1-\alpha}} \left(\frac{2-\alpha}{\alpha}J - 1\right) L^{-\frac{\lambda}{1-\alpha}}$$

where $\lambda = 1 - \alpha - \beta$ and

$$J = \frac{(4-\alpha)\alpha}{(2-\alpha)(4-\alpha^2)}\left[1 + \sqrt{1 - \frac{3\alpha(2-\alpha)(4-\alpha^2)}{(4-\alpha)^2}}\right]$$

At loan rate $r^*(L)$, the firm will purchase machinery of labor intensity

$$(8)\quad n = \left(\frac{asJ}{w}\right)^{\frac{1}{1-\alpha}} L^{-\frac{\lambda}{1-\alpha}}$$

Also, the expected revenues of the bank at this loan rate are

$$(9)\quad \hat{\mu}_R(L) = \left(\frac{asJ^{\alpha}}{w^{\alpha}}\right)^{\frac{1}{1-\alpha}} \left(-\frac{4-\alpha^2}{2\alpha^2} J^2 + \frac{4-\alpha}{\alpha} J - \frac{3}{2}\right) L^{\frac{\beta}{1-\alpha}}$$

Now, in Appendix B it is shown that an equilibrium cannot exist if Q displays increasing returns to scale with respect to the size of investment L and the end-of-period labor input N, i.e. if $\lambda \equiv 1 - \alpha - \beta < 0$. In particular, at any loan rate and loan size for which the bank's expected profits $\delta = \mu_R - (1+h)L$ were nonnegative, it would always be possible to increase both the expected profits of the bank and those of the borrower by making a loan of larger size. Since the implications of constant returns to scale ($\lambda = 0$) were discussed in Section III.A., we may confine our attention now to the case in which Q displays decreasing returns to scale with respect to L and N ($\lambda > 0$).

2. Before showing how equilibrium is determined in this case, we must explain in greater detail how the expected profits of the bank and the borrowing firm vary with the terms of the loan. Consider first the bank. The function $r^*(L)$ indicates the loan rate at which the bank's expected revenues μ_R are maximized, given the size of the loan. This function is plotted in Figure 7; since we are assuming $\lambda > 0$, equation (7) implies that it must have negative slope. Now, at any point on the curve, the bank's expected profits from a loan are

$$\hat{\delta}(L,h) = \hat{\mu}_R(L) - (1+h)L$$

Since $\lambda = 1 - \alpha - \beta > 0$, it is clear from the expression for $\hat{\mu}_R(L)$ in equation (9) that $\hat{\delta}(L,h)$ will attain a maximum at a unique and finite value of L. We shall let $L_1(h)$ refer to this value of L and $\breve{\delta}(h)$ to the maximized value of the bank's expected profits. Both functions are decreasing in h. In Figure 7, the maximum value of δ is assumed to occur at point B. As we move away from B along the curve r*(L), the bank's expected profits will decrease monotonically. Also, as the loan rate is increased at a given value of L, δ will rise monotonically until the loan rate becomes so high that default is certain (i.e. until $r = \hat{r}(L)$).

For each value of δ, there will exist a locus of points in r-L space at which the bank's expected profits, $\delta(r,L,n^*(r,L),h)$, are equal to δ. We shall refer to each iso-profit locus as $\phi(h,\delta)$, to indicate that the location of the curve depends on both the level of expected profits δ and on the opportunity rate h. As indicated in Figure 7, each iso-profit curve becomes vertical at the two points of intersection with the locus r*(L). Also, the closer is an iso-profit locus to the point B at which $\hat{\delta}(L,h)$ attains a maximum, the higher will be the level of expected profits δ to which the curve corresponds.

Consider next the position of the borrowing firm. When $\lambda > 0$, there will at each loan rate r exist a finite loan size D(r) which maximizes its expected profits $u(r,L,n^*(r,L))$. This maximum will be unique, with $\frac{du}{dL} \gtrless 0$ as $L \lesseqgtr D(r)$. Solving the first order condition $\frac{du}{dL} =$

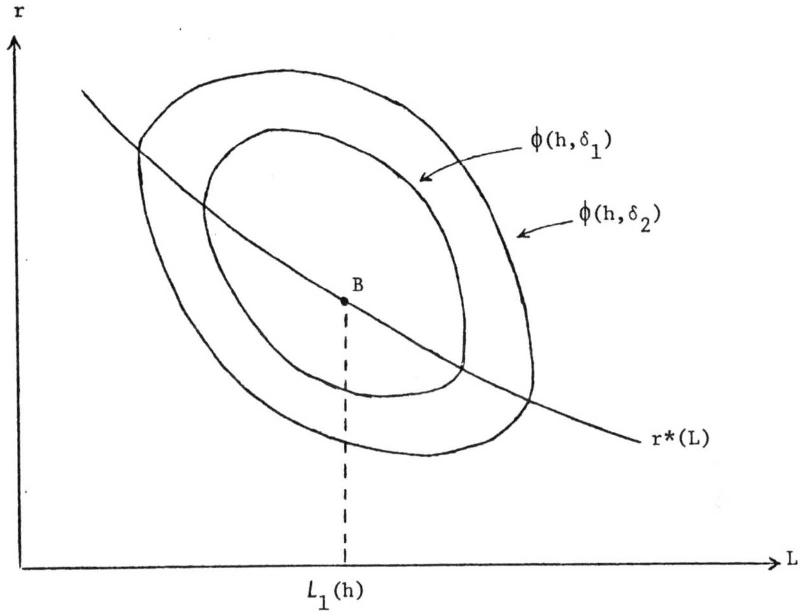

$\delta_1 > \delta_2$

Figure 7

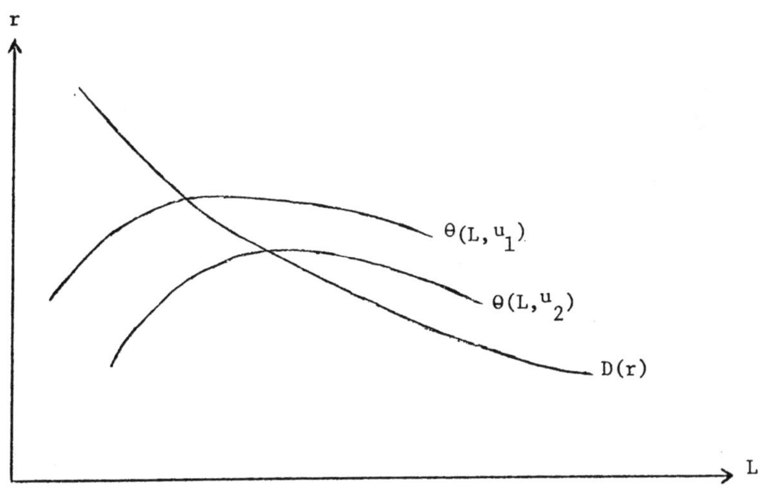

$u_1 < u_2$

Figure 8

$u_L = 0$ and making use of equation (6), we obtain the borrower's inverse demand curve, $D^{-1}(L)$:

$$(10)\quad 1+r = \left(\frac{as}{w^{\alpha}}\right)^{\frac{1}{1-\alpha}} \left(\frac{\alpha}{1+\lambda}\right)^{\frac{\alpha}{1-\alpha}} \frac{\beta}{1+\lambda} L^{-\frac{\lambda}{1-\alpha}}$$

It will be noted that this expression is identical to that given for $1+r^*(L)$ in equation (7), but with the constant J replaced by the fraction $\frac{\alpha}{1+\lambda}$. Thus, the borrower's demand curve will also be negatively sloped and will lie above the locus $r^*(L)$ if $\frac{\alpha}{1+\lambda} > J$, coincide with it if $\frac{\alpha}{1+\alpha} = J$, and lie below it if $\frac{\alpha}{1+\lambda} < J$. As in the case of the bank, we can for each value of u define an iso-profit curve $\theta(L,u)$. Given any L, however, there will in this case exist only one loan rate at which the borrower's expected profits $u(r,L,n^*(r,L))$ are equal to u. Since $\frac{\partial u}{\partial r} < 0$, each of these iso-profit curves will have positive slope to the left of the point of intersection with the borrower's demand curve and negative slope to the right of that point (see Figure 8). Also, the higher is the borrower iso-profit locus, the lower will be the level of expected profits u to which it corresponds.

3. How is a competitive equilibrium determined? First, equilibrium condition (E.3a) states that a bank must have no incentive to alter terms of its loans. This condition will be satisfied by any combination of r and L--say r_1 and L_1--that solves the problem

$$\max_{r,L} \delta(r,L,n^*(r,L),h) \text{ subject to}$$

$$u(r,L,n^*(r,L)) \geq u(r_1,L_1,n^*(r_1,L_1))$$

From the properties of the curve $r^*(L)$ mentioned earlier, it is not difficult to show that this maximization problem is equivalent to

(11) $\max_{r,L} u(r,L,n^*(r,L))$ subject to

$$\delta(r,L,n^*(r,L),h) = \delta(r_1,L_1,n^*(r_1,L_1),h)$$ [10]

In other words, a particular combination of r and L will satisfy condition (E.3a) if and only if it represents a point on a bank iso-profit locus at which the expected profits of the borrower attain a maximum. In terms of Figure 9, this requirement is satisfied both by point B, at which the expected profits of the bank attain their highest possible value, $\hat{\delta}(h)$, and by points such as C, at which a borrower iso-profit locus $\theta(L,u)$ and a bank iso-profit locus $\phi(h,\delta)$ are tangent.[11] We shall define $L_2(h,\delta)$ to be that value of L which solves the maximization problem (11) and yields expected profits δ to the bank. In Appendix B it is shown that this value is unique and that it is a decreasing function of both the opportunity rate h and the level of expected profits δ.

As stated in condition (E.3b), equilibrium also requires that no bank have an incentive to alter the number of loans that it makes. This means that δ^*, the expected profits yielded by each loan in equilibrium, must equal c, the cost to the bank of administering a loan. Finally, from (E.4) we know that the equilibrium opportunity rate h must equal $\Omega(SL)$, where $S \leq M$ is the number of firms receiving loans.

We can now see that two quite distinct types of equilibrium may occur: one in which some firms are unable to obtain loans because banks are already earning the maximum possible expected profits per loan

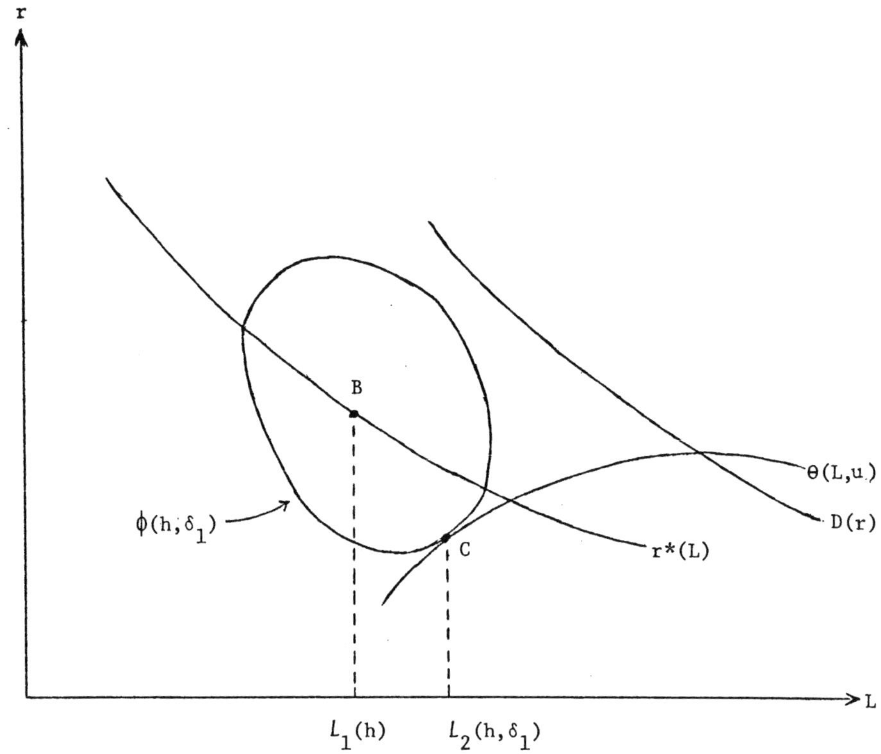

Figure 9

(subject to the constraint that the borrower is free to choose n), and another in which all M firms with investment projects are able to obtain credit. The first type of equilibrium will prevail if h, L, and S satisfy

$$(12)\qquad \begin{aligned} L &= L_1(h) \\ h &= \Omega(SL) \\ \delta(h) &= \delta^* \\ S &< M \end{aligned}$$

and the second type of equilibrium when

$$(13)\qquad \begin{aligned} L &= L_2(h,\delta^*) \\ h &= \Omega(SL) \\ S &= M \end{aligned}$$

If the bank's maximum possible expected profits per loan are equal to δ^* at opportunity rate h', it is clear from $\partial L_2/\partial h < 0$ that $L_2(h,\delta^*)$ must exceed $L_1(h')$ at all lower values of h. Since the opportunity rate is a nondecreasing function of the total volume of lending ($\Omega' \geq 0$), this means that the two types of equilibrium are mutually exclusive. More precisely, if there exist an h, L, and S satisfying the first set of conditions above, there will not exist some other combination of those variables satisfying the second set.[12]

The determination of equilibrium is illustrated in Figures 10 and 11.[13] As already indicated, both L_1 and L_2 are decreasing functions of h. As we move down the curve $L_1(h)$, the expected profits of the bank increase. At opportunity rate h' and loan size L', δ is assumed to equal δ^*. At this point, the two curves converge. At higher values of h, the function $L_2(h, \delta^*)$ is undefined while at lower h, $L_2(h, \delta^*)$ exceeds L'.

The first type of equilibrium, in which some firms are denied credit, is depicted in Figure 10. Equilibrium occurs at E_1, the point on the curve $L_1(h)$ at which the expected profits of the bank are equal to δ^*. At this point, $L_1(h)$ intersects a curve $\Omega(SL)$ corresponding to a value of S less than M. Figure 11 illustrates the second type of equilibrium, in which all M firms are able to obtain loans. In this case equilibrium occurs at E_2, the point of intersection of the curves $\Omega(ML)$ and $L_2(h, \delta^*)$.

We have already noted, and Figures 10 and 11 confirm, that the two types of equilibrium described above are mutually exclusive. But what factors will determine which of the two equilibria prevail?

(1) First of all, the likelihood of an equilibrium with Type II rationing will be greater, the larger is the number of firms M with investment projects or the higher is the opportunity rate h which must be paid at each volume of total lending L_T. In terms of Figure 11, either an increase in M or an upward shift in the function Ω will shift up the curve $\Omega(ML)$; if the new curve intersects $L_1(h)$ at a point above E_1, Type II rationing must occur.

(2) An equilibrium in which some firms are denied credit will also be more likely the higher is the cost c of administering each loan. An increase in c will increase the level of expected profits δ^* which each loan must yield to the bank in equilibrium. Since $\frac{d\tilde{\delta}}{dh} < 0$, this de-

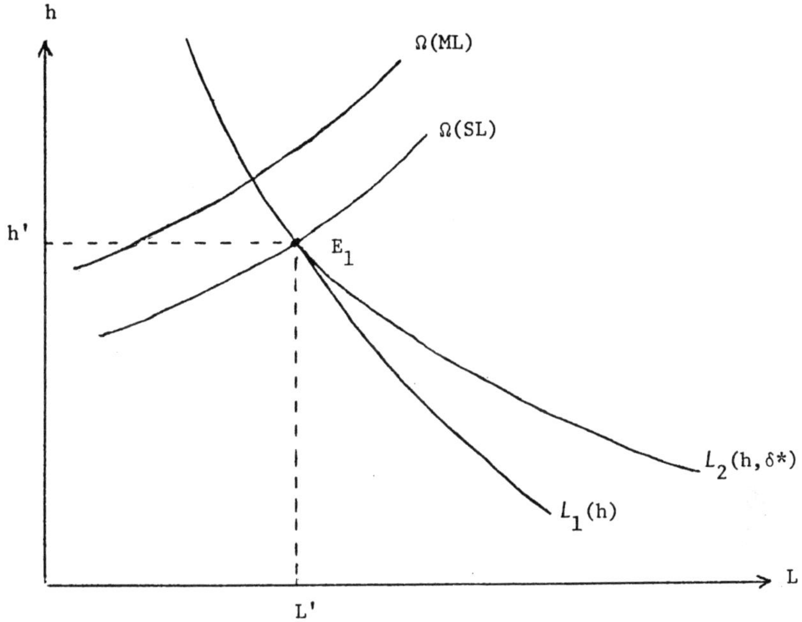

Figure 10: Fewer than M firms
receive credit

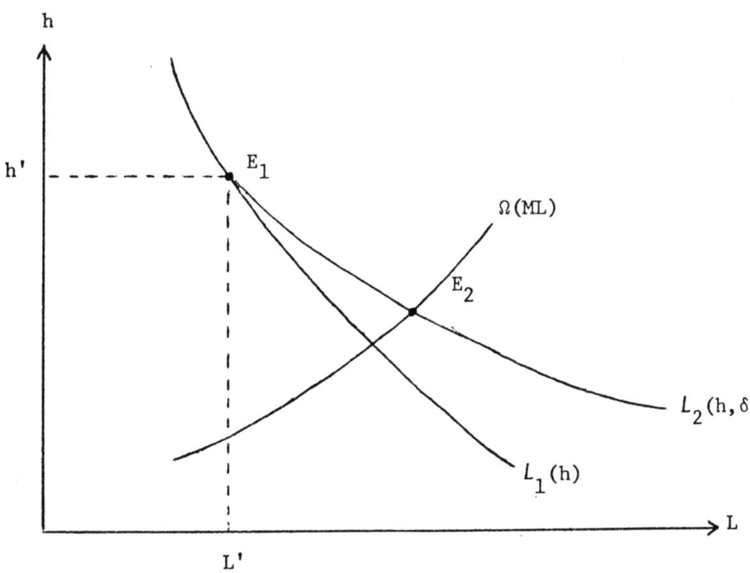

Figure 11: All firms receive credit

creases the opportunity rate h' at which $\gamma(h) = \delta^*$ and shifts the point E_1 downward along the locus $L_1(h)$; if E_1 now lies below the point of intersection of $L_1(h)$ and $\Omega(ML)$, the new equilibrium must be one in which fewer than M firms receive credit. If administrative costs are zero, Type II rationing cannot occur, since the bank's maximum possible expected profits per loan are always positive.

(3) Finally, the likelihood of an equilibrium with Type II rationing will be greater the higher is the wage rate w, the lower is the maximum possible end-of-period price s, and the lower is the shift parameter a in the production function $Q = aL^{\beta}N^{\alpha}$. An increase in w or a decrease in a or s will have two effects: it will shift in the curve $L_1(h)$ and it will reduce the maximum level of expected profits $\gamma(h)$ which the bank can achieve at each h. The first effect tends to reduce the loan size at which $\gamma(h) = \delta^*$, while the second effect tends to increase it. It is not difficult to show that the second effect will always dominate the first, causing the point E_1 to shift downward and to the right.[14]

It is important to realize that the description of market equilibrium which we have given is not limited to the particular case of the putty-clay model under consideration. The conditions which must be met for equilibrium to be determined in the manner we have described may be summarized as follows:

(1) At each loan size, there exists a unique loan rate $r^*(L)$ at which the bank's expected revenues μ_R attain a maximum, given that the borrower is free to choose γ. At any L, the expected revenues of the

bank decrease monotonically as we increase the loan rate above $r^*(L)$ or reduce it below $r^*(L)$.

(2) Along the locus $r^*(L)$, the bank's expected revenues are a strictly concave function of the size of the loan.

(3) For any value of δ, there exists a unique loan size which maximizes the expected profits of the borrower subject to the constraint that the bank's expected profits equal δ. Also, this value of L is lower the higher is the opportunity rate h.

It can be shown that these three conditions are satisfied not only in the particular case we have been examining in this section, but also in an example to which we referred briefly in Section II--the case in which $x = aL^{\alpha}e^{-\lambda p}$ with probability p, where $\alpha < 1$ and $\lambda > 1$. The first two conditions ensure that the functions $L_1(h)$ and $\gamma(h)$ exist and that they have negative slope, while the third condition enables us to define the function $L_2(h,\delta)$ and ensures that it, too, will be decreasing in h. Whenever these conditions are met, there will be two possible types of market equilibrium, one in which all firms are able to obtain loans and another which is characterized by Type II rationing. As explained above, the likelihood that the equilibrium will be of the latter variety will be higher the larger is the number of firms M with investment projects, the higher is the opportunity rate h corresponding to each total volume of lending, and the higher is the cost of administration c.

4. In Section I.C. we considered the implications of Type II rationing for the effectiveness of monetary policy in the limiting case

in which the size of each investment project is fixed. It was shown in this case that monetary policy would have an impact on total lending and investment if and only if the initial equilibrium was characterized by Type II rationing. We now show that Type II rationing will also render monetary policy more effective when project size is variable.

As before, we may view monetary policy as affecting the market for bank loans through shifts in the opportunity rate schedule $\Omega(L_T)$. Let us suppose first that the initial equilibrium is one in which all M firms receive credit (Figure 12). In this case any downward shift in the function Ω or any upward shift in Ω which leaves $\Omega(ML')$ less than h' will affect the size of each investment project but not the total number of projects which are financed, M. In either case the effect of the shift in Ω on total lending will be partially offset by a change in the equilibrium opportunity rate h. For example, a tight monetary policy will tend to decrease total lending by reducing the amount of deposits banks can attract at the initial deposit rate h_1^* (i.e. by reducing the value of L_T at which $\Omega(L_T) = h_1^*$). But if banks reduce the size of each loan while paying an unchanged opportunity rate they will earn excess expected profits $\delta > c$. Competition among banks for deposits will therefore drive the opportunity rate up to h_2^*. This rise in h tends to increase the desirability of bank deposits to wealthholders, partially offsetting the initial decrease in their relative attractiveness brought about by the tightening of monetary policy. In the same manner, the expansionary impact of an easy monetary policy will

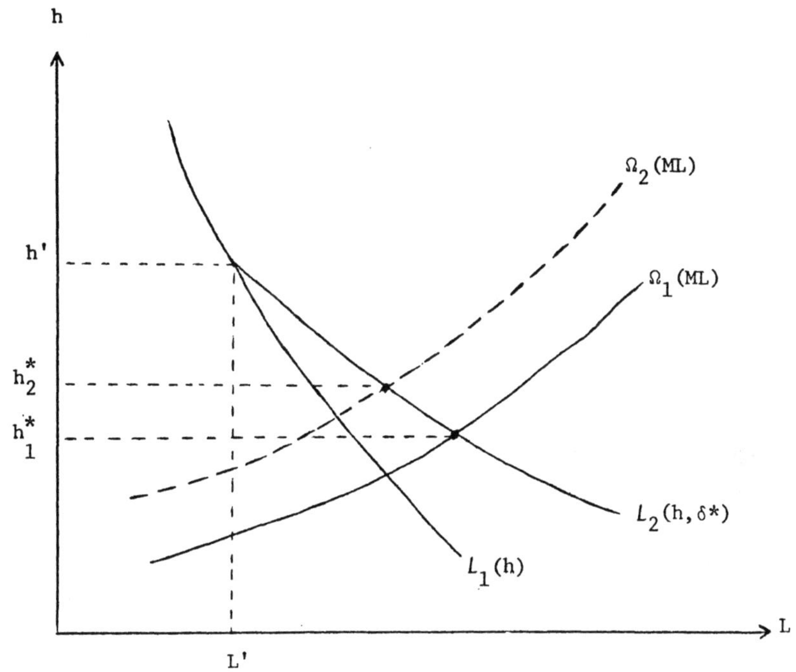

Figure 12

be dampened by an accompanying decrease in the equilibrium opportunity rate.

The reason monetary policy is more effective when the initial equilibrium is characterized by Type II rationing is that these offsetting movements in the opportunity rate do not occur. In terms of Figure 10, any upward shift in Ω or any downward shift in Ω which leaves $\Omega(ML')$ greater than h' will leave the equilibrium opportunity rate, the loan rate, and the size of each investment project unchanged, affecting only the number of firms S that receive credit. Equilibrium still occurs at the point E_1, but this point will now be intersected by a Ω schedule corresponding to a different value of S--a lower value if monetary policy has been tightened and a higher value if monetary policy has been eased.

As in the previous case, a tight monetary policy will reduce the amount of deposits which banks can attract at the initial opportunity rate. In the present case, however, banks will respond by making fewer loans rather than by reducing the size of each loan, since they are already earning the maximum possible expected profits per loan. And since the expected profits from each loan will remain only high enough to cover the cost of administration c, banks will not bid up the opportunity rate in an attempt to gain more funds. Thus, when the initial equilibrium is characterized by Type II rationing, the impact of monetary policy on total lending and investment will be felt in full; the impact will not be dampened by offsetting changes in h.[15]

IV. Implications for allocative efficiency

As yet relatively little has been said about the allocative efficiency of the competitive equilibrium. We have seen that the borrower will always choose a higher value of γ--i.e. a riskier project--than maximizes the total expected outcome; for example, in the putty-clay model, each firm will invest in excessively labor-intensive machinery. Of equal importance, however, are (1) the efficiency with which resources are allocated between investment and alternative uses (is total investment too high or too low?) and (2) the efficiency with which resources are allocated among firms (are too few or too many firms receiving loans?). In this section we will focus on the allocation of credit among firms, confining our discussion to the putty-clay model. We are interested particularly in the following question: Given the total volume of lending L_T which actually takes place in competitive equilibrium and the labor intensity of investment n (and thus also the total planned input of labor $L_T n$), could the total expected return from investment be increased by redistributing credit in some way among firms? To be more specific, if the equilibrium is characterized by Type II rationing, could the total expected return to investment be increased by financing a larger number of projects of somewhat smaller size?[16]

To calculate the social return to investment, we must take into account not only the expected income from all projects but also the resources, if any, which are absorbed in the administering of loans. We shall define the total <u>net</u> expected return to investment as

$$W = \sum_{1}^{S} \mu_x(L_i, n) - Sc$$

where S is the total number of firms receiving credit, L_i is the size of the loan received by the ith firm, and c is the cost of administering each loan. For a given labor intensity of investment $\bar{n}$ and a given total volume of lending $\bar{L}_T$, the optimal distribution of credit will then be the solution to the problem

$$\underset{S,\{L_i\}}{\text{Max}} \quad W \text{ subject to } S \leq M \text{ and } \sum_{1}^{S} L_i = \bar{L}_T$$

When there are no costs of administration and when end-of-period output Q displays constant returns to scale in L and N, the solution to this problem is trivial. Since in this case $W = \sum_{1}^{S} L_i \mu_x(1,\bar{n}) = \bar{L}_T \mu_x(1,\bar{n})$, the net expected return from a given volume of total lending will be independent of the manner in which that total is distributed among the M firms with investment projects. Thus, in the case of constant returns to scale, the competitive equilibrium will not allocate resources inefficiently among firms.

The more interesting case is that in which Q displays decreasing returns to scale in L and N. For a given volume of total lending, the quantity $\sum_{1}^{S} \mu_x(L_i, n)$ will in this case be maximized by granting loans of equal size to all M firms, since the average expected outcome $\mu_x(L,\bar{n})/L$ will be a decreasing function of project size.[17] Thus, if costs of administration could be ignored, any equilibrium characterized by Type II rationing would involve an inefficient allocation of resources among firms. When these costs are taken into account, maximization of W still requires that those firms which do receive credit receive loans of equal size. However, since total costs of administration will increase with the number of loans S, it is no longer clear that credit should be granted to all M firms.

Since loans must be of equal size, our maximization problem may be restated as

$$\max_{S,L} W = S[\mu_x(L,\bar{n}) - c] \text{ subject to } S \leq M \text{ and } SL = \bar{L}_T$$

The necessary conditions for an optimum then include

(14) $$\mu_x(L,\bar{n}) - L\frac{\partial}{\partial L}\mu_x(L,\bar{n}) - c \geq 0$$

(15) $$[\mu_x(L,\bar{n}) - L\frac{\partial}{\partial L}\mu_x(L,\bar{n}) - c](M-S) = 0$$

The expression in (14) represents the net effect on W of reducing loan size and increasing the number of loans by just enough to maintain total lending at a constant level; (15) states the obvious requirement that this net effect equal zero if fewer than M firms are to receive credit.

In the particular case examined in Section III.B., we saw that the bank's maximum possible expected revenues can be expressed as the function $\hat{\mu}_R(L)$, with $d\hat{\mu}_R/dL > 0$ and $d^2\hat{\mu}_R/dL^2 < 0$. Also, at the optimal loan rate $r^*(L)$, the total expected project outcome can be expressed as $\hat{\mu}_x(L) = b\hat{\mu}_R(L)$ where b is a constant greater than one.[18] But if credit is being rationed in equilibrium we know that the equilibrium loan size must maximize the bank's expected profits $\hat{\delta}(L) = \hat{\mu}_R(L) - (1+h)L$ at the prevailing h, and that this maximum must be just sufficient to cover the administrative cost c. Thus,

$$c = \hat{\mu}_R(L) - (1+h)L = \hat{\mu}_R(L) - L \frac{d}{dL} \hat{\mu}_R(L) < \hat{\mu}_x(L) - L \frac{d}{dL} \hat{\mu}_x(L)$$

Now, as we move to the right along the locus $r^*(L)$, the borrower's optimal labor intensity will fall, since equation (8) implies $dn/dL < 0$. Since $\frac{\partial}{\partial n} \mu_x(L,n) < 0$ at $n = n^*(r,L)$, it follows that

$$\frac{d}{dL} \hat{\mu}_x(L) = \frac{\partial}{\partial L} \mu_x(L,n) + \frac{\partial}{\partial n} \mu_x(L,n) \frac{dn}{dL} > \frac{\partial}{\partial L} \mu_x(L,n)$$

Thus, if credit is being rationed in equilibrium, $\mu_x(L,\bar{n}) - L \frac{\partial}{\partial L} \mu_x(L,\bar{n}) - c$ will be positive, violating condition (15). This means that the net expected return to investment can be increased--given the equilibrium labor intensity of investment and the total planned input of labor--by distributing the same total amount of credit among a larger number of firms.

The results of this section point up a second important distinction between Type I credit rationing, in which each firm receives a smaller loan than it desires, and Type II rationing, in which some firms are denied credit altogether. As we noted in the Introduction, and as is shown in Chapter I, the first type of rationing has no adverse implications for the efficiency of resource allocation. The second type of rationing, by contrast, may involve a suboptimal allocation of credit among firms.

V. The problem of second loans

There is one remaining item of business with which we must deal in this chapter. In Section I.B. we indicated that an incentive to make second loans might exist in a market equilibrium described by conditions (E.1)-(E.4), even if the bank making the first loan always had priority over the borrower's assets in the event of default. To rule out this possibility, we assumed that a bank could either require its customers not to seek additional financing for a project or insist that they obtain prior consent for any second loan. In this section we show first that a second loan which is acceptable to the borrower will be worthwhile to the bank which makes it only if it reduces the expected profits of the bank which granted the first loan. We then prove that an incentive to make second loans cannot exist if those borrowers who receive credit in equilibrium receive loans as large as they desire, i.e. if there is no Type I rationing. Finally, we establish through a specific example that banks _can_ have an incentive to make second loans when this is not the case.

Suppose that a bank has made a loan to a firm at terms r_1 and L_1, and that the firm now takes out a second loan from another bank at terms r_2 and L_2. Suppose also that the bank making the first loan has priority over the firm's assets in the event of default. From the point of view of the borrower, the two loans will be equivalent to a single loan of size $\bar{L}$ at interest rate $\bar{r}$, where

$$\bar{L} = L_1 + L_2, \quad \bar{r} = \frac{L_1}{\bar{L}} r_1 + \frac{L_2}{\bar{L}} r_2$$

Thus, a borrower will choose the same value of γ, say $\bar{\gamma}$, that he would if he received only one loan at terms $\bar{r}$ and $\bar{L}$. Furthermore, the combined expected profits of the banks from the two loans will equal the expected profits $\delta(\bar{r},\bar{L},\bar{\gamma},h)$ that either bank would realize from a single loan to the same customer at terms $\bar{r}$ and $\bar{L}$. Letting $\delta_1(r_1,L_1,L_2,\bar{\gamma},h)$ be the expected profits of the bank making the first loan and $\delta_2(r_1,L_1,r_2,L_2,\bar{\gamma},h)$ the expected profits of the bank making the second loan, we thus have

$$(16) \qquad \delta_1(r_1,L_1,L_2,\bar{\gamma},h) + \delta_2(r_1,L_1,r_2,L_2,\bar{\gamma},h) = \delta(\bar{r},\bar{L},\bar{\gamma},h)$$

For a bank to have an incentive to make a second loan of size L_2 at interest rate r_2, it is necessary that

$$(17) \qquad u(\bar{r},\bar{L},\bar{\gamma}) \geq u(r_1,L_1,\gamma_1)$$

$$(18) \qquad \delta_2(r_1,L_1,r_2,L_2,\bar{\gamma},h) > \delta^* = c$$

where γ_1 is the project characteristic the borrower would select if he took out only the first loan. Condition (17) ensures that the customer will be willing to accept the second loan and condition (18) that the bank will wish to make it.

Now suppose that the terms of the first loan, r_1 and L_1, satisfy equilibrium conditions (E.3a) and (E.3b). In this event $u(\bar{r},\bar{L},\bar{\gamma}) \geq u(r_1,L_1,\gamma_1)$ must imply $\delta(\bar{r},\bar{L},\bar{\gamma},h) \leq \delta(r_1,L_1,\gamma_1,h) = \delta^* = c$. From equation (16) it is then clear that the expected profits of the bank making the second loan can exceed δ^* only if $\tilde{\delta}_1 < 0$, i.e. only if the expected profits of the bank which made the first loan fall below zero. However, if the project characteristic γ is unchanged $(\bar{\gamma} = \gamma_1)$, and if an increase in project size at a given γ always shifts out the cumulative distribution function of the project outcome x--as will be the case, for example, when $x = \psi(L,\gamma,y)$ with $\psi_L > 0$--the taking out of a second loan must <u>raise</u> the expected profits of the bank which made the first loan; $\tilde{\delta}_1$, that is, will exceed δ^*. Thus, if γ were technologically fixed, or if a bank could commit the borrower to a given value of γ in the loan contract, we could rule out the possibility that banks would want to make second loans in an equilibrium described by conditions (E.1)-(E.4).

In this chapter, however, we are assuming that the borrower cannot be prevented from choosing whatever project characteristic γ he wishes. If the borrower selects a higher value of γ when he takes out the second loan--i.e. if he makes the project riskier--the expected profits of the bank making the first loan may fall or even become negative. Thus, by offering loan terms r_2 and L_2 which cause the borrower to increase γ, it would appear that a bank might be able to earn sufficient expected profits from a second loan to make it worthwhile. We now show that this can happen--that $\tilde{\delta}_2$ can exceed δ^*--only if the borrower is initially receiving a smaller volume of credit than he desires and is therefore willing to take out a second loan at a higher rate of interest:

Proposition 4. Let r_1, L_1, and γ_1 satisfy equilibrium conditions (E.1)-(E.4). Then if $\max_{\gamma} u(r_1,L,\gamma) \leq u(r_1,L_1,\gamma_1)$ for all $L > L_1$, there cannot exist an incentive for a bank to make a second loan to any firm.

Proof: To prove that no bank can have an incentive to make a second loan, we must show that there do not exist an r_2 and L_2 satisfying conditions (17) and (18). Now, a bank's expected profits from a second loan at terms r_2 and L_2 are

$$(19)\qquad \gamma_2 = \int_{z_1}^{z_1+z_2} (x-z_1)F_x(x,\bar{L},\bar{\gamma})dx + z_2 \int_{z_1+z_2}^{x_M} F_x(x,\bar{L},\bar{\gamma})dx$$

$$- (1+h)L_2 < z_2 \int_{z_1}^{x_M} F_x(x,\bar{L},\bar{\gamma})dx - (1+h)L_2$$

where $z_i \equiv (1+r)L_i$ and $\bar{\gamma}$ maximizes $u(\bar{r},\bar{L},\gamma)$. Now, since $\bar{L} > L_1$ implies $\max_{\gamma} u(r_1,\bar{L},\gamma) \leq u(r_1,L_1,\gamma_1)$, and since $\max_{\gamma} u(r,\bar{L},\gamma) <$ $\max_{\gamma} u(r_1,\bar{L},\gamma)$ for all $r > r_1$, condition (17) can be satisfied only at an $\bar{r} \leq r_1$. Since $\bar{r}$ is merely a weighted average of r_1 and r_2, this implies $r_2 \leq r_1$. From (19) we then obtain

$$(20)\qquad \gamma_2 < L_2\{(1+r_1) \int_{z_1}^{x_M} F_x(x,\bar{L},\bar{\gamma})dx - (1+h)\}$$

But the expected profits of the bank which made the first loan are

$$(21)\qquad \gamma_1 = \int_{x_m}^{z_1} xF_x(x,\bar{L},\bar{\gamma})dx + z_1 \int_{z_1}^{x_M} F_x(x,\bar{L},\bar{\gamma})dx - (1+h)L_1$$

Substituting this into (20) yields

$$\gamma_2 < L_2\{\frac{1}{L_1}[\gamma_1 - \int_{x_m}^{z_1} xF_x(x,\bar{L},\bar{\gamma})dx]\} < \frac{L_2}{L_1}\gamma_1$$

Thus, $\gamma_1 \leq 0$ implies $\gamma_2 < 0$. Since equilibrium condition (E.3) implies $\delta(\bar{r},\bar{L},\bar{\gamma}) \leq \delta(r_1,L_1,\gamma_1) = \delta^*$, it follows from equation (16) that condition (18) is violated. This completes the proof.

From the above proposition we know that banks cannot have an incentive to make second loans unless the equilibrium loan terms r_1 and L_1 lie to the left of the borrower's demand curve D(r).[19] We have previously seen, however, that an equilibrium with Type II rationing can occur only at a point on the locus r*(L), i.e. at a loan rate which maximizes the bank's expected revenues μ_R given L. Thus, if the locus r*(L) either coincides with the borrower's demand curve or lies to the right of it, there cannot exist an incentive to make second loans in any equilibrium which involves Type II rationing; in the putty-clay model examined in Section III.B., we saw that this would be the case for all values of the parameters α and λ such that $\frac{\alpha}{1+\lambda} \leq J$. Of course, even if r*(L) lies entirely to the right of D(r), an equilibrium in which all firms receive credit may occur at a point to the left of D(r). Thus, the condition $\frac{\alpha}{1+\lambda} \leq J$ allows us to rule out the possibility of second loans only for equilibria characterized by Type II rationing.

We have established conditions under which the incentive to make second loans can be ruled out. It remains to show that there are other circumstances in which such an incentive will exist. This is most easily seen by considering once again the putty-clay model of Section III.B., in which $Q = aL^{\beta}N^{\alpha}$ with $\alpha + \beta < 1$. Suppose that a firm has taken out a loan of size L_1 at interest rate r_1 and let u_1 be its expected profits at those terms. Then from (16), the expected profits which a bank can earn by making a second loan that leaves the borrower exactly as well off as before will be

$$\gamma_2 = \delta(\bar{r},\bar{L},\bar{n},h) - \gamma_1(r_1,L_1, L_2,\bar{n},h)$$

$$= \delta(\Theta(\bar{L},u_1),\bar{L},n^*(\Theta(\bar{L},u_1),\bar{L}),h)$$

$$- \gamma_1(r_1,L_1,\bar{L}-L_1,n^*(\Theta(\bar{L},u_1),\bar{L}),h)$$

where $n^*(\bar{r},\bar{L})$ is the borrower's optimal labor intensity of investment when he borrows a total amount $\bar{L}$ at an average interest rate $\bar{r}$ and $\Theta(\bar{L},u)$ is the average loan rate at which $u(\bar{r},\bar{L},n^*(\bar{r},\bar{L})) = u$.

We are interested in what happens to $\gamma_2 = \delta - \gamma_1$ as the size of the second loan is increased from zero and the interest rate on that loan is adjusted to keep the borrower's total expected profits unchanged at u_1. But if the terms on the first loan satisfy equilibrium condition (E.3a), the total change in δ from a marginal increase in $\bar{L}$ above L_1 must be $d\delta/d\bar{L} = 0$. Thus, at $\bar{L} = L_1$, the total change in γ_2 will be $d\gamma_2/d\bar{L} = d\delta/d\bar{L} - d\gamma_1/d\bar{L} = -d\gamma_1/d\bar{L}$. In other words, the expected profits from a very small second loan will be equal in magnitude and opposite in sign to the change in the expected profits of the bank which made the first loan.

In the particular case examined in Section III.B., the change in $\tilde{\delta}_1$ which results from a rightward movement along the borrower iso-profit curve $\Theta(L,u_1)$ can be decomposed into two parts, one positive and the other negative. To see this, note that the project outcome in this case can be expressed in the multiplicative form

$$x = \bar{L}^{\frac{\beta}{1-\alpha}} \max\{0,\ pa(\frac{as\bar{v}}{w})^{\frac{\alpha}{1-\alpha}} - w(\frac{as\bar{v}}{w})^{\frac{1}{1-\alpha}}\}$$

where $\bar{v} = \frac{w}{as}\bar{L}^{\lambda}\bar{n}^{1-\alpha}$. Suppose that as we increase $\bar{L}$ we first reduce $\bar{r}$ so as to induce a decrease in $\bar{n}$ just sufficient to hold the variable $\bar{v}$ constant.[20] Then from the expression above it follows that the entire probability distribution of the project outcome will shift outward, producing an unambiguous increase in $\tilde{\delta}_1$. As Appendix B makes clear, however, a downward adjustment in $\bar{r}$ just sufficient to hold $\bar{v}$ constant will leave the borrower with a higher level of expected profits than he enjoyed in the initial position, before the increase in $\bar{L}$. To return to the initial iso-profit curve $\Theta(L,u_1)$, $\bar{r}$ must now be increased. This second effect involves an increase in $\bar{n}$, and by shifting probability weight into the tails of the distribution of the project outcome, it tends to reduce $\tilde{\delta}_1$.

In Appendix C it is shown that as we begin to increase $\bar{L}$ above L_1, the second effect will be more likely to outweigh the first the lower is the value of v in the initial position. Furthermore, if $c = 0$ and if the terms on the first loan satisfy equilibrium conditions (E.3a) and (E.3b), the initial value of v will decrease as $\beta/(1-\alpha)$ falls toward zero and will eventually become sufficiently small that $d\tilde{\delta}_1/d\bar{L} < 0$. Thus, if $c = 0$ and β is small relative to $1-\alpha$, there will exist a second loan which renders the expected profits of the first bank negative and which yields expected profits $\gamma_2 > 0$ to the second bank, while leaving the total expected profits of the borrower unchanged. If the administrative cost c is positive, there may still exist an incentive for second loans, but such an incentive will be less likely the higher is c.

A major conclusion which emerges from this section is that a bank may wish to prevent a borrower from seeking additional financing from other sources, even if the bank has absolute priority over the borrower's assets in the event of default. We have seen that the problem arises because the terms of the additional financing may make it worthwhile for the borrower to select a riskier project; from Proposition 4 we also know that the lender need be concerned about this prospect only if he has provided the borrower with a smaller loan than the borrower desires.

In those cases in which an incentive for second loans does exist, our approach in this chapter has been to assume that the bank can require prior consent for any additional loans the borrower might want to take out. This assumption ensures that second loans will never be made, because any second loan made at terms acceptable both to the bank which made the first loan and to the borrower could not be worthwhile for the bank which made the second loan (i.e. could not yield expected profits γ_2 sufficient to cover costs of administration c). Of course, this assumption requires that banks be able to monitor and enforce those provisions in the loan contract relating to a firm's future borrowing practices but not those relating to specific features of the investment project (i.e. γ). As was noted in Section I.A., loan agreements often do include limits on the amount of additional borrowing which the firm can undertake; and in most instances, the bank could probably verify compliance by simply checking the periodic financial statements which the borrower is almost always required to provide. Thus, the distinction we have made between the two types of provisions is not an unreasonable one.

VI. Conclusions

We have seen that the problem of moral hazard will arise in the market for bank loans under two conditions: (1) the bank is unable to exercise direct control over certain characteristics of the borrower's investment project by specifying them in the loan contract; (2) by altering those characteristics in appropriate fashion the borrower can increase the riskiness of the project outcome, in the sense of shifting probability density from the center of the distribution to the tails, but after some point further increases in risk can be achieved only at a sacrifice in the total expected income from the project. An important case in which the second condition is met is what we have referred to as the "putty-clay-model. In this case the firm must decide when it makes its investment how much labor, raw materials, or other factors of production it will employ at the end of the period with its newly installed capital, even though it does not know what the price of its output will be at that time. As we have seen, the borrower can in such cases increase the riskiness of his investment project by choosing a higher end-of-period input of labor or other factors--e.g. by using his loan to acquire machinery of greater labor intensity.

The moral hazard problem arises under the two conditions stated above because the terms of the loan influence the borrower's choice of project characteristics and thus indirectly affect the probability distribution of the outcome of the project. As long as there is a risk of default, the bank's expected revenues from a loan will depend on the probability distribution of the project outcome; thus, in negotiating the terms of the loan--e.g. the rate of interest on the loan and the size of the loan--the bank will want to take into account not only the direct effect which those terms have on its expected revenues but also the indirect effect which they have through their influence on the borrower's choice of project characteristics. We have referred to this as a problem of "moral hazard" because it is analogous to those situations in insurance markets in which the terms of a policy affect the insured's probability of having an accident, for example, by causing him to behave more carelessly.

The central point of this chapter is that the phenomenon of moral hazard can lead to equilibrium credit rationing, in the sense that some firms receive credit in equilibrium while other, identical firms do not. The reason this can occur is that increases in the loan rate will cause a borrower interested in maximizing expected profits to alter the characteristics of his investment project in such a way as to increase the risk of the project and reduce the total expected outcome. Such a change in project characteristics will tend to reduce the bank's expected revenues from a loan, and if this effect is sufficiently strong it may offset the increase in the total amount due from the borrower. When this is the case, any firm which has not received a loan will find that it cannot obtain one by offering to pay a higher rate of interest than banks are currently charging. If a bank could commit the firm to the same set of project characteristics it believes will be chosen by its current customers, and if the bank could somehow be certain that the firm would live up to the agreement, it would be happy to accommodate the firm at the higher rate of interest. But since we have assumed that this is not possible, an equilibrium may well occur in which banks ration credit by refusing to lend to certain firms. In general, such an equilibrium will be more likely to occur the larger is the number of firms seeking credit, the lower is the relative attractiveness of bank deposits to wealth holders, and the higher is the cost of administering each loan.

The type of credit rationing we have been concerned with in this paper has been seen to have important implications for both the effectiveness of monetary policy and the efficiency of resource allocation. When the initial equilibrium is characterized by rationing, an easing or tightening of monetary policy can have a significant impact on lending and investment even if the size of individual investment projects is completely unresponsive to changes in the cost of borrowing; the reason is that changes in monetary policy will affect the number of firms which are able to obtain loans, increasing the degree of rationing in the case of monetary contraction and decreasing it in the case of monetary expansion. Also, if some firms are receiving credit in equilibrium while other firms with identical projects are not, the allocation of resources may be inefficient, in the sense that the net expected return from investment could be increased by distributing the same volume of credit more evenly among firms. It is significant that the alternative concept of credit rationing, in which borrowers are able to obtain credit but receive smaller loans than they desire, has neither of these implications.

Appendix A

This Appendix is concerned with the case in which

$$x = \max\{0, \psi(L,\gamma,y), \quad \psi_y > 0, \quad \psi_{\gamma y} > 0$$

$$\psi(L,\gamma,y_{min}) \leq L, \quad \psi_{\gamma\gamma} < 0$$

$$\psi_\gamma(L,\gamma_{max},y) < 0 < \psi_\gamma(L,\gamma_{min},y)$$

where y is a random variable with cumulative distribution function G(y) and density function g(y). We first establish that Assumptions A.1-A.5 are satisfied. It is then shown that if $0 < g(y_{max}) < \infty$ and $g'(y_{max})$ is finite, the partial derivative $\partial\gamma^*/\partial r$ cannot approach zero as r approaches $\hat{r}(L)$. Finally, we determine the competitive equilibrium for the case in which ψ displays constant returns to scale with respect to L and γ.

1. a) Since $\psi_y(L,\gamma,y) > 0$, the equation $x = \psi(L,\gamma,y)$ defines an inverse function $\psi^{-1}(L,\gamma,x)$, with

$$\frac{\partial\psi^{-1}}{\partial\gamma} = -\frac{\psi_\gamma}{\psi_y}, \quad \frac{\partial\psi^{-1}}{\partial x} = \frac{1}{\psi_y}$$

Thus,

$$\text{(A.1)} \qquad \frac{\partial}{\partial x}\psi_\gamma(L,\gamma,\psi^{-1}(L,\gamma,x)) = \psi_{\gamma y}\frac{\partial\psi^{-1}}{\partial x} = \frac{\psi_{\gamma y}}{\psi_y} > 0$$

Also, since $F(x,L,\gamma) = G(\psi^{-1}(L,\gamma,x))$,

$$\text{(A.2)} \qquad F_\gamma(x,L,\gamma) = \frac{\partial}{\partial\gamma}G(\psi^{-1}(L,\gamma,x)) = G'\frac{\partial\psi^{-1}}{\partial\gamma} = -G'\frac{\psi_\gamma}{\psi_y}$$

Let $y^*(\gamma,L)$ be that value of y for which $\psi_\gamma(L,\gamma,y) = 0$; since $\psi_{\gamma y} > 0$, this value must be unique. Also, let $\tilde{y}(\gamma,L) = \max\{y_{min}, \psi^{-1}(L,\gamma,0)\}$. Then from equations (A.1) and (A.2) it is clear that Assumption A.1 is satisfied, with

$$\bar{x} = \psi(L,\gamma,\tilde{y}) = x_m \text{ for all L and } \gamma \text{ such that } \psi_\gamma(L,\gamma,\tilde{y}) \geq 0$$

$$= \psi(L,\gamma,y^*) \text{ for all L and } \gamma \text{ such that } \psi_\gamma(L,\gamma,\tilde{y}) < 0 <$$

(A.3) $$\psi_\gamma(L,\gamma,y_{max})$$

$$= \psi(L,\gamma,y_{max}) = x_M \text{ for all L and } \gamma \text{ such that}$$

$$\psi_\gamma(L,\gamma,y_{max}) \leq 0$$

b) From (A.2) and the fact that $\psi_\gamma(L,\gamma_{max},y) < 0 < \psi_\gamma(L,\gamma_{min},y)$, it follows that Assumption A.3 must hold. Also, since $x_m = \max\{0,\psi(L,\gamma,y_{min})\}$ and $\psi(L,\gamma,y_{min}) \leq L$, Assumption A.2 is satisfied.

c) To see that Assumption A.4 holds, we observe from (A.3) that $\bar{x}$ is a continuous function of γ with

$$\frac{\partial \bar{x}}{\partial \gamma} = 0 \text{ for L and } \gamma \text{ such that } \psi_\gamma(L,\gamma,\tilde{y}) > 0 \text{ and}$$

$$\psi(L,\gamma,y_{min}) < 0$$

$$= \psi_\gamma(L,\gamma,y_{min}) > 0 \text{ for L and } \gamma \text{ such that } \psi_\gamma(L,\gamma,\tilde{y}) > 0 \text{ and}$$

$$\psi(L,\gamma,y_{min}) > 0$$

$$= \psi_\gamma(L,\gamma,y^*) + \psi_y(L,\gamma,y^*)\frac{\partial y^*}{\partial \gamma} = \psi_y \frac{\partial y^*}{\partial \gamma} \text{ for L and } \gamma$$

$$\text{such that } \psi_\gamma(L,\gamma,\tilde{y}) < 0 < \psi_\gamma(L,\gamma,y_{max})$$

Thus, since $\psi_\gamma(L,\gamma,y^*) = 0$ implies $\frac{\partial y^*}{\partial \gamma} = -\frac{\psi_{\gamma\gamma}}{\psi_{\gamma y}} > 0$, $\frac{\partial \bar{x}}{\partial \gamma}$ is nonnegative in all three cases--i.e. $\bar{x}$ is nondecreasing in γ for all L and γ such that $\bar{x} < x_M$.

d) $F(x',L,\gamma_2) = F(x',L,\gamma_1)$ implies $\psi^{-1}(L,\gamma_2,x') = \psi^{-1}(L,\gamma_1,x')$ and, at $x = x'$,

$$\text{(A.4)} \qquad \frac{\partial}{\partial x}[F(x,L,\gamma_2) - F(x,L,\gamma_1)] =$$

$$= G'\{\frac{\partial}{\partial x}\psi^{-1}(L,\gamma_2,x) - \frac{\partial}{\partial x}\psi^{-1}(L,\gamma_1,x)\}$$

We have seen that $\frac{\partial \psi^{-1}}{\partial x} = \frac{1}{\psi_y}$. But, since $\psi_{\gamma y} > 0$, $\gamma_2 > \gamma_1$ must imply

$$\psi_y(L,\gamma_2,\psi^{-1}(L,\gamma_2,x')) > \psi_y(L,\gamma_1,\psi^{-1}(L,\gamma_1,x'))$$

Thus, the right-hand side of (A.4) must be negative for $G' > 0$--i.e. $\gamma_2 > \gamma$ and $0 < F(x',L,\gamma_2) = F(x',L,\gamma_1) < 1$ imply $\frac{\partial}{\partial x}[F(x,L,\gamma_2) - F(x,L,\gamma_1)] < 0$ at $x = x'$. Assumption A.5 follows immediately.

2. Proposition. Suppose that $u(r,L,\gamma)$ attains a unique maximum with respect to γ at each r lying within some neighborhood of $\hat{r}(L)$, and let $\gamma^*(r,L)$ be the borrower's optimal γ given r and L. Suppose also that $0 < g(y_{max}) < \infty$ and that $g'(y_{max})$ is finite. Then if $\lim_{r\to\hat{r}} \frac{\partial \gamma^*}{\partial r}$ exists, it is positive.

Proof: By differentiating the expression for $u(r,L,\gamma)$ in equation (5) we obtain

$$\frac{\partial^2 u}{\partial \gamma^2} = \int_{\hat{y}}^{y_{max}} \psi_{\gamma\gamma}(L,\gamma,y)g(y)dy + \frac{g(\hat{y})[\psi_\gamma(L,\gamma,\hat{y})]^2}{\psi_y(L,\gamma,\hat{y})}$$

and

$$\frac{\partial^2 u}{\partial r \partial \gamma} = -\frac{\psi_\gamma(L,\gamma,\hat{y})g(\hat{y})L}{\psi_y(L,\gamma,\hat{y})}$$

Thus,

$$\text{(A.5)} \qquad \frac{\partial \gamma^*}{\partial r} = -\frac{\partial^2 u/\partial r \partial \gamma}{\partial^2 u/\partial \gamma^2} = \frac{L}{\psi_y(L,\gamma^*,\hat{y})B + \psi_\gamma(L,\gamma^*,\hat{y})}$$

where

$$B = \frac{\int_{\hat{y}}^{y_{max}} \psi_{\gamma\gamma}(L,\gamma^*,y)g(y)dy}{\psi_\gamma(L,\gamma^*,\hat{y})g(\hat{y})}$$

Now at $\hat{r}(L)$, $\underset{\gamma}{\text{Max}}\ \psi(L,\gamma,y_{max}) = (1+r)L$. Thus

$$\lim_{r \to \hat{r}} \hat{y}(r,L,\gamma^*(r,L)) = y_{max}$$

$$\lim_{r \to \hat{r}} \psi_\gamma(L,\gamma^*,\hat{y}) = 0$$

Since both the numerator and denominator of B approach zero as r goes to $\hat{r}$, we must apply L'Hopital's rule to evaluate the limit. Differentiating the numerator of B with respect to r and using $\frac{\partial \hat{y}}{\partial \gamma} = -\frac{\psi_\gamma}{\psi_y}$

and $\frac{\partial \hat{y}}{\partial r} = \frac{L}{\psi_y}$, we obtain

$$\text{(A.6)} \qquad -\psi_{\gamma\gamma} g(\hat{y}) \frac{L}{\psi_y} + \{\int_{\hat{y}}^{y_{max}} \psi_{\gamma\gamma\gamma}(L,\gamma^*,y)g(y)dy + \psi_{\gamma\gamma} \frac{\psi_\gamma}{\psi_y}\} \frac{\partial \gamma^*}{\partial r}$$

Differentiating the denominator of B with respect to r we get

$$\text{(A.7)} \qquad \psi_{\gamma y} g(\hat{y}) \frac{L}{\psi_y} + \psi_\gamma g'(\hat{y}) \frac{L}{\psi_y} + \{- \frac{g'(\hat{y})\psi_\gamma^2}{\psi_y} + g(\hat{y})[\psi_{\gamma\gamma} - \psi_{\gamma y} \frac{\psi_\gamma}{\psi_y}]\} \frac{\partial \gamma^*}{\partial r}$$

Suppose $\lim_{r\to\hat{r}} \frac{\partial \gamma^*}{\partial r} = 0$. Then as $r \to \hat{r}$ the limit of (A.6) will be $- \psi_{\gamma\gamma} \frac{L}{\psi_y} g(y_{max})$ and the limit of (A.7) will be $\psi_{\gamma y} \frac{L}{\psi_y} g(y_{max})$. Since $0 < g(y_{max}) < \infty$ by assumption, both expressions are nonzero and finite. Thus

$$\lim_{r\to\hat{r}} B = - \frac{\psi_{\gamma\gamma}}{\psi_{\gamma y}}$$

which is positive but finite. But (A.5) then implies $\lim_{r\to\hat{r}} \frac{\partial \gamma^*}{\partial r} > 0$, which is a contradiction. Since $\lim_{r\to\hat{r}} \frac{\partial \gamma^*}{\partial r} \geq 0$, it follows that $\lim_{r\to\hat{r}} \frac{\partial \gamma^*}{\partial r}$ must be positive.

3. If $\psi(L,\gamma,y)$ is homogeneous of degree one in L and γ, so also must be the bank's expected revenues $\mu_R(r,L,\gamma)$ and the borrower's expected profits $u(r,L,\gamma)$. This leads to the following result:

<u>Proposition.</u> Suppose that ψ displays constant returns to scale with respect to L and γ. Consider any $L_1 > 0$ and let r_1 and γ_1 be

values of r and γ which maximize the bank's expected revenues $\mu_R(r,L_1,\gamma)$ subject to the constraint that γ maximize the borrower's expected profits $u(r,L_1,\gamma)$. Then for any $k > 0$, r_1 and $\gamma = k\gamma_1$ will maximize $\mu_R(r,kL_1,\gamma)$ subject to the constraint that γ maximize $u(r,kL_1,\gamma)$. Also, $\mu_R(r,kL_1,k\gamma_1) = k\mu_R(r,L_1,\gamma_1)$--i.e. the bank's maximum expected revenues are proportional to the size of the loan.

Proof: Since ψ displays constant returns to scale with respect to L and γ, it must be true for any $k > 0$ and y that $\psi(kL,k\gamma,y) = k\psi(L,\gamma,y)$. But this implies $\hat{y}(r,kL,k\gamma) = \hat{y}(r,L,\gamma)$ and $\tilde{y}(kL,k\gamma) = \tilde{y}(L,\gamma)$. From the expressions for μ_R and u in (4) and (5) it is then clear that

$$(A.8) \qquad \mu_R(r,kL,k\gamma) = k\mu_R(r,L,\gamma)$$

$$(A.9) \qquad u(r,kL,k\gamma) = ku(r,L,\gamma)$$

for all $k > 0$.

Now consider any $r_2 \neq r_1$ and let γ_2 be any value of γ which maximizes $u(r_2,kL_1,\gamma)$. Then from (A.9)

$$u(r_2,L_1\,\frac{\gamma_2}{k}) = \frac{1}{k}\,u(r_2,kL_1,\gamma_2)$$

$$\geq \frac{1}{k}\,u(r_2,kL_1,\gamma) = u(r_2,L_1,\,\frac{\gamma}{k})$$

for all γ. That is, $u(r_2,L_1,\gamma)$ attains a maximum at $\gamma = \frac{\gamma_2}{k}$. But since r_1 and γ_1 are assumed to maximize $\mu_R(r,L_1,\gamma)$ subject to the constraint that γ maximize $u(r,L_1,\gamma)$, this implies

$$\mu_R(r_2, L_1, \frac{\gamma_2}{k}) \leq \mu_R(r_1, L_1, \gamma_1)$$

From (A.8) it then follows that

$$\mu_R(r_2, kL_1, \gamma_2) \leq \mu_R(r_1, kL_1, k\gamma_1)$$

That is, r_1 and $\gamma = k\gamma_1$ maximize $\mu_R(r, kL_1, \gamma)$ subject to the constraint that γ maximize $u(r, kL_1, \gamma)$.

According to this proposition, any loan rate r* which maximizes the bank's expected revenues μ_R at one loan size must also maximize μ_R at all other loan sizes. Now, if $1+\rho^*$ is the maximum value of μ_r at L = 1, the bank's maximum expected revenues at any other loan size can be expressed as $(1+\rho^*)L$. But since the borrower's expected profits $u(r, L, \gamma)$ are homogeneous of degree one in L and γ, they too will be proportional to the size of the loan at loan rate r*. This implies that a market equilibrium will exist only if the opportunity rate h is equal to ρ^*: If $h > \rho^*$, the bank's expected profits from a loan, $\delta = \mu_R - (1+h)L$, will necessarily be negative. And if $h < \rho^*$, the bank would always be able to increase both its own expected profits and those of the borrower by charging loan rate r* and increasing the size of the loan; that is, equilibrium condition (E.3a) will be violated.

Since competitive equilibrium requires that the opportunity rate h equal ρ^*, the equilibrium loan rate can only be a value of r which maximizes μ_R at each loan size. At any other loan rate, the bank's opportunity cost of making a loan would exceed its expected revenues. Also, since $\delta = \mu_R - (1+h)L = 0$, an equilibrium will exist only if administrative costs c are zero.

The total volume of credit L_T will be determined by the requirement that $\rho^* = h = \Omega(L_T)$. However, equilibrium condition (E.3a) will be satisfied at all loan sizes. Furthermore, equilibrium condition (E.2) cannot be used to rule out the possibility that some firms will fail to receive credit. The equilibrium may be characterized by Type II rationing, because no bank will be able to increase its expected profits by making a loan at a higher rate or by granting a loan of different size: an increase in the loan rate would reduce μ_R by inducing the borrower to choose a riskier project, while an increase or decrease in loan size with r held constant would merely change expected revenues in the same proportion as the opportunity cost of making the loan.

Appendix B

In this Appendix we prove several propositions about the putty-clay model for the case in which $Q = aL^{\beta}N^{\alpha}$ and p has a uniform probability distribution. It is shown first that an equilibrium cannot exist when Q is characterized by increasing returns to scale (i.e. $\alpha + \beta > 1$). We prove next that the function $L_2(h,\delta)$ exists, i.e. that the expected profits of the borrower attain a unique maximum along a bank iso-profit locus. Finally, we establish that L_2 is decreasing in h and in δ.

1. If n is always chosen to maximize the borrower's expected profits u(r,L,n), equation (6) can be used to express r as a function of n and L. This in turn allows us to express the bank's expected revenues μ_R and the firm's expected profits u in terms of n and L alone. Letting $v = \frac{w}{as} L^{\lambda} n^{1-\alpha}$, with $\lambda \equiv 1 - \alpha - \beta$, we then obtain

$$\text{(B.1)} \qquad \gamma(L,v,h) = L^{\frac{\beta}{1-\alpha}} H_1(v) - (1+h)L$$

$$\text{(B.2)} \qquad \tilde{u}(L,v) = L^{\frac{\beta}{1-\alpha}} H_2(v)$$

where

$$H_1(v) = \left(\frac{asv^{\alpha}}{w^{\alpha}}\right)^{\frac{1}{1-\alpha}} \left\{- \frac{(4-\alpha^2)}{2\alpha^2} v^2 + \frac{4-\alpha}{\alpha} v - \frac{3}{2}\right\}$$

$$H_2(v) = \left(\frac{asv^{\alpha}}{w^{\alpha}}\right)^{\frac{1}{1-\alpha}} 2\left(\frac{\alpha-v}{\alpha}\right)^2$$

It is not difficult to show that $\tilde{p} < \hat{p} < s$ implies $\frac{\alpha}{2-\alpha} < v < \alpha$ and that the probability of default is $1 - 2\frac{\alpha - v}{\alpha}$. Also, $H_2' < 0$ and $H_1' \gtrless 0$ as $v \lessgtr J$, where J is the constant defined in the text and lies below α.

Equilibrium condition (E.3) states that a bank must have no incentive to alter the terms or the number of its loans. This requires that δ be nonnegative and that r and L solve the maximization problem

$$\max_{r,L} \delta(r,L,n^*(r,L),h) \text{ subject to } u(r,L,n^*(r,L)) \geq \bar{u}$$

where $\bar{u}$ is the value of u at the equilibrium loan terms. Now, choosing r and L to solve this maximization problem is clearly equivalent to choosing L and v to maximize $\gamma(L,v,h)$ subject to the constraint $\tilde{u}(L,v) \geq \bar{u}$. From (B.2), however, it is clear that $\tilde{u}(L,v)$ is nondecreasing in L. Thus, the solution to the maximization problem can occur only at an L and v for which $\partial\gamma/\partial L \leq 0$. At any other point, it would always be possible to raise the expected profits of the bank without reducing the expected profits of the borrower by increasing L and holding v constant.

Partially differentiating (B.1) with respect to L we obtain

$$\text{(B.3)} \qquad \frac{\partial\gamma}{\partial L} = \frac{\beta}{1-\alpha} L^{-\frac{\lambda}{1-\alpha}} H_1(v) - (1+h)$$

But (B.1) also implies

$$H_1(v) = [\delta + (1+h)L]\, L^{-\frac{\beta}{1-\alpha}}$$

Substituting this into (B.3) yields

$$\text{(B.4)} \qquad \frac{\partial\gamma}{\partial L} = \frac{\beta}{1-\alpha}\frac{\delta}{L} - \frac{\lambda}{1-\alpha}(1+h)$$

In the case of $\lambda \equiv 1 - \alpha - \beta < 0$, equation (B.4) implies $\frac{\partial \gamma}{\partial L} > 0$ for all L and v such that $\gamma(L,v,h) \geq 0$. Thus, an equilibrium cannot exist if Q displays increasing returns to scale in L and N.

2. As was noted above, $H_1' \gtrless 0$ as $v \lesseqgtr J$, where J is the constant defined after equation (7) in the text. We can thus define a function $\tilde{\phi}(L,h,\delta)$ indicating that value of $v < J$ for which $\gamma(L,v,h) = \delta$; since $H_2' < 0$, this will also be the value of v that maximizes $\tilde{u}(L,v)$ subject to the constraint $\gamma(L,v,h) = \delta$. By differentiating equation (B.1) with respect to L we obtain

$$\text{(B.5)} \qquad \tilde{\phi}_L = \frac{1}{H_1'} L^{-\frac{\beta}{1-\alpha}} \left(1 + h - \frac{\beta}{1-\alpha} L^{-\frac{\lambda}{1-\alpha}} H_1\right)$$

Any value of L that solves $\max_{L,v} \tilde{u}(L,v)$ subject to the constraint $\gamma(L,v,h) = \delta$ must satisfy $\frac{\partial}{\partial L} \tilde{u}(L,\tilde{\phi}(L,h,\delta)) = 0$. Totally differentiating equation (B.2) with respect to L yields

$$\text{(B.6)} \qquad \begin{aligned} \frac{\partial}{\partial L} \tilde{u}(L,\tilde{\phi}(L,h,\delta)) &= \frac{\beta}{1-\alpha} L^{-\frac{\lambda}{1-\alpha}} H_2 + L^{\frac{\beta}{1-\alpha}} H_2' \tilde{\phi}_L \\ &= \frac{\beta}{1-\alpha} L^{-\frac{\lambda}{1-\alpha}} H_2 + \frac{H_2'}{H_1'} \left(1 + h - \frac{\beta}{1-\alpha} L^{-\frac{\lambda}{1-\alpha}} H_1\right) \end{aligned}$$

Differentiating again with respect to L and simplifying we obtain

$$\text{(B.7)} \qquad \begin{aligned} \frac{\partial^2}{\partial L^2} \tilde{u}(L,\tilde{\phi}(L,h,\delta)) &= \frac{\lambda\beta}{(1-\alpha)^2} L^{-1-\frac{\lambda}{1-\alpha}} \left(\frac{H_2' H_1}{H_1'} - H_2\right) \\ &\quad + H_1' L^{\frac{\beta}{1-\alpha}} \tilde{\phi}_L^2 \frac{d}{dv} \left(\frac{H_2'}{H_1'}\right) \end{aligned}$$

Now, by differentiating the expressions for $H_1(v)$ and $H_2(v)$ following equations (B.1) and (B.2), we obtain

(B.8) $$\frac{H_1'}{H_2'} = \frac{\alpha^2}{4} \frac{(1-v)(\frac{2-\alpha}{\alpha} v - 1)}{(\alpha-v)(\frac{2-\alpha}{\alpha} v - \alpha)} - 1$$

Since $\alpha < 1$, this expression is increasing in v, implying $\frac{d}{dv}(\frac{H_2'}{H_1'}) < 0$. Also, $H_2' < 0$ and, for $v < J$, $H_1' > 0$. Equation (B.7) therefore implies $\frac{\partial^2}{\partial L^2} \tilde{u}(L,\tilde{\phi}(L,h,\delta)) < 0$. This means that the value of L which solves $\operatorname{Max}_{L,v} \tilde{u}(L,v)$ subject to $\tilde{\delta}(L,v,h) = \delta$ is unique and can be represented by the function $L_2(h,\delta)$.

3. The partial derivative of $L_2(h,\delta)$ with respect to h is

(B.9) $$\frac{\partial L_2}{\partial h} = - \frac{\partial^2}{\partial L \partial h} \tilde{u}(L,\tilde{\phi}(L,h,\delta)) / \frac{\partial^2}{\partial L^2} \tilde{u}(L,\tilde{\phi}(L,h,\delta))$$

Differentiating equation (B.1) with respect to h yields $\tilde{\phi}_h = L^{\frac{\lambda}{1-\alpha}}/H_1'$. From equation (B.6) we then obtain

(B.10) $$\frac{\partial^2}{\partial L \partial h} \tilde{u}(L,\tilde{\phi}(L,h,\delta)) = \frac{H_2'}{H_1'} + \frac{d}{dv}(\frac{H_2'}{H_1'}) L\tilde{\phi}_L$$

Now, from (B.6) and $H_2' < 0$ it is clear that $\frac{\partial}{\partial L} \tilde{u}(L,\tilde{\phi}(L,h,\delta)) = 0$ implies $\tilde{\phi}_L > 0$. We also know that $H_1' > 0$ for $v < J$ and $\frac{d}{dv}(\frac{H_2'}{H_1'}) < 0$. Thus, equation (B.9) implies $\frac{\partial^2}{\partial L \partial h} \tilde{u}(L,\tilde{\phi}(L,h,\delta)) < 0$. Since $\frac{\partial^2}{\partial L^2} \tilde{u}(L,\tilde{\phi}(L,h,\delta)) < 0$, it then follows from (B.9) that $\frac{\partial L_2}{\partial h} < 0$, as asserted.

Similarly, by differentiating the relationship $L^{\frac{\beta}{1-\alpha}} H_1(v) - (1+h)L$

$= \delta$ with respect to δ, we find that $\tilde{\phi}_\delta = L^{-\frac{\beta}{1-\alpha}}/H_1'$. Together with equation (B.6), this implies

$$\text{(B.11)} \qquad \frac{\partial^2}{\partial L \partial \delta} \tilde{u}(L, \tilde{\phi}(L,h,\delta)) = \tilde{\phi}_L \frac{d}{dv} \left(\frac{H_2'}{H_1'}\right)$$

Since $\partial\tilde{u}/\partial L = 0$ implies $\tilde{\phi}_L > 0$ and since $\frac{d}{dv}\left(\frac{H_2'}{H_1'}\right) < 0$, it follows that

$$\text{(B.12)} \qquad \frac{\partial L_2}{\partial \delta} = - \frac{\partial^2}{\partial L \partial \delta} \tilde{u}(L, \tilde{\phi}(L,h,\delta)) / \frac{\partial^2}{\partial L^2} \tilde{u}(L, \tilde{\phi}(L,h,\delta)) < 0.$$

Appendix C

This appendix is concerned with the incentive for second loans in the putty-clay model described in Section III.B. In particular, it will be shown that the expected profits of the bank which made the first loan may decrease as the size of the second loan is increased above zero and as the interest rate on the loan is adjusted to leave the borrower's total expected profits from the two loans unchanged.

Let $\bar{v} = \frac{w}{as}\bar{L}^{\lambda}\bar{n}^{1-\alpha}$, where $\bar{L} = L_1 + L_2$, the total size of the project, and $\bar{n} = n^*(\bar{r},\bar{L})$, the borrower's optimal labor intensity of investment given that he takes out both loans. Then as in Appendix B we can express the borrower's total expected profits from the two loans as $\tilde{u}(\bar{L},\bar{v}) = \bar{L}^{\beta/(1-\alpha)}H_2(\bar{v})$. Since $\partial\tilde{u}/\partial v = \bar{L}^{\beta/(1-\alpha)}H_2' < 0$, this determines a function $\tilde{\delta}(\bar{L},u)$ indicating the value of $\bar{v}$ at which $\tilde{u}(\bar{L},\bar{v}) = u$. The partial derivative of this function with respect to $\bar{L}$ is

$$(C.1) \qquad \tilde{\delta}_L = -\frac{\partial\tilde{u}/\partial L}{\partial\tilde{u}/\partial v} = -\frac{\beta}{1-\alpha}\frac{H_2}{\bar{L}H_2'}$$

By evaluating the expression for $\tilde{\delta}_1$ in equation (21), we find the expected profits of the bank making the first loan to be

$$(C.2) \qquad \tilde{\delta}_1 = \frac{z_1}{s}\{s - \frac{\hat{p}_1 + \tilde{p}}{2}\} - (1+h)L_1$$

Here $\tilde{p}$ is the price at which the total project outcome is just equal to zero, $\hat{p}_1$ is the price at which the project outcome is just sufficient to pay off the first loan, and z_1 is the principal and interest on the first loan. The sum $\hat{p}_1 + \tilde{p}$ can be expressed as a function of z_1, $\bar{L}$, and $\bar{v}$. In particular,

$$(C.3) \qquad \hat{p}_1 + \tilde{p} = \frac{z_1 + 2w\bar{L}\bar{n}}{a\bar{L}^{1-\lambda}\bar{n}^{\alpha}} = \frac{z_1}{a}\bar{L}^{-\frac{\beta}{1-\alpha}}\left(\frac{as\bar{v}}{w}\right)^{-\frac{\alpha}{1-\alpha}} + 2s\bar{v}$$

Suppose now that we increase the size of the second loan above zero while adjusting the interest rate on that loan so as to leave the borrower's expected profits unchanged at level u_1. Totally differentiating (C.2) with respect to $\bar{L}$ we obtain

$$\frac{d\delta_1}{dL_2} = \frac{d\delta_1}{d\bar{L}} = -\frac{z_1}{2s}\left\{\frac{\partial}{\partial\bar{L}}(\hat{p}_1 + \tilde{p}) + \frac{\partial}{\partial\bar{v}}(\hat{p}_1 + \tilde{p})\delta_L(\bar{L},u_1)\right\}$$

But by differentiating (C.3) and evaluating at $\bar{L} = L_1$, we obtain

$$-\frac{z_1}{2s}\frac{\partial}{\partial\bar{L}}(\hat{p}_1 + \tilde{p}) = \frac{as}{2}\frac{\beta}{1-\alpha}L_1^{-\lambda}n_1^{\alpha}\left(\frac{2-\alpha}{\alpha}v_1 - 1\right)^2$$

where $n_1 = n^*(r_1,L_1)$ and $v_1 = \frac{w}{as}L_1^{\lambda}n_1^{1-\alpha}$. Making use of equation (C.1) and equation (B.8) in Appendix B and again evaluating at $\bar{L} = L_1$, we can also obtain

$$-\frac{z_1}{2s}\frac{\partial}{\partial\bar{v}}(\hat{p}_1 + \tilde{p})\delta_L = L_1^{\frac{\beta}{1-\alpha}}(H_1' + H_2')\delta_L(L_1,u_1)$$

$$= -\frac{\beta}{1-\alpha}L_1^{-\frac{\lambda}{1-\alpha}}\left(\frac{H_1'}{H_2'} + 1\right)H_2$$

$$= -\frac{as}{2}\frac{\beta}{1-\alpha}L_1^{-\lambda}n_1^{\alpha}\frac{(\alpha-v_1)(1-v_1)(\frac{2-\alpha}{\alpha}v_1 - 1)}{\frac{2-\alpha}{\alpha}v_1 - \alpha}$$

Thus, at $\bar{L} = L_1$,

$$\frac{d\gamma_1}{dL_2} = 2as\frac{\beta}{\alpha^2}L_1^{-\lambda}n_1^{\alpha}\frac{\frac{2-\alpha}{\alpha}v_1 - 1}{\frac{2-\alpha}{\alpha}v_1 - \alpha}\{v_1 - \frac{\alpha(1+\alpha)}{2}\}v_1 \tag{C.4}$$

It follows that $d\gamma_1/dL_2 \gtreqless 0$ at $\bar{L} = L_1$ as $v_1 \gtreqless \frac{\alpha(1+\alpha)}{2}$. This critical value lies above $\alpha/(2-\alpha)$, which is the lower bound on v. However, it also lies below J, which is the value of v that prevails when the bank charges the optimal loan rate $r^*(L)$.

Now suppose that c = 0 and that r_1 and L_1 satisfy equilibrium conditions (E.3a) and (E.3b). Then from equations (B.1) and (B.6) in Appendix B it follows that

$$-\frac{H_2(v_1)}{H_1(v_1)}\frac{H_1'(v_1)}{H_2'(v_1)} = \frac{1-\alpha}{\beta} - 1$$

Since $H_2' < 0$, $H_1' > 0$ for v < J, and $\frac{d}{dv}(\frac{H_1'}{H_2'}) > 0$, the expression on the left is decreasing in v_1. Thus, when c = 0, v_1 will be lower the higher is 1-α relative to β, and will approach the lower bound $\alpha/(2-\alpha)$ as β approaches zero. This establishes that the value of $d\gamma_1/dL_2$ at $\bar{L} = L_1$ may be negative.

Footnotes

1 Henceforth we shall refer to δ as the bank's expected profits per loan. It should be remembered, however, that δ is calculated gross of administrative costs.

2 Of course, in deciding whether or not to violate a contract, the borrower will have to consider not only the possible legal penalties but also the effect of a violation on his reputation as a debtor.

3 To ensure that an equilibrium exists, we assume that $\Omega(0) < h'$. When this condition is met banks will always be able to earn expected profits per loan $\delta^* = c$ at some $S > 0$.

It is important to note that the existence of moral hazard in the lending process will lead to a market breakdown if $h' < \Omega(0) < \hat{h}$, where $\hat{h}$ is the opportunity rate at which $\underset{\gamma}{\text{Max}}\ \mu_x(\bar{L},\gamma) - (1+h)\bar{L} = c$. When this inequality holds, there will exist combinations of r and γ which yield both a positive level of expected profits u to the borrower and a level of expected profits δ to the bank sufficient to cover any costs of administration. Thus, if borrowers could be committed to a given set of project characteristics in the loan contract, a market equilibrium would exist. When borrowers cannot be so constrained, however, they will choose projects so risky that banks earn expected profits $\delta < c$ at any interest rate they charge; as a result, an equilibrium will not exist.

4 Assumption A.2 ensures that such values of x do indeed exist, i.e. that the principal and interest z always exceeds the minimum possible project outcome x_m.

5 In an earlier paper, [4], I considered an example in which the probability distribution of the state of the world depends on the project characteristic γ and in which Assumptions A.1, A.2, A.4 and A.5 are satisfied. This is the case of an all-or-nothing investment project in which x equals $\psi(L,p)$ with probability p and zero with probability 1-p, with $\psi_p < 0$ and $0 < p < 1$. Here the probability of failure 1-p corresponds to the parameter γ and the maximum outcome $\psi(L,p)$ corresponds to $\bar{x}$. As shown in Figure 5, each pair of distributions $F(x,L,1-p_2)$ and $F(x,L,1-p_1)$ will obey the single-crossing property. Although Assumption A.3 is not satisfied in this case and although our proofs have been for continuous and not discrete probability distributions, it can be shown that Propositions 1 and 2 will both hold if $p\psi_p/\psi < -1$ for p very close to 1, e.g. if $\psi(L,p) = aL^{\alpha}e^{-\lambda p}$ with $\lambda > 1$.

Although we will have occasion to refer to this example at a later stage, the major focus of this paper will be on the case described in the text.

6 As r approaches $\hat{r}(L)$, $\frac{\partial \mu_R}{\partial \gamma}$ approaches

$$\int_{y_{min}}^{y_{max}} \psi_{\gamma}(L,\gamma^*,y)g(y)dy$$

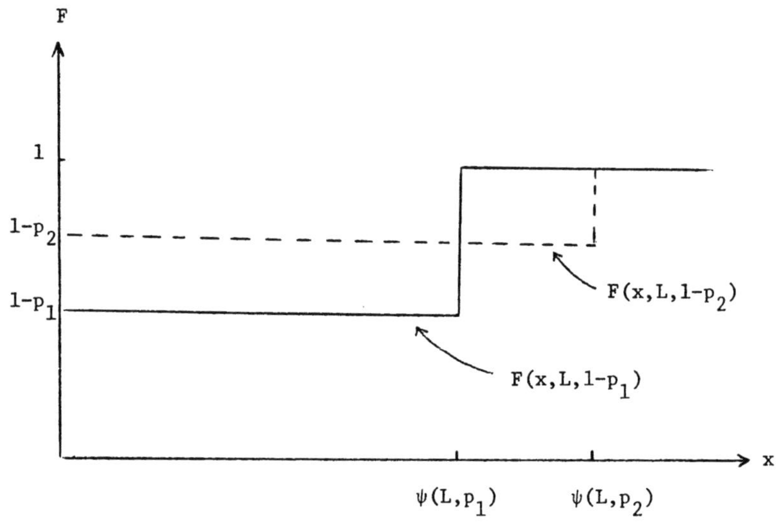

$1-p_2 > 1-p_1$

Figure 5

where γ^* is the value of γ that maximizes $\psi(L,\gamma,y_{max})$. Since $\psi_{\gamma y} > 0$ and $\psi_{\gamma}(L,\gamma^*,y_{max}) = 0$, this integral is negative.

7 More precisely, the firm must determine the amount of labor it will employ at the end of the period if it should decide at that time to produce a positive level of output. At the end of the period the firm can always decide not to produce at all (e.g. if the price of its output is excessively low), in which case it will of course employ zero labor.

8 The derivation given in the Appendix is for the more general case in which the outcome of the project takes the form $x = \psi(L,\gamma,y)$.

9 As we showed in Chapter II, an exactly analogous indeterminacy occurs when a ceiling is imposed on the loan rate, if there is no default risk and administrative costs are zero.

10 Since $\partial u/\partial r < 0$ and $\delta \to 0$ as $r \to h$, any combination of r and L which solves the second problem must also solve the first. For the converse to be true, it is sufficient (1) that δ attain a unique maximum at some point on the curve $r^*(L)$ and decrease monotonically as we move away from that point along the curve; and (2) that δ decrease monotonically at any value of L as we raise the loan rate above $r^*(L)$ or reduce it below $r^*(L)$. The case of constant returns to scale is an example in which the first property is violated, so that the two maximization problems are

not identical (i.e. a solution to the first problem will not be a solution to the second).

11 It should be noted that equilibrium cannot occur at any point above $r^*(L)$, since in this case the expected profits of both the bank and the borrower could be increased by reducing the loan rate.

12 Let h', L', and S' satisfy conditions (12) for the first type of equilibrium. Since $d\tilde{\delta}/dh < 0$ implies $\delta < \delta^*$ for all r, L, and $h > h'$, the condition $L = L_2(h, \delta^*)$ in (13) clearly cannot be satisfied at any $h > h'$. Also if $h < h'$, then $M > S'$, $L = L_2(h, \delta^*) > L_1(h') = L'$, and $\Omega' \geq 0$ imply $h = \Omega(ML) \geq \Omega(S'L') = h'$, which is a contradiction. The only remaining possibility is that $h = h'$. But conditions (13) will be satisfied in this case only if $\Omega(L_T) = h'$ for all L_T between S' and M. This cannot occur at all if $\Omega' > 0$, and if $\Omega' = 0$ it can occur only on a set of measure zero.

13 As in Section I.C., we assume $\Omega(0) < h'$ to ensure that an equilibrium will exist (see footnote 3).

14 By definition, $L_1(h)$ is the value of L which maximizes $\delta = \hat{\mu}_R(L) - (1+h)L$ and $\tilde{\delta}(h)$ is the maximized value of δ. But from equation (9) it is clear that $\hat{\mu}_R(L)$ can be expressed as $bL^{\frac{\beta}{1-\alpha}}$, where b is a constant which is decreasing in w and increasing in a and s. Solving the first order condition $d\hat{\mu}_R/dL = 1+h$, we obtain

$$L_1(h) = \left[\frac{(1+h)(1-\alpha)}{b\beta}\right]^{-\frac{1-\alpha}{\lambda}}$$

$$\gamma(h) = (1+h)^{-\frac{\beta}{\alpha}} \cdot \left[\frac{1-\alpha}{b\beta}\right]^{-\frac{1-\alpha}{\lambda}} \frac{\lambda}{\beta}$$

The second equation can be inverted to derive h as a function of b and δ. Substituting into the expression for $L_1(h)$, we then obtain the value of L at which the bank's expected profits are maximized as a function of b and δ alone:

$$L = \left[\frac{b\lambda}{\delta(1-\alpha)}\right]^{-\frac{1-\alpha}{\beta}}$$

Since this function is decreasing in b, a fall in b must always shift the point E_1, the point on the curve $L_1(h)$ at which $\gamma(h) = \delta*$, downward and to the right (i.e. to a lower value of h and a higher value of L).

15 To demonstrate the impact of monetary policy on total lending more formally, we can rewrite the function Ω as $\Omega(L_T,t)$, where t is a shift parameter. When the initial equilibrium is characterized by Type II rationing, the effect of a marginal shift in Ω on lending is found by totally differentiating the equation $h' = \Omega(L_T,t)$ with respect to t. This yields

$$\frac{dL_T}{dt} = -\frac{\partial\Omega/\partial t}{\partial\Omega/\partial L_T}$$

On the other hand, when the initial equilibrium is one in which all firms receive credit, we totally differentiate the equations $h = \Omega(L_T, t)$ and $L_T = M\mathcal{L}_2(h, \delta^*)$ with respect to t to obtain

$$\frac{dL_T}{dt} = -\frac{\partial\Omega/\partial t}{\partial\Omega/\partial L_T}\left[\frac{-M\dfrac{\partial \mathcal{L}_2}{\partial h}\dfrac{\partial\Omega}{\partial L_T}}{1 - M\dfrac{\partial \mathcal{L}_2}{\partial h}\dfrac{\partial\Omega}{\partial L_T}}\right]$$

The expression in brackets is a fraction between zero and one and represents the dampening effect of the induced change in the equilibrium opportunity rate.

16 The efficiency with which resources are allocated between investment and alternative uses in competitive equilibrium will not be considered here.

17 $NQ_N(L,N) + LQ_L(L,N) < Q(L,N)$ implies $L\dfrac{\partial\mu_x}{\partial L} + N\dfrac{\partial\mu_x}{\partial N} =$

$$\int_{\tilde{p}}^{p_{max}} \{p[LQ_L + NQ_N] - wN\}g(p)dp < \int_{\tilde{p}}^{p_{max}} [pQ - wN]g(p)dp = \mu_x$$

Thus, if Q displays decreasing returns to scale in L and N, so will μ_x.

18 In the notation of Appendix B, $b = [H_1(J) + H_2(J)]/H_1(J)$, where J is the value of v which is optimal for the bank.

19 In this context, $D(r)$ is the value of L that maximizes the borrower's expected profits $u(r,L,\gamma)$, when γ is also chosen so as to maximize u.

20 From equation (6) it follows that increasing $\bar{L}$ while holding $\bar{r}$ constant will cause $\bar{v}$ to rise. Since the borrower's optimal labor intensity $\bar{n}$ increases with $\bar{r}$, this means that the increase in $\bar{L}$ must be accompanied by a decrease in $\bar{r}$ if $\bar{v}$ is to remain unchanged.

References

[1] Diamond, Peter A. and Stiglitz, Joseph E., "Increases in Risk and in Risk Aversion," Journal of Economic Theory, July 1974

[2] Gould, John P., "Adjustment Costs in the Theory of Investment of the Firm," Review of Economic Studies, January 1968

[3] Hayes, Douglas A., Bank Lending Policies, Bureau of Business Research, Graduate School of Business Administration, University of Michigan, 1971

[4] Keeton, William, "An Essay on the Theory of Credit Rationing"

[5] Reed, Edward W., Cotter, Richard V., Gill, Edward K., and Smith, Richard K., Commercial Banking (Prentice Hall, Englewood Cliffs, N.J., 1976)

[6] Rothschild, Michael and Stiglitz, Joseph E., "Increasing Risk: I, A Definition," Journal of Economic Theory, September 1970

[7] Uzawa, H., "Time Preference and the Penrose Effect in a Two Class Model of Economic Growth," Journal of Political Economy, July/August 1969

Biography

William Keeton was born in Houston, Texas on November 22, 1947. In 1964 he graduated from Winchester High School in Winchester, Massachusetts. He attended Yale University from 1964 to 1968, receiving a B.A. in Political Science and Economics and an M.A. in Economics. From 1968 to 1970 he served as a Peace Corps Volunteer in Colombia and from 1970 to 1972 he worked at the Council of Economic Advisers.